Ken W. Purdy's

WONDERFUL WORLD OF THE AUTOMOBILE

Ken W. Purdy's

WONDERFUL WORLD OF THE AUTOMOBILE

Thomas Y. Crowell Company

NEW YORK · ESTABLISHED 1834

Designed by Laurel Wagner
Manufactured in the United States of America by the Vail-Ballou Press, Inc., Binghamton, N.Y.
Library of Congress Catalog Card No. 60-8255

See page 244 for acknowledgments.

Contents

Foreword

THIS BOOK is like no other that I know. It is personal: it concerns only things that interest me about the automobile, and I have written it without regard for established pattern. Some of it touches on individuals whom I have liked or admired, and machines that have intrigued me; some of it is fictional but most of it is fact; the last section concerns the paramount problem of the automobile—the rate at which it is killing us. I have written a great deal about the automobile in the past; I do not intend to write more; this book in a sense is my last word on the subject.

K.W.P.

Ken W. Purdy's

WONDERFUL WORLD OF THE AUTOMOBILE

1 · What's to Talk About?

THE FIRST TOPIC of conversation among Americans is not politics and it is not money. It is the automobile.

Perhaps we would be wiser if we talked less about the automobile and more about politics and literature and other vital matters, since it may be that the automobile is not really terribly important in the eternal scheme of things. But we do not, perhaps primarily because most of us use the automobile as a conversational substitute for other topics.

We talk about the automobile because it is basic to our life in this country, and because it's a substitute for politics and money, and for a third reason: it's fascinating. It was the automobile, not the horse, the steamship or the airplane, that made man free of his environment, made him his own man. We use it as we use nothing else: as simple transport, as an instrument of sport, as an indispensable arm of commerce, as a pleasure-giving device and as an indicator of our place in the tribal pecking-order. The automobile kills 60,000 or 70,000 of us every year, maims perhaps 1,500,000 of us, and we cheerfully accept this hazard. The people and the automobiles are at war, and the people are losing, but they don't care, they love their killer, and they go on producing it in bewildering variety and incredible numbers.

Since the automobile age began, say in 1895, about 3,500 makes of motor cars have been produced. At the moment, about 100 are being made, big and little, front-engined and rear-engined, air- and water-cooled, front-wheel-driven and rear-wheel-driven, drawing power from one cylinder or from two, three, four, six, eight, twelve and costing from $1000 to $25,000. It is the fashion among some authorities to decry the utilitarian aspect of today's automobiles, and to bemoan the passing of the great luxury carriages, but this is nonsense. Ordinary run-of-the-mill sedans today offer more luxury, in some ways, than the most expensive cars of the 1920's did, and if one cannot be satisfied with an off-the-peg purchase, the great Italian coach-builders are prepared, in consideration of $40,000 or $50,000, to run up something to individual taste. Messrs. Rolls-Royce still welcome customers who like to buy a dozen cars at a time, to give as Christmas presents. One can still buy fast cars, too. Enzo Ferrari, of Modena, Italy, has a nice line of 150-mph coupes beginning at around $12,000.

If one is still not pleased with contemporary motorcars, one can join the devoted men and women who buy and restore and use antique automobiles. The fascination of this pursuit (it is distinctly more than a "hobby") is subtle and elusive, but for me the pleasure to be taken from a mint-condition 1912 Rolls-Royce or 1930 Hispano-Suiza, for example, is nostalgic in basis. I am moved to think of the ground over which this noble noble machine has rolled and the persons it has transported. (Yes, I know: the car was probably owned by a slob who profited hugely in the black market of his day, and its cargo was, no doubt, usually trollops in bulk. Do go away; you bother me.) There is fascination, too, in the detail to which restoration can be carried, resulting ultimately in a car much finer than it was when it left its factory. Some owners are clearly obsessive in this regard, and no doubt suffer from the idiocy of minutiae which brings some to engrave the Gettysburg Address upon the head of a pin or build scale-model ships armed with half-inch cannon that will actually fire.

If the automobile itself is fascinating, what of the men who have been drawn to it? Some of them have been, I think, among the most intriguing of earth's children. Durant, Bugatti, Porsche, Portago . . . Consider Portago, for a beginning, a name I always think of as spoken in a shout: PORTAGO!

2 · Portago!

DON ALFONSO CABEZA de Vaca y Leighton, Carvajal y Are, Conde de la Mejorada, Marquis de Portago was twenty-eight when he died at Guidizzollo, a few miles from Brescia and the end of the Mille Miglia (Thousand Mile) automobile race in Italy on the 12th of May, 1957. Portago had been a flier, a jai-alai player, a poloist, a steeplechase rider (the world's leading amateur in 1951 and 1952), an Olympic bobsledder and record-holder, a remarkable swimmer, and he was at his death one of the dozen best racing drivers in the world. He had never sat in a racing car until 1954 but he believed he would be champion of the world before 1960 and most of the men he ran against every week thought that he very well might be—if he lived.

Portago was uniquely gifted. An athlete all his life, he was not a big man, not heavily muscled, but he had unusual strength, great endurance, abnormal eyesight, a quickness of reaction that was legendary among his friends. He was highly intelligent, courteous, and very much aware of the world around him.

Gregor Grant, editor of the British weekly *Autosport,* said just before the 1957 Mille Miglia, "A man like Portago appears only once in a generation, and it would probably be more accurate to say only once in a life-time. The fellow does *everything* fabulously well. Never mind the driving, the steeple-chasing, the bobsledding, the athletic side of things, never mind the being fluent in four languages. There are so many other aspects to the man: for example I think he could be the best bridge player in the world if he cared to try, he could certainly be a great soldier, and I suspect he could be a fine writer."

Portago's death, I suppose, proved out again the two well-worn British aphorisms: "Motor racing is a sport at which you get better and better until you get killed" and the other, less optimistic one: "There are two kinds of racing drivers: those who get killed before they get good, and those who get killed afterward." But whether they will die at the wheel sooner or later or not at all, most men have to serve years of apprentice time before they make the big league: the racing team of one of the major factories. They drive sports cars, stock and not so stock, in rallies and dreary airport events; they cadge rides in scruffy hand-me-down racing cars, hoping to attract a wealthy sponsor's eyes. When—and if—they are invited to Italy or Germany or France or England to sign a racing contract, they have behind them thousands of miles of competition driven in dozens of makes of cars. This is standard, this is usual, and, with most of the other rules, Portago broke it.

Driving relief in his first race, the 1,000 kilometers for sports cars at Buenos Aires in 1954, he did three laps so badly that he dropped the car from second place to fifth—because he had never learned how to shift gears! To the day he died, he had driven few makes of competition automobiles: Maserati, Osca, Ferrari. He never drove the usual sports cars: MG's, Jaguars, and so on. For personal use, before he began to compete, he usually drove American cars: Fords, something else that may have been a De Soto, he wasn't sure. Explaining this, the last time I talked with him, he said, "Automobiles bore me, I know next to nothing about them, and I care less.

"I have no sentimental attachment for a car," he said. "I can hardly tell one from another. Sometimes I make a little scratch on a car, in an inconspicuous place, so I can recognize it the next time I'm in it, so I can remember its defects. I'm not interested in cars. To me they're a means of transportation from Point A to Point B, that, or a machine for racing.

"When I have a racing car that I'm going to drive, I walk up to it and I look at it and I think, 'Now, is this son-of-a-bitch going to hold together for the next five hundred kilometers? What is this thing going to do to me today, how is it going to let me down, or make me lose the race—or perhaps even kill me?' That is the only interest I have in it. As soon as the race is over—I couldn't care less what happens to the car."

Portago's forthright disclaimer of interest in the machines on which his career was based was typical. To the outermost limit which custom and law allowed, the twelfth Marquis de Portago said precisely what he pleased and did exactly as he liked. When he saw a friend in the crowd lining the streets after he had left the Rome check point in his last race, he stood on the brakes, waited for her to run to him, kissed her and held her in his arms, until an official furiously waved him on. Portago was probably the only man in the race who would have allowed himself such a gesture. He would have done it at the risk of his life. He was an avowed romantic, and he had remarked that in another age he would have been a Crusader, or a knight-errant. He often dressed in black, his hair was black and curly, usually long over his neck and ears, clinging to his head like a skullcap, he moved quickly and rarely smiled, he sometimes looked like a juvenile delinquent or a hired killer, but more often like what he was, a Spanish grandee. The remark that he had been born three or four centuries too late was a cliché among his friends.

"Every time I see Fon," one of them said, "I see him in a long black cape, a sword sticking out of it, a floppy black hat on his head, riding like a fiend across some castle drawbridge."

When he began to drive, Portago was not the best-loved figure on the international circuit; nor was he when he died, if it comes to that. Lacking technical skill to balance his bitterly competitive instinct, he was dangerous in his first races, and to most people he seemed arrogant and supercilious. He was reputed to be enormously wealthy; he was a great lady-killer; and, if he was not pugnacious, still he was quick to fight. Most of the other drivers preferred to leave him alone. Nobody expected him to be around long. Many thought he was just another aristocratic dilettante who would quickly lose interest in racing cars, but the few who knew his lineage were not so sure.

His mother, an Englishwoman who brought a great fortune to his father, is a strong-minded woman, and a determined lust for adventure, plus an inclination toward government, runs through the Portago line. Spanish history is studded with the name. In the sixteenth century one of Portago's forebears, Cabeza de Vaca, was shipwrecked on the Florida coast. He *walked* to Mexico City, recruiting an army as he went. Another conquered the Canary Islands, another was a leader in the fight to drive the Moors out of Spain. Portago's grandfather was governor of Madrid, his father was Spain's best golfer, polo player, yachtsman; he was a fabulous gambler, said to have once won $2,000,000 at Monte Carlo, a soldier and a movie actor. He died of a heart attack on the polo field, playing against his doctor's orders. The last king of Spain, Alfonso XIII, was Portago's godfather.

Naturally enough, in the light of his background and his own propensity for high-risk sports, Portago was constantly accused of fearlessness, of nurturing a death wish, and so on. We talked at length about that. We sat in my room in the Kenilworth Lodge in Sebring, Florida, site of the annual Twelve-Hour race. Portago had been punctual and had apologized for being unable to keep his promise that there would be no interruptions—he had placed a phone call to Caracas and he asked if he might tell the operator to put it on my wire when it came through. I wanted to record the interview and I asked him if he would object to a Minifon. He said he would not and he told me about an interview recording he was making for Riverside Records, a house specializing in sports car material. We talked generalities for half an hour and then I turned the machine on. I mentioned a newspaper article that had said something to the effect that he "lived on fear."

"A lot of nonsense," Portago said. "I'm often frightened. I can get frightened crossing the street in heavy traffic. And I know I'm a moral coward. I can't even go into a shop to look around and walk out without buying something. As for enjoying fear, I don't think anybody enjoys fear, at least in my definition, which is a mental awareness of a danger to one's body. You can enjoy courage —the performance of an act which frightens you—but not fear.

"I know that my first ride in a racing car frightened me. That was the Mexican road race, the Carrera Panamericana, of 1953. I had been riding horses in competition for a long time, at least twice a week for five years, but I had to give it up because I put on some weight and I couldn't get rid of it. And I couldn't get by no matter what I tried, and I tried most things: weighing-in with papier-mâché boots and saddle, made to look like leather and weighing nothing, or hiding a five-pound weight on the scale so that the whole standard of weight for all the riders would go up.

"I enjoyed riding, particularly I enjoyed jumping. There are interesting things you can do with a horse. A horse, you know, is very stupid. Not being much of a thinker, a horse likes to do whatever he sees another horse doing. So if you can come up to a jump say half a length ahead of another rider, when you lift your horse for the jump, his will go too, but being half a length behind, he usually won't make it. I think having ridden is helpful in many sports, and perhaps peculiarly in automobile racing, where a sense of balance is so important. I think flying may help, too. I learned to fly when I was seventeen, but I gave it up after a bit. It bored me. After all, you just sit there. It's interesting only when you're near the ground. I flew under a bridge once for a five hundred dollar bet. And while I guess I was a good pilot I certainly was a lousy navigator. I was always coming down at strange airports to ask where I was. Once, in a fog, I landed on top of a cow.

"To get back to the Mexican road race, I met Harry Schell and Luigi Chinetti at the Paris auto show in 1953 and Chinetti asked me to be his co-driver in the Mexican race. All he really wanted me for, of course, was ballast. I didn't drive a foot, not even from the garage to the starting line. I just sat there, white with fear, holding on to anything I thought looked sturdy enough. I knew that Chinetti was a very good driver, a specialist in long-distance races who was known to be conservative and careful, but the first time you're in a racing car you can't tell if the driver is conservative or a wild man, and I didn't see how Chinetti could get away with half of what he was doing. We broke down the second day of the race, but I had decided by then that this was what I wanted to do more than anything else, so I bought a three-liter Ferrari.

"I was fortunate, of course, in being able to buy my own car. I think it might have taken me five or six years longer to make the Ferrari team if I had had to look around for a sponsor and all that. I was lucky, having enough money to buy my own car—even if I'm not 'enormously wealthy.' In those years I was perpetually in debt." (Portago earned perhaps twenty thousand dollars a year as a driver and had a five-figure income from a trust fund, but his mother, now Mrs. Olga Martin-Montis, controlled the family fortune, which was of American origin and reputedly runs well into nine figures. At her death it would have been divided between Portago and his sister Soledad.)

Harry Schell, today one of the fifteen internationally ranked Grand Prix drivers, went with Portago to the Argentine for a 1,000-kilometer sports-car race.

"Harry was so frightened that I would break the car he wouldn't teach me how to change gear, so when after 60 laps (the race was 101 laps) he was tired and it was my turn to drive, after 3 laps, during which I lost so much time that we dropped from second to fifth place, I saw Harry out in the middle of the track frantically waving a flag to make me come into the pits so that he could drive again. We eventually finished second overall and first in our class, or rather, Harry did. I didn't learn to change gears properly until the chief mechanic of Maserati took me out and spent an afternoon teaching me." (Portago had driven since childhood, but changing gears on a passenger car bears little relation to shifting on a 175-mile-an-hour competition car, on which missing a down-shift can wreck engine or transmission or both and kill the driver as well.)

Schell and Portago ran the three-liter Ferrari at Sebring in 1954. The rear axle broke after two hours. Portago sold it and bought a two-liter Maserati, the gear-shifting lesson thrown in, and ran it in the 1954 Le Mans twenty-four-hour race with Allesandro de Tomaso co-driving. They led the class until five in the morning, when the engine blew up. He won the Grand Prix of Metz with the Maserati—"but there were no good drivers in it"—and ran with Chiron in the Twelve Hours of Rheims, Chiron blowing up the engine with twenty minutes to go while leading the class. He ran an Osca in the Grand Prix of Germany, and rolled it. "God protects the good, so I wasn't hurt," he said.

In 1954 Portago broke down while leading the first lap of the Mexican road race in a three-liter Ferrari, and won his class, an overall and a handicap race in Nassau. He bent an automobile occasionally and he was often off the road, but he was never hurt until a 1955 race at Silverstone in England when he missed a gear-shift from fourth to third and came out of the resulting crash with a double compound break in his left leg.

The crash had no effect on Portago's driving; he continued to run a little faster on the circuit and to leave it less frequently. At Caracas in 1955 he closed on Juan Manuel Fangio, then champion of the world and one of the greatest drivers of all time, until he was only nine seconds behind him, and finished second. He was a member of the Ferrari team in 1956, an incredibly short time after he had begun to race. It was as if he had signed with the Yankees three years after seeing his first baseball game. He won the Grand Prix of Portugal in 1956, a wild go-round in which the lap record was broken seventeen times, the last time by Portago. He won the Tour of France, the Coupes de Salon, Paris, the Grand Prix of Rome and was leading Moss and Fangio at Caracas when a broken gas line put him out of the race. After Caracas that year I asked Stirling Moss, then No. 2 in the world, how he ranked Portago.

"He's certainly among the ten best in the world today," Moss said, "and as far as I'm concerned, he's the one to watch out for."

In Cuba, just before the 1957 Sebring, Portago was leading Fangio by a respectable margin when a gas line let go again.

"I don't think anyone else will be champion of the world as long as Fangio competes," Portago told me. (He was right. Fangio retired holding a unique record: he had been champion five times.) "If the absolute limit of road adhesion on the car through a certain bend is 101.5 miles an hour, the old man will go through at 101, every time. I may go through at 99, in which case I'll be well beaten, or at 102, in which case there'll be an accident. Moss is of course better than I am, too. If I pass Moss, I wonder what's the matter with his car! But I'm learning still, I think I get a little better with every race."

Portago's closest friend was Harry Schell, an American who has lived most of his life in Paris. They spent much time together. Each appeared to be tense—more accurately, taut—something that was not in any way allied to nervousness but was instead a peculiar expression of awareness. Like Portago, Schell walks rapidly, he turns his head constantly, he seems to be trying always to see something that is just out of sight, to hear something that is just out of earshot.

I said as much.

"It sounds corny," Portago said, "but I think that because racing drivers are very near to death every Sunday in the season, they are more sensitive to life, and appreciate it more. I'm sure I love life more than the average man does. I want to get something out of every minute, I want no time wasted. You know, people say that race drivers are daredevils who don't care whether they live and you've seen stories about me and my flirting with death and all that. Nonsense, all nonsense. I want to live to be one hundred and five, and I mean to. I want to live to be a very old man. I'm *enchanted* with life. But no matter how long I live, I still won't have time for all the things I want to do, I won't hear all the music I want to hear, I won't be able to read all the books I want to read, I won't have all the women I want to have, I won't be able to do a twentieth of the things I want to do. And besides just the *doing*, I insist on getting something out of what I do. For example, I wouldn't race unless I was sure I could be champion of the world."

"Can you imagine yourself driving when you're Fangio's age?" I asked him. (Fangio was then forty-six.)

Portago smiled. His mouth was unusually small, and straight lined, and his smiles were brief, but warm enough. "Never," he said. "Certainly not. In any case I'll stop when I'm thirty-five; and, if I'm champion of the world, sooner."

"And then?"

"Well, I'm very ambitious, and . . ." The phone rang beside me. It was Portago's Caracas call and I handed the instrument to him. I had passed the open switchboard in the lobby an hour before, when he had placed the call, and I had overheard the operator, so I knew to whom the call was going and I knew it would be personal.

"I'll take a walk," I told him. "Call me."

"Please," he said. "Don't go. Please. Anyway I'm going to speak Spanish."

As it turned out, the call was a report that the party in Caracas was unavailable.

"Forgive me," he said. "I didn't mean to be rude, I didn't mean to suggest that naturally you wouldn't speak Spanish. I'm sorry."

I told him that he was right, in any case. "We were talking about what you intend to get out of automobile racing," I said.

"Well, I haven't told this to a great many people," Portago said. "You see, Spain has had no new national hero for many, many years. That is what the championship of the world means to me. When I give up racing I'm going to Spain and go into politics." Later he said, "I think I might reasonably aspire to be Foreign Minister of Spain." And a few days later, from Paris, Portago sent a photograph of himself and Fangio and the Pretender to the Spanish throne. On it he had written, "With Fangio and Don Juan, the *future king* of Spain."

Portago was married in 1949 to Carol McDaniel, an enchanting and beautiful woman, and their children are Antonio and Andrea. Two hours after he had met Carol McDaniel, Portago told her he intended to marry her. They spent most of their eight years of married life in France. Carol Portago brought to her husband a social stability that was new to him. She became an intimate of the Duke and Duchess of Windsor and she could move with grace in circles to which only Portago's name gave him entree. "Carol, in a sense, tamed Fon," one of their friends has said. "To the degree that anyone could, she brought him into the twentieth century. I think he regretted not having been born in the 1700's, lots of us thought that, and I believe that Carol helped him fit into his own time."

Portago had discovered early in life that women responded to daring as to nothing else—to daring, to indifference, to arrogance and certainty and sensitivity, and in one sense at least women were more important in his life than anything else.

"The most important thing in our existence is a well-balanced sex life," he said to me. "Everybody knows this is true, but nobody will admit it—of himself. But if you don't have a happy sex life, you don't have anything."

"It's the first thing the historians suppress when they write the lives of great men," I said, "and it was often an astonishingly big factor in their lives."

"Of course," Portago said. "Look at Nelson, look at Napoleon."

"Well, look at George Bernard Shaw," I said, "who gave it up altogether, and married on condition his wife never mention sex to him."

"A freak," Portago said. "A very untypical writer. Look at Maupassant. A prodigy, in more ways than one. Well, as for me, making love is the most important thing I do every day, and I don't care who knows it."

Portago was willing to maintain his opinions under most circumstances, whether by debate or a right cross. I had heard that he had once challenged a man to a duel, but he denied it. He had fenced rarely, he said. He was taught boxing by Edmund Nelson, who died with him in the Mille Miglia. Nelson was a British ex-professional boxer who was just out of the merchant marine and working in New York's Plaza Hotel when Portago, still in his teens, resided there. It was Nelson who taught Portago bobsledding. The first time Portago went down the St. Moritz run he went down steering, and he took 15 seconds off the time of the then champion of Switzerland. It was Nelson who said, "I know Fon says he'll live forever, but I say he won't live to be thirty."

It is not on record that Portago lost many fights. He was always in condition. He ordered milk at most of the world's best bars. He smoked constantly, but never inhaled. His reactions were freakishly fast, beyond normal to an extent that even he apparently did not appreciate. He once remarked after a car had spun with him, "It went very slowly. There was lots of time to think." Another time, in speaking of steeplechasing, he said, "When your horse falls after a jump, you look around for another horse to hide behind."

One time in Paris Portago stepped off a curbstone as a Citroën went past much too close, Portago felt, to the feet of the lady he was with. He flipped a cigarette at the driver so quickly and so accurately that he hit him in the face with it. The man got out and Portago knocked him down twice. He handled his own defense in the consequent law proceedings and was thoroughly trounced by the plaintiff's attorney.

"I hate to fight," he told me. "I'll do anything honorable to get out of a fight, but I get into situations in which there is no way out. I was with some friends, they were shipping people, and a man called them 'a bunch of bloody pirates.' I'm afraid I hit him. Another time I suggested to a man on a dance floor that it might be nicer for everybody if he put his cigar away when he danced. He'd already burned a friend of mine with it. When I started to leave the place, later, two of this cigar-lover's friends stood in my way and wouldn't move. What could I do, once I'd asked them please to let me by? I lowered the boom on them."

Among the men whom Portago found it necessary to knock down was a columnist who has not even yet forgiven him. His airy indifference to the maxim "Never hit a reporter" insured that his attention to women other than his wife would have maximum attention in the public prints. At least one of the women concerned demonstrated a semiprofessional ability in publicity in her own right. Just before Portago's death, columnists predicted that he and his wife would be divorced. Portago was volatile, violent, headstrong. Carol Portago is tranquil, firm-minded, strong-willed, and their life together produced some heady moments. Some time after Portago's death I asked her if there had been substance in the rumors of divorce.

"Like so much else that was printed about Fon," Carol Portago said, "that has no connection with reality. Fon's attitude toward divorce was very Spanish, very Catholic: to him divorce was anathema, it was impossible, unthinkable.

"Another thing: there was very little that was sneaky about Fon. He moved quite beyond commonplace deception. I knew him, I think, better than anyone else, and there was very little indeed in his life that I did not know about. We could talk about anything, and we did. I can assure you that some of the explanations, excuses, that he gave me at one time or another when we talked about something that he had done were strange and wonderful, often hilarious, but one could not laugh at him because he was absolutely sincere. All one can say about it, really, is that he was unable to resist a beautiful woman, any more than he was able to resist any other kind of challenge. This was a facet of his nature, and not by any means the most important. Most of his attachments were completely casual. One was not, but even that had ended, to all intents and purposes, before his death.

"After all, the essence of Fon's whole personality was his maleness. He was totally a man, and he was almost ferocious in his determination to live by his own rules.

"As for me, the more time that has passed since his death, the closer I have seemed to come to despair. I miss him very much more now than I did even a few months ago."

Portago and I talked of a good many things that don't matter much now, during our time in that room. It had rained hard during the night, but the sun was steaming it off, and outside we could hear cars slowing for the corner around the hotel that led to the circuit. Two team Maseratis came past, the mechanics who drove them blipping their engines incessantly to keep the plugs clear. A tractor-and-trailer load of oranges stalled in the intersection and one of the Maseratis began to steam.

"Genuine Italian-type sports cars," I said. "Suitable for summer touring."

Portago grinned. "This is an easy course in one way," he said. "There's only one genuine fast bend in it. [A fast bend is a gentle corner which must be taken, if one is earnest, with the car sliding all four wheels, just on the knife-edge of control-loss.] But the flat corners, the way it ruins brakes . . . A race I don't like is the Mille Miglia. No matter how much you practice you can't possibly come to know 1,000 miles of Italian roads as well as the Italians, and, as Fangio says, if you have a conscience you can't drive really fast anyway, I mean over 150 miles an hour. There are hundreds of corners in the Mille Miglia where one little slip by a driver will kill fifty people. You can't keep the spectators from crowding into the road, you couldn't do it with an army. It's a race I hope I never run in."

"I have a quotation in a story, a piece of fiction that won't be published until next summer," I told Portago, "something that I think you might have said: that of all sports, only bullfighting and mountain climbing and motor racing really try a man, that all the rest are mere recreations, games that children can play. Would you have said that?"

"I couldn't agree with you more," Portago said. "You're quite right. I've thought of bullfighting, of course, but the trouble is that you must start when you're a child, otherwise you'll never really know the bulls. And the only trouble with mountain climbing for me is lack of an audience! Like most drivers, I'm something of an exhibitionist."

Portago and I had promised ourselves a certain length of time. We had run an hour past it when he stood up and I shut off the wire recorder. We said good-bye. I saw him three times more, briefly, before the 1957 Sebring was over. In April he wrote me from Paris to say that he had won at Montlhery, beating sports cars with a *gran turismo* (fast touring) car, and breaking the lap record. He said he was going to run in the Mille Miglia and at Monte Carlo. Finally, the day before the race, a cable came from Brescia, asking if I could use his first-person account of the race. Obviously an earlier depression had left him as the beginning of the race neared. Previously he had written to Dorian Leigh, an internationally famous beauty who had been his friend: ". . . As you know, I did not want to run in the Mille Miglia. Until I returned from my first practice, I thought I was going to run a *gran turismo* car. Now it appears that I will have to drive the 3.8 sports. [Portago loathed the 3.8 Ferrari, and conceded a superstition about it: he felt that the car was malevolent.] This may mean that my 'early death' will come on Sunday. . . ."

Clearly, the man was distressed, but there was nothing of significance in his fear. Most race drivers, and many of the best of them, are frightened before a race. One of the immortals of American racing commonly vomited while enduring the hard hour before the start. I remember talking with another ranking American driver just before a race a few years ago. He was rational enough, but his eyes were glazed, and when I tried to pick up the threads of the conversation that evening, I discovered that he not only did not recall the subject of our talk, he did not believe he had spoken to me at all. Most drivers hated the Mille Miglia, arguing that sheer chance counted too heavily in determining whether one finished or crashed, lived or died. Juan Manuel Fangio at least once refused to run in it. Minimally a driver should not run a car he dislikes in so brutal an event, and while the 3.8 may not have possessed the evil personality with which Portago believed it was endowed, still it was not the most successful of Commenatore Ferrari's creations.

Portago told a reporter that he was intent only on finishing, which implied a disinclination to drive really fast. But when he slid down the starting ramp at Brescia in the early morning, Edmund Nelson hunched enigmatically beside him, the big red car bellowing under them, Portago, true to his mold, forgot whatever fear he had felt, threw away whatever resolutions he had made, and began to go. He was, fantastically, fourth at the first check point. He drove all day, through the mountains and the plains, flat-out and when a broken half-shaft put Peter Collins out at Parma, Portago began to try for second place. He was straining for a sight of Von Trips' car, lying second to Taruffi, 900-odd miles of the race already run, when a tire blew, or a half-shaft went, at something between 125 and 150 miles an hour on the straight at Guidizzollo, and the 3.8 lifted its wheels off the road and left him helpless. The car killed Portago, it nearly destroyed his body. Nelson died with him, and so did ten of the spectators who always lined the very edges of the roadways when the Mille Miglia was run.

Except for the final seconds after he had lost the car, seconds that must have seemed so long to him, Portago's last hours were happy. He was doing what he wanted to do, and doing it far better than the form chart indicated he possibly could. He was surely thinking, as he screamed down the Valley of the Po toward Brescia and the finish, that he might conceivably win the race. (The great Piero Taruffi won it, in the fifth decade of his life, and with twelve previous attempts behind him.)

Most men die regretting the errors they have made in the multiple choices that life forces upon us, and Portago knew, in the fraction of time in which he could think about it, that error was killing him. Motor racing, like every other endeavor, rigidly reserves the ultimate reward for those who are talented, lucky—and totally devoted. Portago was enormously talented, he was luckier than most, but he did not have, in fullest measure, the vital ability to concentrate obsessively upon a single purpose. The gods, in which he did not believe, or fortune, or fate or something else for which we have as yet no name somehow guards those who do own this thing. Portago knew what it was, as many men do not, he often spoke of it—"you must have the mental strength to concentrate absolutely . . ."—but he could not maintain it. Rather, he had not learned how to maintain it. Few do. Someone said of Fangio, "I can concentrate as well as he does, for one lap. But the old man can do it for three hours."

A wiser man than Portago might have stayed out of the Mille Miglia, even if the absence required an illness of convenience. He had not made even one practice circuit of the course, but he tried to outdrive men who could not remember how many dozens of times they had run it. Perhaps saddest of all, he overruled the Ferrari depot at Florence when he was urged to take two new rear tires for the run to Brescia. He said he could not spare the time, although Ferrari mechanics have changed two wheels in less than forty seconds.

But in a sense none of these things were mistakes, because Portago had no choice. There was no caution in him. A refusal to count odds was the essence of his nature. Usually he won, but he was intelligent and he knew that averages would almost certainly trip him ultimately. Knowing this, he still preferred to accept the hazard. That was his nature, the core of his being, and he could do nothing to alter it. Had he been cautious, we would never have heard of him. Portago's determination to take what he wanted out of the world, on his own terms and no matter what the price, present or potential, made him what he was: the absolutely free spirit.

"If I die tomorrow," he told me the day before Sebring, "still I have had twenty-eight wonderful years."

I cited to him the Spanish proverb, "In this life, take what you want—but pay for it."

"Of course," he said. "Of course, that's exactly it. You must pay. I remember someone who wrote about the British in the First World War, about the terrific mortality rate among young officers who had to lead bayonet charges against fixed machine guns, and most of them, or many of them, were aristocrats in those days. They had a life expectancy at the front of thirty days or something like that. And this man—he was a journalist, I can't remember his name—said, I remember, 'In war, the British aristocrats pay for the privileges they enjoy in peacetime.' You pay . . . you try to put it off, but you pay. I think, for my part at least, I think the game is worth the candle."

Portago was not a great racing driver, although it is certain that he would have been, had he lived. He was not an artist, he left nothing of beauty behind him and nothing of use to the world. He moved no mountains, wrote no books, bridged no rivers. He saved no lives, indeed he took innocents with him to death. He could be cruel. If he wished to indulge himself he would do it, though the act hurt and humiliated others who had done him no harm nor in any way earned his enmity.

Yet they had flinty hearts who did not mourn his death. At the least he was an adornment in the world, an excitement, a pillar of fire in the night, producing no useful heat or light, perhaps, but a glory to see nonetheless. At most he was an inspiration, for, with the mere instruments of his life set aside—the steeplechasing, the motor racing, wealth, women, world roaming—he stated again what cannot be too often stated: If anything at all is meant for us, we are meant to live life, there is no folly like the folly of the hermit who cowers in his cave, and a dead lion is a greater thing than a live mouse.

The accomplishments of the twenty-eight years of Don Alfonso Cabeza de Vaca y Leighton may make only a small monument for him, or none at all, but he knew what greatness knows, and we are the poorer for his going.

3 · The Incredible Nuvolari

TAZIO NUVOLARI, who died in Italy in 1953 with three decades of professional racing behind him, was almost certainly the greatest automobile driver who ever lived. Only the great Mercedes-Benz driver of the 1930's, Rudolph Caracciola, and the contemporary Juan Manuel Fangio can be mentioned in the same breath with him, and neither was the innovator that Nuvolari was.

Most of those who remember him—and everyone who ever saw him remembers him well—think that of all the peaks in the life that Tazio Nuvolari lived with such dash and *brio,* the 1935 Nürburg Ring race was the highest. Rated an also-ran because he was driving an outmoded Alfa-Romeo against two full teams of Mercedes-Benz and Auto-Union monsters, Nuvolari beat them all, driving a car that was incontrovertibly 15 miles an hour slower than the slowest of them. Actually he beat them twice: a disastrously clumsy refueling pit stop let cars that hadn't been able to keep him in sight get past him as he stood in the pits, so that he had to go out and catch them all over again.

It was an almost incredible performance, but I think that Nuvolari exceeded it twelve years later, in the first postwar Mille Miglia, a race that he did *not* win.

The truly great are so ranked by the rest of men because they react violently to the stacking of great odds against them. The also-rans, the little men, are beaten down by adversity, and we never hear of them; and many of the near-great might have been otherwise remembered if luck had thrown crushing force against them, or if they had had the will to look for challenge and overcome it. Nuvolari was happy when the odds were hopelessly high against him; he sought out such situations, and he was lucky enough, once or twice, to find them. The 1947 Mille Miglia was one.

The event itself was nearly postponed out of existence. The Mille Miglia had been run last in 1941, on a closed circuit, not over the road, and in some quarters there was small enthusiasm for running it again. Too, Italy had been bombed and fought over from end to end, the country was politically torn and its economy was in chaos. Gasoline was almost unobtainable and new tires brought $150 on the black market, when they could be found at all. Still the Brescia Automobile Club managed to get permission to close a thousand miles of road, from Brescia down the Adriatic coast to Fano, across to Rome, then up to Leghorn, Florence, Bologna and all the way to Turin in the north and back to Brescia through Milan. The government was persuaded to set aside 20,000 gallons of precious 80-octane gasoline, and Pirelli undertook to provide tires for 245 cars at $20 each. (Only 153 cars started; the other entrants took their tires and their gasoline and went away happy.)

Nuvolari was fifty-five in 1947, and he was a sick man. It was almost impossible for him to drive in circuit races because the exhaust fumes hanging in the air so irritated his respiratory tract that he would often hemorrhage. But he had won the Mille Miglia twice, in 1930 and again in 1933, and he wanted very much to win it a third time. He signed with the new firm of Cisitalia to drive an open two-seater running an 1100-cc engine. Piero Taruffi, who was to win the last Mille Miglia, the 1957 running, was on the same team. The Cisitalia was the hope of Italy in those days. The engine was basically FIAT, much worked up by Taruffi and Dusio, whose brain child Cisitalia was. The Mille Miglia version developed about 60 horsepower at 5,600 rpm and would show 120 miles an hour, given a little time to work up to it. The frame was made of light welded tubing and the body was stark.

The Mille Miglia is traditionally run in April or May, but the 1947 event was twice postponed and it was eight o'clock on the evening of the 21st of June when the first little FIAT 500 buzzed out of Brescia. The last car left at three next morning. Biondetti, with a 3-liter Alfa-Romeo, was the logical favorite, but it was for Nuvolari, who left an hour ahead of him, that the crowd screamed the loudest cheers and crowded farthest into the road. On form Biondetti certainly had the best chance: his car had 140 horsepower, and he was a seasoned specialist in over-the-road events, well able to use it.

When the cars came through the control at Padua, 100 miles out, three 1100-cc FIATS were leading, the first one, Gilera driving, posting an average of 83.1. By Pesaro, 250 miles from Brescia, the average was down to 72.6, Bassi's FIAT leading, and an Alfa second. Crossing the Italian peninsula from Pesaro to Rome, Nuvolari began to gain time. The country was mountainous, the roads narrow and winding; in this terrain the comparative lack of power to be beaten out of the small Cisitalia engine didn't matter so much as skill and the willingness to watch a wheel slide to within inches of the unfenced precipices, and Nuvolari began to pass everything in sight. The first car into Rome was a Lancia Aprilia, but it was well down in the ruck on elapsed time, and the loudspeaker announced that Nuvolari was now leading. He was 7 minutes ahead of Biondetti in the big Alfa-Romeo, he was 15 minutes ahead of the third man and 20 minutes ahead of the fourth. In Rome the drivers found pouring rain, and the weather worsened steadily from there on. One after another, leading cars began to go out: Cortese, driving a new Ferrari, blew a gasket; Villoresi burned out bearings on his new Maserati; Dusio and Taruffi of the Cisitalia team had both retired before Rome.

Running north to Florence along the coast, Nuvolari held much of the time advantage he had piled up before Rome. He needed it, for from Florence onward the roads were good, and comparatively straight, and torque and inches would tell. He came into Florence still leading the entire field: he had run 721 miles in 10 hours 13 minutes, an average just one-tenth under 70 miles an hour. Biondetti was within seconds of him now. The worst of the mountain roads were ahead, and the weather had become incredibly bad: rain was falling in sheets and in places the wind blasted it horizontally across the roads. Wind and thunderstorms had put down telephone wires along the route, and the drivers no longer knew their standings. At Asti, 958 miles out, Nuvolari was still leading. But the cars were now boring through a full tropical cloudburst, and the twisting roads, the up-hill-and-down terrain in which Nuvolari's unearthly skill outweighed the bigger engine of Biondetti's Alfa, were all behind him. Ahead lay the Turin-Milan-Brescia *autostrada,* flat and straight. On this last stretch, every advantage lay with Biondetti—not only because of the extra horsepower available to him, but because he was riding in a closed car. Nuvolari was sitting in a puddle and had been for hundreds of miles; the water sloshed around in the little Cisitalia as it would in a mobile bathtub. And the full brunt of the storm centered in the north, between Turin and Brescia. Some drivers, even veterans —Balestrero was one—pulled up and quit under trees, under bridges, anything to get out of the rain falling like lead. "I couldn't see six inches ahead of my windshield," one of them said. "It was like driving on the bottom of a lake."

Out of Turin, Nuvolari was 5 minutes behind Biondetti but somehow he held him on the autostrade, driving flat out, running on knowledge of the road, instinct and his incredibly fast reactions. But, nearing Milan, the engine was swamped and the magneto quit. Nuvolari and his co-driver, Carena, piled out and changed it. Holding a coat over the engine, working by feel in the howling blackness, it took them over 15 minutes to hook up the new magneto. They came into Brescia at 4:30 Sunday afternoon, 16 minutes and 4 seconds behind Biondetti after 16 hours of driving. Nuvolari stopped the car and slumped over the wheel. He could barely raise his head. They lifted him out of the car, carried him into a hotel and sent for a doctor. Giving away 80 horsepower and nearly two liters of engine, driving an open car through one of the worst storms in Italian history, he still would have won, or come within seconds of winning, had the Cisitalia's magneto held up. It may have been the greatest single drive in the history of automobile racing.

4 · The Wacky World of Motor Sport

IT WAS IN 1936, when I was laboring ten hours a day on the staff of a Massachusetts newspaper for a stipend which would not today tempt a high-school boy to cut a lawn, that I was first exposed to what the British motoring magazines refer to simply as The Sport. The publisher of our little gazette, a Harvard graduate of recent vintage, undertook to stage a road race in the town as a promotion device. To this end he summoned from Yale and Harvard, then the twin hubs of what little American road racing there was, a covey or pride of sports-car owners. They stormed into town the next week end, driving or towing their exotic machinery. Even the tow cars were extraordinary: I remember an immaculate 12-cylinder boat-tail Auburn roadster pulling an Alfa-Romeo.

The types in the drivers' seats were new to me. They were *sportif*, to say the least. They were of a race apart. They spoke only to each other, and in their native tongue: "I shouldn't turn that over five thou, old boy, the big-ends won't stand up to it." They treated their mounts like new-born children. I remember standing in one of the garages, mouth agape, as a Bugatti owner heated a gallon and a half of castor oil on a portable electric burner he had brought in his tow car. He had a candy thermometer in the reeking stuff, and he peered steadily at it. Just as it rose to the temperature he wanted—180° F, as I recall it—he snatched the instrument out, grabbed the kettle and turned to me to say, "Do stand aside, please. This oil mustn't cool before I get it into the engine." He had about three feet to cover before reaching the filler-pipe, and I marveled at his fear that the temperature of the oil would decline half a degree before he could decant it.

Alas, all was in vain: the city council forbade the race.

It must have been one of those same types whom I saw, about ten years later, standing outside the Time-Life building in New York. A brand-new MG idled at the curb, and the dashing *pilote,* pulling on a pair of pierced-back chamois driving gloves, was about to board it when one of the staring yokels (an MG would draw a crowd in New York in 1946) asked him what the letters stood for. [Morris Garages.]

"MG?" he drawled, affecting surprise. "Why, 'Mighty Good,' of course."

"Where can you buy one?" the fellow said.

"You can't *buy* one," he was told. "They're available only as gifts."

I encountered this gambit on other occasions. It was not uncommon. Alarmed at the growing interest of the peasants in their hobby, many sports-car owners consistently refused to divulge price or dealer's name. Their effort was in vain. Before long, sights to make the blood run cold in the veins of a founding member of the Automobile Racing Club of America were to be seen on New York City streets: a fellow driving an Invicta while wearing a fedora hat, for example. It was enough to make one reach for the hara-kiri knife.

The easiest target for snobbery was of course the Detroit automobile, and I contributed my share, and then some, to that movement. Detroit had it coming, though, in those years. The 1949 family sedans, for example, were not very good automobiles, and those of us who had access to the public prints denounced the men who made them in terms that might perhaps have been better reserved for wife-beaters and poor-box looters. Whether our strictures had anything to do with it I refuse to say, but Detroit automobiles *did* change. In 1949 anyone who could drive a little 54-horsepower MG with fair enterprise could run away and hide from a big Buick. Today, unless you're driving something very good indeed, you are best advised not to make faces even at a butcher's boy driving a Ford panel truck. He may very well blow you off—half a side of beef and fifty pounds of sausage in the back end notwithstanding. And if you are convincingly to rebuke the owner of a Chevrolet Corvette, you had best be mounted on an imported *bolide* in the $10,000-and-up category: say a Mercedes-Benz 300SL or a Ferrari America. Even so, you may not make it.

Yes, the time to sneer at Detroit is not now, and one of the surest marks of a new boy is a snide, "Oh, well, a Detroit car may *go,* but it won't handle, you know. You'll kill yourself in a bend with it." Not many of us drive well enough to take, say, a Plymouth Fury to the point where it will break loose in a gentle bend. The present American cars handle, all right. If you're skeptical, go out on a parkway some six o'clock in the morning and run past the first state trooper you see. He'll convince you.

Most of the attitudes that comprise the sports-car *mystique* were imported from Britain. One of them has it that the owner of an open car must never, never put the top up in anything short of a blizzard or a full gale. I knew one such type who gave his wife two black eyes in observance of this convention. It wasn't that he struck her. He just drove two hundred and fifty miles on a cold autumn day with the top down *and* the windshield folded flat. The wind-buffeting blacked her eyes—or so he told me with much amusement. She was a long-suffering girl. It was her husband's custom, of a Sunday, to polish his car. It glistened like cut glass when he began, but there were always little things to do, like running melted wax under the rubber strips on the running board to guard against corrosion. His wife's assigned task was to polish the engine, using a small cork dipped in a mixture of metal-polish and abrasive, applying it with a nicely controlled twist of the wrist. It didn't usually take her more than four hours to do the whole engine.

Indeed, there were some odd types in The Sport. I have seen a man mumble and flush when it was pointed out to him that he had wrongly placed his left leg in entering a vintage racing car. Poor fellow, he had thought the idea was to squirm into the narrow seat in whatever way was effective, when what he had done was equivalent to mounting a horse on the off-side. A man of genuine *sang-froid* would have carried it off, saying something like, "That's all very well for the 3½-liter, old boy, but *this* is a 4-liter."

I remember seeing this ploy effectively implemented by an Englishman who came into a filling station driving a friend's Alfa-Romeo. It was a racing model, and most Alfa racing types had the accelerator mounted between the clutch and brake pedals instead of to one side. The car came into the station very fast and, just when it should have braked, the engine howled and it leaped forward. The driver managed, just, to stop it six inches short of a brick wall. As he jumped out he said to the owner, standing by, white and shaking, "You ought to have a look at that throttle return-spring, old boy." It was perfectly obvious that he had stepped on the gas thinking it was the brake pedal, but no one accused him of the *gaffe*.

As amusing as anything else in the wacky world of motor sport, if one can maintain detachment, is the convention that everyone —well, very nearly everyone—who owns a sports car and is a member of an accepted club is an altogether splendid fellow. I have heard some notable nonsense spouted to state the point. It is a fallacy, of course, common to all special-interest groups. I remember how hurt were the members of a crossbow club when one of the members axed his father. "But he was *one* of us," they said. "He was a Guildsman." The phenomenon doesn't appear with as much strength in The Sport now as it did, say, ten years ago, when sports-car people felt themselves a minority under siege by the barbarians, and needed to reassure each other that there were no fifth columnists within the fort. So-and-so might be a louse who would sell you a car that had been twice around the world, the hard way, and swear that the 5,469 miles on the odometer represented, to his certain knowledge, every foot it had run since it left the factory, but as long as the Better Business Bureau didn't cite him as a thief and a monster, no one else would mention his little failings. Such and such might be an anti-Semite and a thing that would steal money from its own mother, but as long as he was publicly opposed to Detroit Iron, the man-eating shark, and Professionalism in the Club, he'd get along —and the one I'm thinking of did.

Competition drivers of this nice-nelly persuasion could be seen on the circuits saluting each other like knights in tourney, and anyone who really went in and disputed a corner soon learned, by noting the coolness with which he was afterward received, that he had done something Horrid. I heard one such told that he should not, after all, old boy, act like a dirt-track driver. (It was widely held at this time, and indeed right up to July, 1959, that track drivers, and track cars, were unworthy of mention in the same breath with pukka sports or Grand Prix cars and the chauffeurs thereof. But in the month cited, Rodger Ward, an Indianapolis winner who has driven on everything but slate roofs, ran an Offenhauser midget against a field of quite good sports cars, and one *monoposto* G.P., at Lime Rock, and beat them all two tries out of three. The shock was profound, and the rafters rang with it for months.)

For a long time the attitude toward professionalism of the Sports Car Club of America, the biggest in the country, resembled that of the lawn-tennis czars. If a race promoter said, out of the corner of his mouth, that he'd give you fifty dollars toward replacing the tires you'd wear down in his event, and you got caught taking it, you could be sure that you'd have your club pin ripped off and your steering wheel broken over your head. Meanwhile, there were drivers who knew not harassment, but were heaped with honors, who were making very good salaries for driving sports cars and who had every appurtenance of professionalism known to locomotive engineers except membership in a union. Everyone knew who they were, but it wasn't considered polite to say anything about it. They were nice fellows for the most part and the men who hired them were nice fellows for the most part. It was hard to think of them as doing anything wrong, since the anti-professionalism rule was so obviously idiotic. Presently, the SCCA allows limited professionalism.

An offense which might be called Disrespect for the Machinery was also frowned upon, and still is by new boys. I knew a driver whose habitually contemptuous term for his own or others' cars contributed to his unpopularity. He called them "lumps," and he was never seen to roll his eyeballs while comparing an Italian supercharger housing with sculpture of Praxiteles' time. This earned him black marks, and he never did achieve entry into the inner circle, granted he offended the ruling powers in other ways. He was an amusing man, intelligent, a superior driver in the early days and a kindly fellow when the mood was on him, but he had no more control over his temper than he had over the tide levels in the Bay of Fundy. He liked to say what he thought at the instant it occurred to him and his vocabulary was rich in four-letter words and novel permutations of them. Portago's contempt for Fine Machinery was held against him by some, and I remember the shock with which someone told of having heard Phil Walters asked what kind of car he would like best for a long trip. Walters, an ex-midget chauffeur, drove on the Briggs Cunningham team and he was for years probably the best road-circuit driver in America. His starry-eyed questioners, expecting that he would cite some exotic, fussy, hard-sprung, gear-howling European model, were nonplussed when he said, "An air-conditioned Cadillac, what else?"

Walters, who isn't active any more, was in my view the most rewarding American driver to watch. He had all the technical equipment in abundance, but so had others; Walters had more than that. He was incredibly smooth, easy, unruffled. He looked mildly about him with an air of bland composure, but he was brutally competitive. His strong sense of humor often showed through his driving. Once at Watkins Glen he came down the straight past the pits behind a driver notorious for his disinclination to go really fast. The man was making elaborate signs in explanation of the various mechanical faults he claimed were preventing his car from running properly, signs ostensibly to his pit-crew but actually for the benefit of the crowd. Just before he pulled over and blasted past, Walters made a sign too: he held up the little finger of his right hand. I remember a hot day on another course when he came through a rough S-bend which other drivers were treating with great respect. He was driving with his left hand and holding a Coke to his lips with his right. It would have been bravado in someone else; in Walters it meant that he was thirsty.

It was interesting to watch Walters with Bill Frick beside one. Frick, a superior mechanic and a good driver in his own right until an accident severed a muscle in one of his arms, could predict Walters' every move. Together they had campaigned midgets and stock cars for years when Walters was known as "Ted Tappet" and they made so formidable a team that promoters used to pay them off for first place before a race now and again, on condition they'd take second or third; it was monotonous for the customers to see Tappet win all the time.

Frick is a unique personality. He is a free spirit. "Who needs you?" is a phrase that comes readily to his lips. He combines a short temper and a low boiling point with consideration and remarkable politesse, a rare combination. He is a remarkably gifted mechanic, I suppose one of the six best in the country. I once took him a Grand Prix Bugatti engine in a basket and, although he loathed that particular type of engine, he set it up so perfectly that the car broke a course record for its class *five years later,* without another mechanic having laid a wrench on it since the day it had left Frick's shop in Rockville Centre.

I can't go on indefinitely about Frick just because I am fond of him, and anyway the two best Frick stories I know are unprintable; one because it involves the construction of a mechanical device so fiendish in purpose that it must be kept from the general public, and the other because it's just unprintable, although Willy's role in the incident, I hasten to say, was above impeachment. I will, however, in closing, state Frick's Law: All You Need Is the Money.

I remember so many amusing things from the wacky world of

the motor sport, and I would like to get them all down—but it would take two hundred pages—and forget them and stop writing about automobiles. The walls of my house sag under the weight of the literature. I no longer subscribe to twenty motoring magazines a month, but even so they accumulate, and last year I threw away twelve hundred pounds of back issues. I would like to burn my clipping files, and try to forget why the bumpers of the only automobile ever represented on a coin—a Chinese *yuan* of Kweichow Province—are wrapped in burlap. It is not necessary to know that, or to know that it was a Viennese janitor who cranked the engine of Siegfried Marcus' car when it made its historic run in 1865, or that the first automobile to do sixty miles an hour was an electric called "*La Jamais Contente.*"

I did burn the only copy of a speech written to be delivered at a sports-car club meeting years ago, but I remember the first few lines and I would just as soon not. The speech was to be in answer to another, prior knowledge of which I had been given. I thought it was an outrageous speech, and much of it was an attack on a man I considered unassailable. I spent a night writing a reply, thirty minutes of invective. It began: "Mr. —— has delivered himself of an address so full of heat, so barren of light, and so irresponsible in content that I think it must constitute an argument in favor of atheism: a righteous deity would have struck him dead. However, he and his colleagues on the rostrum appeared well pleased with it, to judge from their attitudes as I see them now. But then, they are a strange lot, to put the matter in a kindly way. I am reminded, looking at them, of a line from the film 'Nothing Sacred.' A man is speaking of a group of people for whom he has little liking, and he says, 'The Hand of Almighty God, reaching down into the mire, couldn't elevate one of them to the depths of degradation.' "

That was how the speech began. Further on, it got rough. I showed it to the one other person most nearly concerned, and while he said that he didn't think it was his right to ask me not to give it, still he believed that it would turn the meeting, a big one, into a donnybrook, with chairs flying through the air, and that he doubted the club would recover in ten years, if ever, from the schism it would institute. So I took the negative decision, which pained me because it required me to stand still and get my brains knocked out. Perhaps it was the right thing to do. I'm still not quite sure.

I remember pleasanter things, the first two races at Watkins Glen, for example, over the original course running down the main street of the village. It was an insanely dangerous course in the light of what we now know about safety precautions, but no one realized it then. Everyone enjoyed himself hugely, and in the dusk we sat on the lawn of the Fontainbleu, looking down to the purple lake through the still air, and tried to think of a good reason for leaving.

I remember the look on the face of a man who had put an automatic transmission into a Cadillac-Allard and had had it select reverse gear, quite by itself, while he was motoring toward the racecourse at 40 miles an hour to try it out at midnight. He leaned against the car after it had been hauled back on the road and tried not to think of his fate had the malfunction occurred ten minutes later, at 120 miles an hour. And the time a wild-eyed driver, two hundred pounds and berserk, held another driver against a garage wall by the throat, screaming that he would kill him, while his friend, a much smaller man, stroked the back of his head as he would a puppy's and said over and over, "Now, now, Pete, now, now," until he finally let go and went away, still white with rage. And the night at Sebring when Piero Taruffi, who must have been fifty then, pushed a stalled Lancia a terrible distance over the circuit and into the pits—at a fast dogtrot. The effort should have killed him, but they picked him up off the cement and in a little while he was talking.

I remember another day on the Sebring circuit, in a little French car a friend had been asked to try out. It had a five-speed gearbox and an engine about as big as a 12-volt battery, and my friend sat there, his foot flat on the floor, shifting gears interminably, and shrieking, with every shift, "So, go! So commence, you little son-of-a-bitch!" He was trying to catch a two-seater sports car ahead of us, an impossible proposition, but he managed it, by refusing to brake for a corner until disaster was staring us dead in the eye.

I remember standing in a cold rain in a Norwalk freight yard and staring in sick fascination at the rotting wreck of a T-head Mercer Raceabout I had bought sight unseen and listening incredulously as Connie Lofink, a specialist mechanic on old cars, said, "I think it's the best one I ever saw in my life." We restored it completely and I enjoyed it hugely before I sold it, like an idiot, and to the wrong man, at that.

And the night I was sitting in a Grand Prix Bugatti at 70 or 75 miles an hour and suddenly it came to me that I didn't know where I was or which way the road went or even if I was on a road at all, and I didn't care; the sensation seemed to be that of free flight, and I reached over and shut off the headlights and went on through the darkness for a long time, through what seemed endless tree-shrouded countryside, until the delight changed suddenly into terror. And the quiet pleasures of Le Gourmet on 55th Street in New York when Rene and Maurice Dreyfus had it, and Le Chanteclair now, and Bobby Said's incredible menage in Pound Ridge, with the four-people bathtub and the cheetah, big as a great Dane, stalking around the barroom downstairs, muttering to herself and stopping now and then to glare through the window at the puma and the ocelot on the screened porch. Stirling Moss was there for breakfast one Sunday on his way home from Venezuela and we spent a long time trying to decide how many troy ounces of gold were in the trophy he'd won, and how much it was worth in pounds sterling. A good deal: it was uncomfortable to hold in one hand. A huge parrot, hanging upside down in the cage built into the living-room wall glared at us with his button-bright eye and cackled, "Where's Charley? Where's Charley?"

That was a bright and sunny morning and we sat on the high porch and looked at the lake with its tiny island. On the lawn, the cheetah, tethered, calculated the length of its leash and suddenly uncoiled in a savage rush for a snooping dog. Alas, she was a foot short and could only glare after him as he howled away.

Louise King was there that morning. Bobby would introduce her to Peter Collins some time later, in Miami. Charlene Said was there, and Hans Tanner and Tony Morewood. Hans is in Italy as I write this, Tony Morewood and Louise Collins in England, Charlene in New York, Bobby in Siam, Stirling in Nassau. There are no Ferraris or Maseratis or Porsches in the garage and the fenced acre where the cats used to disappear behind rocks no bigger than their heads, to rush in mock savagery at Charlene, come to exercise them, is empty. The cheetah, I suppose, is dead.

5 · The Spectacle at Sebring

THERE ARE only two American automobile races sanctioned by the world-governing body of the sport, The Federation Internationale de l'Automobile, and listed as events carrying world championship points. One is the annual Five-Hundred-Mile race in Indianapolis, established in 1911 and run almost every year since. The other is the Sebring Twelve-Hour race, formally the Grand Prix of Endurance for the Amoco Trophy.

Indianapolis is a metropolis, long associated with automobile activity, situated in the center of the country. It's a logical site for a big race. Sebring, population under 10,000, is hidden away in south-central Florida, inaccessible even by feeder air line. In 1950 it was notable only as the seat of Highland County. Last year reporters representing Argentinian, American, British, Belgian, Cuban, French, German, Italian, Mexican, Swedish and Swiss publications covered the race, and automobiles jammed into the town carried the license plates of almost every state in the union except Alaska and Hawaii.

For thousands of American sports-car buffs the annual pilgrimage to the little Florida town is as regular as Christmas, and, in the minds of many Europeans, Sebring crowds New York,

Chicago and Hollywood on the list of well-known American place names. Says Baron Huschke von Hanstein, manager of the German Porsche team: "We have at least five first-rate European drivers ask us to bring them for every seat in our entry."

Ten days before the date of the race, usually the third Saturday in March, the men and women who will drive the sixty-five starting cars begin to drift into Sebring. The big factory teams, such as Ferrari of Italy, come in force, led by the team racing manager and a senior engineer. They may bring three $25,000 automobiles, built purposely for this race, dozens of crates of spares, scores of tires. There'll be six drivers, among the best in the world, and a crew of mechanics expert enough to change two wheels in forty seconds or replace a faulty fuel pump in seven minutes.

Other entrants will arrive with one car, a box of tools, a sleeping bag and just enough money for one thin meal a day. Rich or poor, their pattern of behavior will be the same: work on the car, drive it to the 5.2-mile circuit, try it out, bring it back, work on it some more, try it again, sleep a little, work some more. Ten minutes before the start on Saturday, with the cars lined up at 45-degree angles to the course, one or two cars may have wan-looking, red-eyed mechanics still desperately tinkering with them almost to the instant the starter's count booms down over the PA system, "ten, nine, eight, seven . . ." and the drivers, standing on their painted crosses on the far side of the roadway, spring to jump in, punch the starter buttons and get away.

A Sebring start is the most exciting spectacle in American sport, duplicated in drama in only one other place in the world, Le Mans, France, where the system originated. Instead of starting off in evenly spaced rows as at Indianapolis, the cars come out in a roaring high-speed traffic jam, nose-to-tail, wheel-to-wheel. They are parked in gear, and the first car away will be the one whose helmeted driver is the fastest sprinter and quickest to throw himself into the seat, depress the clutch, hit the starter button and jam his foot onto the accelerator. However fast he is, the other sixty-four will be only split seconds slower, and as the howling mass of cars funnels under the Amoco Bridge in front of the grandstand, the onlooker inevitably believes that he is about to see the biggest accident in history. But somehow the cars get through, rarely even touching one another, to disappear around the first bend, and four minutes or so later the growing scream of a single engine announces the appearance of the leader, the field strung out for a mile behind him.

For the next twelve hours, until ten o'clock at night, in bright sunshine or tropical rainfall, the cars will boom around the twisting 5.2 miles of concrete and blacktop. By that time the winning car may have covered 1000 miles, in the course of which 2500 brake applications and 3500 gearshifts will have been made, every one of them timed to a half-second. The winning driver's hands may be blistered, his leg and shoulder muscles jumping with fatigue spasms, his nerves so taut that despite exhaustion it will be hard for him to sleep when he finally finds his way to bed. His monetary reward may be $5000 or a little more, to be split with his co-driver and the owner of the car. But his sense of accomplishment will be enormous and because of Sebring's unique place in American auto racing, his gain in reputation will be great.

The Sebring race had its beginning in 1950 when Sam and Miles Collier of Florida, chief architects of the postwar sports-car-racing revival, decided that the 2300-acre wartime B-17 field would make an ideal site for a distance race. An ex-USAAF officer, Colonel Claude D. Richardson of Sebring, persuaded the Sebring Firemen, a volunteer organization, to sponsor the event. Alec Ulmann of New York, an aircraft industry consultant and a long-time automobile enthusiast, entered the picture when he came to Sebring to do business with Richardson. Ulmann has for some years now been the sole promoter of the event and it was he who persuaded the F.I.A. to add Sebring to the list of races counting toward the world sports-car championship.

There are two championships in international automobile racing, neither of which has ever been held by an American. The sports-car championship is a manufacturer's championship and is based, in 1959, on points to be competed for at Sebring; the Targa Florio road race in Sicily, May 24; the 1000-kilometer race at the Nürburg Ring in Germany, June 7; the Twenty-Four Hours of Le Mans, France, June 20–21; the Tourist Trophy, Great Britain, September 5; and the Grand Prix of Venezuela, November 8. The cars used in these races may be of varying engine sizes: the smallest of motorcycle dimensions, the largest half as big as a Buick; and they must be road-equipped: lights, spare tire, doors, starter and so on.

The drivers' championship is contested in single-seat full racing cars currently held by international agreement to 2,500 cubic centimeters engine capacity (less than half the size of a Ford, although the cars will do 180 miles an hour) and run in races of approximately 200 miles designated as the Grand Prix of the host country: Grand Prix of Belgium, Grand Prix of Italy, and so on, with the Grand Prix of Europe held every year in a different country. These races are generally termed Grandes Epreuves and as a rule no country can have more than one. The American Grande Epreuve is Indianapolis, but this is a courtesy listing, since the Indianapolis authorities allow big engines which do not conform to the international formula used by the rest of the world. A Grand Prix of the United States of America was run on the Sebring circuit on December 12, 1959, the first time Grand Prix cars have run in the United States since 1937, and this year, for the first time, an American driver, Phil Hill of California, was in serious contention for the title. The 1958 champion, Mike Hawthorn of England, was killed in a road accident, and the previous champion, Juan Manuel Fangio of Argentina, retired after winning the title five times.

In February of 1957 *The Wall Street Journal* said that automobile racing had become the biggest American spectator sport, and it is the revival of road racing, as distinct from track racing, that has made it so. This is no new thing: the biggest crowds ever brought together for sporting events in this country used to watch the old pre-First World War Vanderbilt Cup races on Long Island—crowds as big as 500,000. These were road races in the classic traditions of Europe, where the automobile and automobile racing had their beginnings. William H. Smyth, chairman of the U.S. Auto Club's road-racing division, thinks it likely that

American road racing will attain a comparable scale within a few years.

In the period between the wars the American automobile changed from an exotic plaything into a commonplace convenience, and racing was restricted to dirt and board tracks. Abroad, the road race remained paramount. Europeans consider track racing to be a bore for drivers and spectators alike. They argue that the merry-go-round pursuit race of identical machines offers little opportunity for the full expression of driving skill, and they believe that the racing automobile should be run in its natural environment, the standard two-lane road. European courses are laid out with right- and left-hand bends and curves of varying severity; they run up and down hill and dale, and even a torrential downpour of rain will not stop an important event; competent drivers are expected to be able to go just as fast on a slippery, rain-soaked road as they are on a dry one. Some, like the legendary Rudolf Caracciola, who drove for Mercedes-Benz, or the Englishman Stirling Moss, currently the world's greatest driver, have run even faster in the rain.

Part of Sebring's fascination lies in its adherence to these conditions. There are seven sharp corners in the 5.2 miles of the Sebring circuit, and five curves, or bends. One of the bends can be taken at around 110 miles an hour; one of the corners can be negotiated at no more than 35; on one straightaway, 140 miles an hour can be reached. Thus the drivers must almost constantly brake, shift, adjust the speed and balance of their cars, and it is in this area that driving skill shows itself. The skill required to drive really fast on such a course is of so high an order that the present list of officially designated "International" drivers numbers only sixteen men, and of these perhaps only six are capable of extending a big car to its absolute limit in reasonable security.

Because sports-car road racing is done in two-seater automobiles, most of which are suitable for ordinary touring use, and on circuits that at least superficially resemble regular highways, its spectator appeal is most compelling. It's easy for the onlooker vicariously to identify himself with the driver. Police expect their catch of speeders to rise in the hours immediately before and after a race as a Walter Mitty-like transference convinces the ordinary driver that his skill is greater than he knew. It is not, of course. Only the most knowledgeable of spectators at a road race even begin to comprehend the level of skill attained by top-ranked drivers. Indeed, some drivers operate in such heights of virtuosity that only the most expert of their peers can understand what they are doing, while conceding the impossibility of imitation. Tazio Nuvolari, an Italian who is acknowledged to have been the greatest driver who ever lived, was such a one. So was Juan Manuel Fangio, and so is Stirling Moss.

The essence of really fast driving is the "drift" or four-wheel slide. A drift is not a skid, a slide by either the front or the rear wheels alone. In a drift all four wheels slide more or less equally. A Grand Prix driver drifts all gentle or "fast" bends, rather than attempting to drive the car around them with the rear wheels tracking those in front. The drift is faster. The driver provokes it deliberately, turning the steering wheel to point the car off the road on the inside of the bend, and perhaps jabbing the brake pedal to break rear-wheel traction with the road surface. He thereafter steers with the accelerator pedal: more accelerator will increase the angle of drift by spinning the rear wheels, thus lessening their grip on the road so that centrifugal force will move the rear of the car outward; less accelerator, by allowing traction to increase, will move the rear wheels closer into line with the front wheels. Since to drift a car is to balance it on the edge of control loss, the maneuver is delicate and dangerous. Still, all really fast driving is done on the very limit of road adhesion. Richard Seaman, a first-rank driver in the late 1930's, put it best when he said that to drive a 600-horsepower car on dry concrete produced exactly the same sensation as driving a fast passenger car on a frozen lake.

To drive in this fashion and live, it is desirable to have the characteristics shared by many Grand Prix drivers: motor reactions about three times faster than average; abnormally acute vision, and an almost freakish sense of spatial relationship which allows a driver always to know exactly what his attitude is, which way he is pointing. This latter ability has the effect of slowing the passage of time.

Not many of the 120-odd drivers who competed at Sebring last year have gifts of that order. Those who have it are instantly identifiable once the field has sorted itself out: the Americans Phil Hill, John Fitch, Carroll Shelby; Jean Behra of France; the Britons Stirling Moss, Roy Salvadori; Olivier Gendebien of Belgium; Joakim Bonnier of Sweden; Wolfgang von Trips of Germany.

From the extraordinary ability of these men the level descends to drivers who are best advised to go slowly and take no chances. In no other race is there such disparity of skills as is displayed at Sebring. David Ash of New York, who has started and finished more races at Sebring than anyone else, has said, "There is probably no other American race in which absolute concentration is so important. Sebring is highway driving raised to the nth power: in addition to handling your own car you must constantly anticipate what drivers of differing abilities will do with theirs." Some American drivers compete almost nowhere else the year around and while they can stay out of the way as long as no extraordinary reactions are demanded of them, their behavior in emergency is often a cross for the top-line pilots to bear. This range of driving ability, combined with the mixing of cars with a top speed as low as 100 miles an hour with those capable of 160, producing a constant, fast traffic-jam situation in the early hours, makes Sebring unique among all U.S. races.

For all its apparent danger, only two drivers have been killed at Sebring in the nine years of the race. A driver was killed in 1956 in an Arnolt-Bristol when he "lost" his automobile in the tricky S bends which come just after the cars have left the wide airport runways for the narrow blacktop road, and a driver died in night practice for the 1959 running when he apparently forgot where he was on the circuit and ran his very fast Maserati straight through a hairpin corner.

Few of the thousands who pour into Sebring every March would admit to thinking of the possibility of disaster. They drive into town keen with the sense of carnival and reunion. Sebring greets them in no special way. It's a sleepy little town, its main business street divided into two sections by a tree-lined circular park. At one end of the business district is the Sebring Hotel, a typical commercial house, its lobby balcony the race press headquarters and drivers' information center, rarely empty from eight a.m. to midnight during the week of the race. Past the Sebring, a few blocks of palm-lined street finds Kenilworth Lodge, a shiny white resort hotel belted with a huge old-fashioned verandah. Hard left around the Kenilworth is the road to the circuit, six miles distant.

A ride around the Sebring circuit begins in front of the main grandstand and the concrete pit structures. The car whips under the Amoco Bridge, one of three offering access to the infield, and appears to be headed straight for the grass of the airport. It drifts along the line of luminescent cone markers through a left-hand bend, then a 925-foot straight, another left-hand bend, a short straight of 580 feet, a right-angle left-hand corner on to the blacktop road, a thousand feet of straight into the lurching S's under the MG Bridge, then a long fast bend and a short straight marked with signs indicating 400, 300, 200 and 100 yards before a hairpin corner. From a speed of 100 mph or so the car is dragged down to 35 as the brakes squeal under heavy applications and the engine howls through the gears.

Around the hairpin, the driver is flattened in his seat by acceleration through a 3625-foot straight before more braking and gearshifting take the car through right- and left-hand corners on to two short straights connected by a bend, and a right-angle to the main runway, nearly a mile long. A right-angle turn leads into another wide runway, 3890 feet of it, then a horseshoe turn around the timing building—where during the race one timing expert for each car will clock its passage—under the Martini-Rossi vehicular bridge and down the pit straight again. The fastest the lap has ever been done was in the 1958 race when Stirling Moss took an Aston Martin around in 3 minutes 20 seconds, an average speed of 93.6 miles per hour. An ordinarily competent driver, alone on the course in a standard passenger car, might hope to get around in 6 minutes, an average of 52 mph.

The quick trip around the circuit is the order of the day for the Sebring visitor—after he's found a place to sleep. The town's five hotels cannot begin to handle the influx, and motels fifty miles away are likely to be booked solidly. Between five hundred and seven hundred Sebring householders rent rooms on a fixed price schedule. A few of them no longer collect the room rent: the same visitors have been coming for so long that they're received as friends. The two biggest hotels, Kenilworth Lodge and Harder Hall, are resort houses on the American plan with prices up to a stiff forty dollars a day, and they are usually fully reserved well in advance. There will be half a dozen big cocktail parties given in the two or three days just before the race, notable mostly for restrained drinking and the presence of remarkably attractive women. The Race Ball on Thursday night, marked by the crowning of a Race Queen and similar folderol, is a subway jam set to very loud music. Comparatively few of the drivers have time or inclination for much merrymaking. Those attached to the big teams are concerned with getting the maximum amount of practice; the others are trying to make their automobiles run as they should.

One of the smallest cars at Sebring last year was a Turner powered by an Austin A-35 engine and entered by Fred Lieb, a technician at the Huntsville, Alabama, missile base. Lieb left Huntsville on the Tuesday before the race, first borrowing a trailer for the car and making a tow bar for it. He drove all night Tuesday through a pouring rain, arrived in Sebring Wednesday at three in the afternoon. His was a reserve entry, good only if another car was dropped, and he had no garage facilities assigned to him. He prepared the car—it's the one he drives to work every day—in a citrus grove near Lake Wales, thirty miles from Sebring. A kindhearted Negro truck mechanic stayed up half the night to help him, the work including such Draconian measures as pouring fuller's earth into the clutch to stop its tendency to slip. He had no place in the race until eleven o'clock Friday night, when he was given the spot vacated by the Maserati crash, but when Honorary Starter James Melton dropped the flag at ten o'clock Saturday morning, the little car was ready to go. Lieb was ready too, and in good shape for a man who'd had very little sleep for four nights, nor much but sandwiches to eat. His co-driver was one of the three women in the race, Miss Sierra ("Smoky") Drolet. The Turner astonished no one by its performance, but Lieb and Miss Drolet finished the race in forty-third positon, beating out five bigger cars, and running 665.6 miles to do it. (The overall winner, the Hill-Gendebien Ferrari, ran 312 miles farther in the same time.) Lieb and his pit crew of devoted friends won nothing, of course; they had packed up and were long on their way home when the prize-giving ceremony began on Sunday morning, but they had had an enormous amount of fun, and they had tasted the indefinable risk-flavored magic of flat-out motor racing.

In point of fact, motor racing is not nearly as dangerous as it appears to be, and most drivers consider that competition with their peers is not as risky as normal highway travel. Because they are spectacular, racing accidents receive disproportionate publicity, but in a year that may see the deaths of ten drivers, four or five hundred mountain climbers will die, and water sports will take as many as 6500.

Every night of the week preceding the race, Sebring is loud with the exhausts of drivers eager to show their acquaintance with the *mystique* by blipping their engines busily while waiting for traffic to clear, by double-clutching down-shifts for corners, and by parading the main street at 15 miles an hour in second gear. Now and then, around midnight, someone will really try, and insomniacs in the Kenilworth will hear the high scream of a small engine wound out, sometimes followed by the slower rumble of a police car in hot pursuit. Early in the morning of race day you can see the real thing: the green British cars, the silver Germans, the blood-red Italians on their way to the circuit, driven by tired mechanics, who always seem to be small men. These blip the engines up and down because they must: the cars are supposed to be sports cars, suitable for over-the-road driving, but the factory teams, from which the winner will come, enter machines that are really two-seater Grand Prix automobiles, running ferociously powerful, highly tuned engines that will boil the radiators or foul out plugs if allowed to idle. They are designed to run efficiently only one way: flat out.

Mixed in with the genuine factory cars are the others, the cars entered by a factory and sold to private owners who, in effect, buy with the automobile an entry they could not otherwise get, and the privately owned cars of many makes, Morgan, Porsche, Stanguellini, Ferrari, MG, Lancia, Alfa-Romeo, Austin-Healey, all carrying the badges of the competitor: white racing number, taped headlight lenses, wheels stripped of hubcaps. An American car has won only once at Sebring: a Cunningham, in 1953, driven by Phil Walters and John Fitch. The car was one of those built by Briggs Cunningham of Connecticut primarily to compete in the Le Mans, France, Twenty-Four-Hour race. In 1957 Chevrolet entered a team of Corvettes under the leadership of Fitch, an international driver and the only American ever to be a member of the Mercedes-Benz team. One of the Corvettes was a special high-performance design. It did not finish the race, won that year by a Maserati.

The procession to the circuit starts before seven, and by eight has reached full density as cars carrying 25,000 spectators join in. Delay is rare: state police, auxiliaries and volunteers funnel the cars into the circuit as fast as the three-dollar tickets can be grabbed by the gatekeepers. Most of them park within the grounds, but outside the circuit, in the carnival atmosphere of exhibits and hot-dog and orange-juice stands, all of them run not by professionals but by Sebring civic groups whose one-day profits almost suffice to support their projects the year around. Bank deposits in the town rise $1,000,000 to $1,500,000 during race week.

A track crossover and an incredibly steep vehicular bridge take five or six hundred people into the ten-dollar-admission paddock area behind the pits. Perhaps seventy-five will spend one hundred dollars to headquarter for the day in the pavilion of the Automobile Racing Club of Florida, an organization set up by Ulmann to sponsor the race. Choice food and liquors will be served to them throughout the twelve hours of the race. The night before, others will have hauled in trailers big enough to be called mobile homes, air-conditioned, stocked with food, fitted out with canopied roof-top observation platforms. Some will fly in: as many as four hundred aircraft may land at the Sebring Air Terminal during the week end, and in 1958 the field registered eighty-four landings in one hour. Most of the paddock ticket holders base themselves on their parked cars, eating box lunches put up by the hotels, or sandwiches, hot dogs and plate dinners sold in the enclosure. They spend much of the race period on their feet, walking inside the circuit from corner to corner. The corners are the places to see drivers at work. At the big horseshoe turn, for example, one can safely stand close enough to the cars to see how much faster the rear wheels turn under acceleration than the front ones; the less skillful the driver, the greater the difference. When Juan Manuel Fangio won in 1957 he was consistently faster through this turn than anyone else, but despite the tremendous excess power of his car, the biggest-engined in the race, his rear wheels spun very little.

Track drivers are inclined to sneer at such niceties, arguing that a winning driver should stick his foot into the firewall and steer; they are apt to consider road-race drivers "gentlemen amateurs" and their mounts "sporty-cars." The Grand Prix drivers, on the other hand, think of the track experts as brave men of limited skill, like tightrope walkers. In point of fact, the two groups practice different but allied trades, like jockeys who ride steeplechase and flat races. The Grand Prix driver has a heavier armament of skills only because he has had to acquire them to survive. The use of brakes is a near-science with some G.P. drivers, for example, but Indianapolis drivers use the brakes only in emergency or when they come into the pits.

Each kind of driver is superior on his home grounds. One Indianapolis winner who publicly derided Fangio's ability found, when he competed at Sebring, that he couldn't keep the Argentinian in sight, couldn't even stay on the same lap with him. The best an Indianapolis winner has done at Sebring is to place third. The late Bob Sweikert, Indy winner in 1955, did that, co-driving with an experienced road racer, and having asked Fangio if he might ride with him for coaching during practice. In 1957 and

'58 a 500-mile race for both kinds of drivers was run at the Monza circuit in Italy and both times the Americans won overwhelmingly. The Monza trials were not considered conclusive, however, because the cars were not evenly matched in engine capacity; the European cars were designed for road-circuit use and because the race was run strictly under Indianapolis conditions: counterclockwise on a banked track (Indianapolis cars will not take a right-hand corner, being weighted on the left side), the race to be stopped in case of rain, and so on.

The 1959 Sebring running deeply discouraged drivers unused to running in the rain. Rain fell almost every day before the race. The circuit was dry on Saturday morning when sixty-four cars snarled away from their starting positions. (The sixty-fifth got under way a minute or so later.) But in midafternoon a gentle rain began and shortly grew into a typical Florida pelter. The blacktop section of the circuit, normally crowned, was slippery but puddle-free; the flat runway sections developed standing ponds, some of them two or three inches deep. Cars boring through this water threw speedboat rooster-tails and the driver of a car close behind often had to choose between slowing up or driving in a steady waterfall.

Denise McCluggage, probably the best American woman driver, handling a 750-cc Osca with Isabell and Alessandro de Tomaso, wrote about it later in the New York *Herald Tribune:* "In the wet, after the rains collect, it's a lake. The car hits it and planes—going forward completely sideways perhaps, riding on the water, not touching the pavement at all. Then it slows enough to break through the sheet of water, touch pavement again, get a grip—you hope before leaving the road—and send you off in the right direction . . . the puddles tug the wheels this way then that, the back wheels alternately buzz in the water, then grip the pavement. . . ."

The race turned into a Ferrari and Porsche procession after mechanical failure and disqualification forced the British Aston Martin and Lister-Jaguar entries out, the Italian cars finishing first and second, the Germans third, fourth and fifth, the two makes splitting the next six positions. A Lister-Jaguar was twelfth.

Phil Hill and Olivier Gendebien won first prize and the Amoco Trophy. A two-cylinder, front-wheel-drive Deutsch-Bonnet won the handicap Index of Performance award. At ten o'clock the finishing gun boomed out, the Columbia Broadcasting System announcers interviewed the winners, wet and weary photographers fought with officious volunteer policemen to get closer, champagne corks popped. By midnight the circuit lay silent again on the Florida plain.

6 · The Enchantment of Risk

At 3:45 on the morning of Sunday, May 24th, 1903, the first of 275 automobiles left Versailles to begin the great Paris-Madrid race. They were to run through Chartres, Tours, Angouleme, to Bordeaux; then to Bayonne, Vittoria, Burgos, Valladolid and Madrid, where great preparations had been made to receive them. France, indeed all Europe was full of enthusiasm for *l'automobile,* and the great city-to-city road races had conveyed the fever of high-speed motoring to millions. Races had been run from Paris to Marseilles, Marseilles-Nice, Bordeaux-Biarritz, Paris-Nice, Paris-Roubaix, Nice-Salon-Nice, Paris-Vienna, Paris-Amsterdam, but Paris-Madrid was to be best of all.

Only scholars and devotees remember now the names of most of the starting cars: Mors, De Dietrich, Turcat-Mery, Gobron-Brillie, Serpollet, Passy-Thellier, Motobloc, Richard-Brasier. Of names we know today only Renault and Mercedes were represented. But all automobiles were wonderful in 1903, and 100,000 wildly excited Parisians jammed the roads to Versailles during the Saturday night before the race, on foot, bicycle, carriage, automobile, candlelighted Chinese lanterns bobbing over their heads, and they crowded close to touch the cars as they passed. The cars nosed their way through the mobs, foot-long orange flames slashing from their open exhausts, chain drives clattering, drivers sitting head-high to the crowds, mechanics crouched low beside them.

The English sportsman Charles Jarrott was first off the mark, in a 45-horsepower De Dietrich. The huge, bearded Chevalier René de Knyff, driving a Panhard, was second, and then Louis Renault in a car of his own make. From then on, minute by minute, big cars, small cars and finally motorcycles were sent away, the last man getting off just as Louis Renault reached Tours, 135 miles from Versailles.

It would be hard to find drivers today who would undertake to push replicas of the Paris-Madrid cars to the limit over 750 miles of badly surfaced road, dust-laden and indifferently marked. Lightness and more lightness had been the universal motto and the chassis of many of the cars were dangerously weak: their builders had used the lightest and thinnest material available and then removed metal by drilling. Chassis frames, even pistons were drilled out, and brake pedals and gear levers were steel lace.

Light as they were, many of the cars carried big and powerful engines: a Mercedes covered the first 17½ miles in 17 minutes and Louis Renault's little car was timed, over a straight stretch, at ninety miles an hour. The hazards of the road, high speed and the flimsiness of the automobiles aside, were frightful: there were an estimated 3,000,000 people lining the course, and the force of *gendarmerie* and army men assigned to protect them was hopelessly inadequate; the dust churned into the air by the passing wheels hung so heavily that following drivers steered by setting course on the tops of the telegraph poles bordering the road. Accidents began almost at once. Marcel Renault, Louis' brother, lost control of his car at Couhe-Verac, was crushed under it, and killed. The Englishman Barrow hit a tree head-on at eighty miles an hour. Another Englishman, Leslie Porter, on a Wolseley, overshot a curve and drove straight into the wall of a house. Tourand, attempting to avoid a child on the road, killed the child, his mechanic and a soldier. Louis Renault was first man into Bordeaux, having been on the road for five hours and a half. Every driver, as he pulled into the control, had a new horror to relate.

No accurate total of dead and injured was ever compiled, but it was known that at least twenty people had been killed, and the French government stopped the race at Bordeaux. The Spanish government withdrew its permission for travel over the roads of Spain. The cars that had arrived at Bordeaux were not allowed to move again under their own power; they were towed by horses to the railroad station and shipped to Paris. In the public press, a hue and cry arose at once and demands for the abolition of automobile racing echoed in political halls.

More than half a century later, on the 12th of May, 1957, 301 automobiles began to stream out of Brescia, Italy, in the black early morning hours, to run down one coast of Italy to Rome and up the other to Brescia again in the famous Mille Miglia sports-car race. Uncounted millions of people lined the roads, roads that were, like the Paris-Madrid routes, supposed to be closed for the day. Still the drivers knew, just as the pioneers had known six decades before, that they would enter and leave every town by driving into a solid wedge of humanity, the narrow end of which would suddenly, miraculously, open an instant before disaster. Because the Mille Miglia was known to be a dangerous race, with heavy spectator and driver fatalities often marring its thirty-year history, the number of entries for 1957 had been reduced and extra precautions for spectator control had been made. Threats of prohibition had been increasingly common in late years, and those to whom the race meant most were anxious to preserve it: the organizers—the chief spirit of whom had said he would run it, if need be, despite any effort of the Italian government to stop him!—the manufacturers, the Italian sports fans for whom racing is a national game. For the Mille Miglia was the last of the great city-to-city road races. All the races that had fanned out of the hub of Paris were long dead, nothing left to tell of them but the memoirs of old men, a few faded posters, some ancient silver cups. The Gordon Bennett races, the Ardennes races, the Vanderbilt Cup in America, all long since abandoned. Great Britain never had allowed open-road racing. The modern Carrera Panamericana, run the length of Mexico, had proven too costly in money and blood to abide. There were two sizable road races still extant in Sicily: the Targo Florio and the Giro di Sicilia, but classic though they were, they were not the real thing: city to city, the cars never running twice over the same piece of road. This is what automobiles were made to do, and this is the only pure form of automobile racing.

Of all the racing community, only the contract drivers for the great houses, the professionals who spend the six months from April to September driving the fastest cars that can be built, had been able to consider the possibility of the Mille Miglia abolition with equanimity. Most of them had come to dislike the race intensely. Juan Manuel Fangio had run Brescia-Rome-Brescia five times and then announced that he would never do it again. Stirling Moss, conceded to be, after Fangio's retirement, the fastest driver in the world, said before the 1955 Mille Miglia, which he won, and won in the fastest time ever posted, that he considered it the most dangerous race of all. Moss *averaged* 95 miles an hour for the 10 hours and 17 minutes he was on the road.

That, then, is the Mille Miglia, one thousand miles of ordinary Italian two-lane roadway for most of its length, carrying about 2980 curves, bends, blind hills and other hazards, a circuit impossible to memorize—and a driver feels secure only on a circuit he has memorized, since no one can safely take a corner at 140 miles an hour unless he knows which way the road bends beyond it. The Mille Miglia is a race for sports cars, not racing cars, but in recent years the distinction between the two has narrowed almost to the vanishing point. The great racing manufacturers, Ferrari, Maserati, Mercedes-Benz, Jaguar, produce "sports" cars that differ from full Grand Prix racing machines only in having room for a passenger and in mounting such amenities as headlights, a starter, a spare tire, perhaps a rudimentary top. The Italian machines are particularly ferocious. Some of them are capable of 200 miles an hour, and their engines are so highly tuned that they cannot be run slowly through more than a few blocks of traffic without stalling or overheating. Viewed against the accepted definition of a sports car, a machine suitable for both competition and ordinary down-to-the-drugstore errand running, they are freaks, but they win races.

The great hazards of the Mille Miglia are four: the ubiquitous, suicidal crowds; the presence in the race of every kind of car in the world, fast and slow, big and little; the tremendous speed of the big cars; and the winding road itself.

The twenty-fourth Mille Miglia went on without serious incident until a Dutch driver went off the road and was killed. A motorcycle policeman, patrolling another part of the course, lost control of his mount and was killed. The race turned into a private contest among the Ferrari drivers, Collins, Taruffi, Von Trips, Gendebien, Portago. Collins' car broke down, Taruffi was leading Von Trips and Gendebien, Portago was fourth when tire failure took the car out of his control, killing him, his passenger and ten spectators.

Editorial denunciation of the sport began within hours and it was bitter and prolonged. Inevitably the critics recalled the horrifying disaster at Le Mans, France, during the running of the 1955 Twenty-Four-Hour race, when Pierre Levegh's Mercedes-Benz left the course at 140 miles an hour and killed more than eighty spectators. The veteran Italian professional who had won the race, Piero Taruffi, announced that he would retire in deference to the wishes of his wife, and in a letter to me said that he doubted that cars would ever again run down the long straight roads of the Adriatic coast and over the mountains back to Brescia again. American newspapers found room on page one for long stories, full of pathos and penny-a-line Freudian theory, explaining the "death wish" that had brought the young Marquis de Portago to an early end, and Mike Wallace, persuading the able American driver and theoretician, John Fitch, to appear on his television program, attempted, although with little success, to treat him as a prisoner in the dock. Otherwise levelheaded citizens argued that automobile racing should be ended, root and branch, by legislation.

It may be that the great city-to-city races have finished a life of more than sixty years—I doubt it—but automobile racing itself is indestructible and talk of abolishing it is nonsense. As long as man has run wheeled things over the earth, he has raced. Individual forms of racing may die out, as racing on the great board-track ovals of the 1920's died out, but man's determination to propel himself faster than his fellow cannot be outlawed.

During the past few years automobile racing *aficionados* made much of limited participation in the sport by the great Detroit firms. In the days before the Kaiser War, every major manufacturer supported racing as a matter of course and as a sure means of publicity. When Detroit switched targets from the male consumer to the female, racing had of necessity to give way to color, upholstery, shape, and the rest of the factors that combine into what we know as "styling."

In the mid-1940's the wheel came round again. Chrysler and Lincoln showed interest in the Mexican road race, and did well in it. Oldsmobile, Ford, Chevrolet actively supported the big stock-car events, and the master executives of Detroit, while piously denying that a horsepower race was in being, flogged their engineers for a few more foot-pounds of torque. The engine of one Big Three model could produce 405 horsepower on the test bench, as much as any contemporary Grand Prix racing car, and more than most. It was quietly made known to the racing community that Chevrolet's sports model, the Corvette, would make a sustained major effort in international racing. Americans who hoped for an end to the absolute domination of road racing by foreign-built machines were set alight with hope, but cooler heads were less optimistic.

Then, on the 6th of June, 1957, the Board of Directors of the Automobile Manufacturers Association recommended an end to all participation in racing by member companies. Indeed, the A.M.A. went further and recommended that no company encourage or assist any form of competition, or publicize any such event, or advertise the speed, engine size, horsepower or acceleration rate of its cars. The unannounced reason for this severe edict was simple: in some two dozen state legislatures, bills were pending which were restrictive of horsepower, engine size, top speed, and so on. Detroit, an admirably well-informed and unified business community, was simply taking the wind out of the legislator's sails. Except insofar as the promising Corevtte racing model was concerned, the move was of little importance to racing as a whole.

Certainly automobile racing is dangerous and the list of drivers who have died at the wheel is a depressingly lengthy one. It is probably the most dangerous of all spectator sports when proper safety measures are not taken and particularly when the audience is unsophisticated. When U.S. road racing was reborn after the Second World War at Watkins Glen, New York, women spectators stood so close to the speeding machines that the air blast swirled their skirts around them. They were in hideous danger and seemed unaware of it. Presently, there is almost no open-road racing left in this country. Spectators watching the comparatively dull track racing have always been reasonably safe except from such freakish hazards as a thrown wheel, and the current tendency in road racing is to use artificial road courses built on private property. On the private course, spectators can be rigidly controlled. Control is necessary, because automobile racing is perhaps the most exciting sport in the world, and it is a commonplace observation that spectators will always try to get almost close enough to the cars to touch them.

Most professional drivers actively dislike the spectators. Barney Oldfield, first of the famous American drivers, thought them little better than ghouls, and a well-known driver now dead once told me that if he were faced with a choice between hitting a tree or a spectator he would unhesitatingly hit the spectator. His reasoning was this: since hitting a tree at speed will almost certainly kill a driver, and a spectator hit by a racing car has about the same chance of survival, then obviously either driver or spectator would die in the hypothetical situation he envisioned. The driver's right to live was the greater, my friend argued, since he was doing what he was supposed to do: driving very fast, after ample public warning that he would do so, while the spectator, by coming close enough to the circuit to be hit, had freely chosen to put himself in a dangerous position. In the average driver's view, the spectator is a necessary evil at best: he provides the money. A top-ranking driver can make $150,000 in a really good year, but I think that most of the internationally ranked drivers would run for the fun of it with almost equal zest. Many of them are in a real sense addicted and could not stop driving under any circumstances. "This is not a game that is essentially a game for boys, like baseball," a ranking driver once said to me. "This is a game in which you must put up a bond for your life every time you go out to play. Because it is the most demanding of all games, it is spiritually the most rewarding, too." He died at the wheel.

I have heard other drivers paraphrase that remark. Typically, the athlete is uncommunicative, but many of the younger Grand Prix drivers are sensitive and articulate men. Stirling Moss, Wolfgang Von Trips, Phil Hill, Harry Schell, Olivier Gendebien, Joakim Bonnier have demonstrated a peculiarly acute awareness of life, an overt determination to take the maximum out of it in excitement, taste, love, music or whatever.

All of them conceded that mastery of a racing automobile on a road course, particularly on a twisting course, or one in the mountains, offers one of life's monumentally sensual experiences. It is an experience hard to describe. The unleashed bellowing of an engine which will move the car from a standing start to 60 miles an hour in 3 seconds, to 100 in 8; the scream of the brakes, producing, in the course of a 350 mile race, enough heat to warm a house through a hard winter; the constant controlled sliding of the automobile (in a well-driven bend, one feels like a man on skis doing a good Christy, Stirling Moss says, and other drivers say the impression is that of driving on glare ice)—all these sensations bear in on one, while, a foot away on either side, similar cars driven by other men scream and scrabble for a footing on the roadway. As in the killing of a bull, or a *rappelle* down a sheer face, Grand Prix automobile racing may infrequently allow one error in judgment to go unpunished, but two, rarely or never. The penalty frequently is death.

The argument will probably never be settled, but I at least do not believe that people watch automobile racing in the hope of seeing men killed. I think that most of the 25,000,000 who watch auto racing every year in this country are drawn to it because racing best defines and distills a basic truth: those who are willing to give up life know best what it is worth.

7 · Oddments and Bet Settlers

In June, 1952, the first official performance figures were recorded for a gas-turbine automobile. The car was a Rover two-seater roadster, made in England (the first such car) and the top speed was 151.96 mph.

The really de luxe high-performance sedans of the classic period, the 1930's, often had an extra speedometer mounted for the rear-seat passengers.

Each of the twenty-four nations that subscribe to the Federation Internationale de l'Automobile's sporting code is assigned a color or combination of colors to use in painting its racing automobiles. Best known are the bottle green of Great Britain and the blood red of Italy. Rarely seen: the pale violet of Egypt, the pearl gray of Luxembourg, the green and white of Bulgaria.

The V-8 engine is an old idea, first made by De Dion Bouton of France in 1907.

A successful British sports car of the 1920's and 1930's, the Frazer-Nash, had no gears. It was driven by chains and sprockets —one for each of the four forward speeds and reverse.

Four-wheel brakes first appeared in 1909 on the Spyker, a Dutch car.

The highest price paid for an automobile will probably never be known, but there is reason to believe that one Type 41 Bugatti did cost $33,000.

There have never been many front-wheel-drive cars on the market, but the idea has never been abandoned, either. Cord, Ruxton, Buccialli were f.w.d. automobiles; the Citroën has used f.w.d. since 1932; SAAB, D.K.W. and others use it now; and there is some reason to believe that Ford will adopt the principle in the next few years.

Automobiles have been made with two wheels, three, six and eight. Best known of these variants was the Morgan Three-Wheeler, of which 40,000 were built in England between 1911 and 1951. With a brave driver, racing Morgans would do 110 miles an hour. There are about six of them in the United States.

The Spanish Hispano-Suiza had the first power brakes, in 1919.

The basic design of the Offenhauser or Meyer-Drake engine, which usually powers about thirty of the thirty-three racing cars that start at Indianapolis every year, goes back to 1921 and has not been essentially changed since. The vibrations set up by the wildly overstressed engine are so severe that drivers compare the sensation to that of riding a pneumatic drill, but the engine is almost unfailingly reliable.

The oldest gasoline-powered automobile still in working order is probably the original Hammel, built in Denmark in 1887.

Mercedes-Benz built a *truck* that would do 106 miles an hour, fully loaded. It was used to transport racing cars in the mid-1950's.

The Nizam of Hyderabad probably owned more Rolls-Royce automobiles than any other individual—more than fifty. He was the richest man in the world, estimated to be worth $2,500,000,-000. The Maharajah of Patiala is said to have bought thirty-five Rolls-Royces at one time just after the Second World War. Perhaps three hundred Rolls-Royces are sold in the United States in a good year, most of them standard sedans at about $13,500. The car is basically a prestige item to the parent company, which is primarily concerned with aircraft and industrial engines. Incidentally, most Rolls-Royces have had six-cylinder engines. A few V-12's were made in the 1930's and a new V-8 is being made now.

The most spectacular of the postwar automobiles was the Pegaso, built in Spain. It was fast, good-looking and amazingly road-worthy, but the complexities of its engine design and its high price, starting at $10,000, pushed it out of the market. There is not, and never has been, any such thing as a handmade production automobile, but the Pegaso did have a great deal of hand-fitting work in its construction.

The naming of an automobile is sometimes peculiarly difficult. The Ford company considered some 100,000 ideas before settling on Edsel, and the Svenska Aeroplan Aktiebolaget was a long time arriving at SAAB. Volvo, the name of another Swedish car, is not a Swedish word: it's the first person singular present tense of the Latin *volvere:* I roll along. D.K.W. stands for *Das Kleine Wunder*, The Little Wonder, or The Dear Little Wonder. The Reo was named after Ransom E. Olds, and so was the Oldsmobile.

The fastest an automobile has run on land under official observation is a bit over 400 miles per hour (by John Cobb of England, in establishing the present Land Speed Record, 394.19, the record is the average of two runs) but 500 is believed to be possible. It will be done on the Utah salt flats, if it's done at all. No place else in the world offers a comparably smooth surface combined with sufficient room for acceleration and braking. Even at 400 mph, Cobb used up almost all the space available.

Nubar Gulbenkian, whose oil fortune is one of the biggest ever amassed by an individual—he is probably a billionaire—preferred the London taxicab to any luxury automobile on the world market. He liked its size, privacy and ride, so he bought one and had a British coachmaker spend eighteen months and $10,000 in refurbishing it to his taste.

The "car of the future" is likely to be an air-sled, or aerodyne, or "ground-effect machine," a wheel-less device supported and driven, a few inches off the ground, by jets of air blasted vertically downward and others aimed horizontally. Full-scale working prototypes exist here and abroad. (The thing works equally well over water and land.)

It is difficult to establish a relationship between success and accident rate among racing drivers. Tazio Nuvolari, who may have been the greatest driver of all time, and was certainly the greatest of the period 1900–1940, had so many accidents he could not remember them all. He broke every major bone in his body, including his neck, and was many times given up by hospital staffs, but he died of illness. Juan Manuel Fangio, five times champion of the world, who recently retired, had only one accident requiring hospitalization in his whole Grand Prix career, and Stirling Moss, presently the ablest driver living, has had only one.

8 · "*Vive les* Plans"

(This piece, and the one that follows it, "Change of Plan," are short stories. Little fiction has been written about automobile racing, which is strange, because it is a remarkably dramatic subject. Because of the fact that the death of Maurice Delafont in "*Vive les* Plans" precisely parallels the death of Jean Behra, the French champion, I am impelled to note that I wrote the story in January, 1957, and that it was first published in July, 1957. Behra died in August, 1959.)

THE BIG SKYROCKET startled Stephanie Talbot. It wasn't really a skyrocket, it was a sort of aerial bomb, a "maroon" the British called it, whooshing a hundred yards into the brass-bright August sky to burst with a flat echoing boom. It meant that there were ten minutes left.

Stephanie was alone. There wasn't much point, for her, in being with someone, trying to talk, at a time like this. She walked along the oil-stained concrete, an aloof little figure in black slacks, black shantung blouse, a green kerchief over her head. She was blonde, pale, and the palms of her hands were wet with perspiration. Stephanie was giving up a man she dearly loved, walking along in the sun, rehearsing what she would say, steeling herself to it, and it was hard to do, moving in the wash of babble and shouts in a half-dozen languages, in the crackling, ripping bite of the exhausts—the *"auspuff"* the Germans call it—of one car after another being warmed up.

She moved past the crowded pit structures with their flat sloping roofs, their counters stacked with tools, stop watches, cans of oil and the rest of the paraphernalia of racing, and came finally to Dennis Marshall's place; "26," the big sign over it read, "Ferrari." Dennis was talking with someone she didn't know. He smiled the man away and turned to Stephanie.

"Hi, darling," he said. "You look ravishing. You look a dear, good, sweet, passionate girl and I adore you. Except that decorum must prevail, I'd certainly kiss you." He kissed her gravely on each cheek. Her hands moved to his shoulders and held him. He looked into her eyes.

"I know, baby," he said. "You're scared green. Shatters me. Here am I, about to have three hours of delirious fun, and maybe pick up two thousand pounds to boot, and you, poor Steph, poor Steph is worried." He shook his head dolefully and a second rocket boomed in the air. "Five-minute gun," he said. "Where's m'hat?" He pulled a white-billed helmet from under the pit counter, gave the curving plastic visor a swipe with his sleeve. "Run over to the bar, Steph," he said. "Have a nice vermouth cassis or something until the cars get sorted out. It's the beginning of these things that shakes one, you know. Go on, now, there's a lamb." He kissed her and walked out to the lean, mean-looking red car standing with the others on the starting grid. She watched him go.

Dennis Marshall wasn't a big man, five nine, perhaps, or barely ten, and only twenty-five years old, but there was more of the virile essence in him than most men ever know. He had a rock-hard body and he moved it with that grace no one's given and few can earn, the price of self-discipline being what it is. He'd been born with fast reaction time. The rest had been sweat and planning. He was one of the three first-ranking automobile racing drivers in the world and in a good year he could make $150,000. He was intelligent, courteous, serene. He's my husband, Stephanie told herself, and I'm his wife, and tonight I'll say good-bye to him and all this.

She didn't go to the bar. She stood beside the pit counter, in the little shade it made, and waited. All the cars were manned now, twenty-odd of them. She knew most of the drivers, all of those in the first three or four rows. They were strange men, terribly strange. She thought Dennis was the only reasonably oriented one in the lot. They were the gayest possible companions, when they weren't talking shop, but they were all mad. She saw Dennis jump out of his car and run over to shout something into Hilary Martin's car. Martin looked up at him. He was a round little butterball of a man, completely preoccupied for hours before a race. You could say hello to him, even stop and talk, and he might never remember seeing you. There was Aldo Caducci, tall, shiny-bald, very gay, and a legendary lady-killer. Next to him, Van Groot, a Dutchman, a rarity in automobile racing. No one knew anything about Van Groot except that he was rich. Patrick Munoz, a Brazilian, twice champion of the world, a man so relaxed that he appeared, in the car or out of it, to be just on the point of falling asleep. There was Borros Spohk, an American who believed that if a man tried hard enough he could live thirty hours a day, and a Swedish count, Helmut Ovden, who had been a devotee of what he called "the blood sports" since his fifteenth birthday. There was the Frenchman Maurice Delafont, a perfectly normal, ordinary man—except that he was fifty, owner of a prosperous business, married to a beautiful woman, had three delightful children, and still went motor racing all year long.

The starter's flag was in the air and Stephanie twisted her hands tightly together and waited. The exhaust noise rose steadily to a shattering roar. The big flag fell and the cars started to move, slowly for the first few feet, many with blue smoke rising from spinning rear wheels, the rubber burning, and then, unbelievably as you watched, they were away, up to 60 miles an hour in the time it took to draw a long deep breath; then 90, 100, all in a solid multicolored pack, mere inches from each other, they howled into the first long curve and were gone. In a bit over five minutes they'd be back. Stephanie pulled and tugged at the clasp of her purse, dredged out a cigarette and lighted it. She could still hear the cars, but they were so distant now that they sounded like airplanes far away. In the next pit a bottle crashed on concrete and a strident woman's voice said, "*Ah, c'est dommage!*" Floating over everything, the impersonal, professional excitement of the public address system.

These few minutes of the first lap were almost the hardest of all for Stehanie. She looked in at the pit. Everything was neatness and order now, the little squares of the graph paper on which the lap charts were kept, the four Swiss split-watches in their mahogany case, the orderly rows of pencils. The voice of the crowd rose almost imperceptibly and began to mount to a shout: the cars were in sight. Stephanie leaned around the pit and stared down the long straightaway to the distant corner where the first car would show itself. It came now, a red one, sliding the corner so that she could see the whole length of it, straightening out with a wicked-looking tremulant tail-wagging, and then seeming to swell in her eyes, without moving, as she looked straight at it. Half a breath and it was level with the pits and she felt the shocking "whack!" as the driver shifted into top. It was Munoz, lifting a limp hand to wave to his pit, twenty feet behind him a green Vanwall car, little Martin, tight and tense, then another red car, Dennis, sitting so far back that his arms were out almost straight in front of him. Once she'd seen Dennis, Stephanie paid no attention to the rest of the cars as they rasped past in loose procession. Silence again. She dropped her cigarette into the dry grass and stepped on it.

Stephanie felt quite apart from the other women who had committed their men to what she thought of as the unspeakable hazards of the race. She was sure she was more in love than any of them were; and she knew exactly what was happening on the 7.7 miles of the road circuit, two cars wide, its black-top softened by the sun. Like many women, Stephanie had a poor graphic imagination; but she did not have to depend upon it to know what the men were daring. Once she had let Dennis show her, two years ago, in Italy; the car a big two-seater open Ferrari of the type called a four-nine.

The road was straight where they started, after Dennis had told her to expect to be frightened, but to force it down; if she could not she was to slap his thigh and he would slow the car. They smiled at each other. He ran the engine up, let in the clutch, and Stephanie's head snapped back. She tried, unsuccessfully, to pull herself forward against the surge of the car's acceleration. Dennis' arms were bare, the muscles standing in ridges. The steering wheel shook in his hands, the uncovered metal of the body vibrated, the noise of the engine was unbearable and Stephanie wanted to scream in sheer terror. The big needle riding the tachometer dial spun around, 3000, 4000, 5000, 6000. Dennis' left hand grabbed the gearshift lever, his left foot hit the clutch, his right stamped on the accelerator pedal and with a crack like a long fat whip being snapped across the sky the engine bit again. The tachometer needle climbed again to 6000 and again his feet danced on the pedals and the soft evening air was split as 400 horsepower slammed into the clutch.

Stephanie was rigid with terror. Ahead of them the road ran out in a right-hand corner. It is impossible to explain how a corner looks running up to a car nearing 200 miles an hour. The car seems to stand still, and the corner rushes into one's face like a train in a nightmare. Stephanie knew they were going to die then and there. The car would sail through the corner and a mile into the woods beyond it. They would leave trees flattened behind them like cornstalks where a hurricane has passed. She couldn't bear to look and she couldn't close her eyes either. She turned to Dennis. He was staring ahead, the brown skin crinkled around his eyes, a small smile rising to his lips. She watched. His toe hit the drilled out skeleton of the pedal and the steel pads of the disk brakes, tight in their calipers, shrieked as they bit into the wheels. His heel came down on the throttle and his left arm flicked as he dropped a gear; the engine screamed, fell off; again the wail of the brakes and the monstrous howl of the engine as he caught third gear. A wash of fuel fumes engulfed them in the cockpit. He flicked the wheel back and forth and the car drifted through the corner, nose pointed in, tail in the middle of the road. Dennis kicked it straight, flattened the accelerator and again Stephanie felt the whole weight of her body thrust inexorably into the leather of the seat-back behind her. She endured it all for three laps of the circuit. The exhaust deafened her; the wind blast plucked at her scalp and tried to tear her tight-clamped lips apart; the incessant struggle to maintain her place in the seat stretched and beat every muscle in her body; engine fumes and the sidewise G-forces in the turns combined to sicken her. She smiled wanly at Dennis as he helped her from the car. She staggered in his arms to a chair. After a while the memory of the physical beating faded. What remained was the face of death hanging to the flying car like its own exhaust smoke.

"There are three sports that try a man," she remembered Helmut Ovden saying, "bullfighting, motor racing, mountain climbing. All the rest are recreations."

The leaders came by again; Munoz, Martin, Dennis, Caducci. The other cars were stringing out behind them. There was no silence now. Every few seconds a car came past, or two or three. Stephanie walked through a narrow place between two pit counters and she felt sheltered immediately, separated from the circuit by the pits, by the odds and ends piled up behind them, tins of oil, cases of mineral water, camp chairs, stacked spare tires and the like. There were parked cars, too, motorcycles, bikes, scooters, occasionally a trailer. The grass was coarse and dusty. Looking a long way across the field she could see another leg of the circuit, little toy cars sliding along it, too far away, too quiet and too small to matter. She felt removed and safe. Still she was oddly bound to do what Dennis had asked her to do, and she looked for the candy-striped tent of the bar. She would have the vermouth cassis he'd suggested, although she didn't want it. She had an uneasy, unspoken conviction that to refuse him anything, just before or during a race, might be fatally unlucky. Fear of his being killed with some small favor ungranted terrified her. She stirred the purplish, bitter-sweet drink. She would have to finish it quickly. She loved the blessed calm away from the circuit, but she could not stand for long not knowing if Dennis was still safe.

By the time the race was half over, an hour and a half gone, it had settled into a deceptively simple pattern. Of the twenty-some cars that had started, four had retired with mechanical trouble, one had been disqualified for accepting help from spectators after going off the road. Munoz, Dennis, Martin and Caducci were all driving on the absolute limit, and they traded the lead back and forth among them. Only the professionals present, and a few knowledgeable spectators, marking the way the cars slid the entire width of the road going into corners and shuddered and danced under maximum acceleration coming out, knew how bitterly the first four places in the race were being contested.

Stephanie knew, and so she marvelled at some of the other women, bright, twittering little things, no more concerned than they'd be at a cricket match or a horse race. She had little to say to them and they had nothing for her. When she wanted to talk with someone she looked for Mme. Delafont, who always came to the races with her husband. Stephanie found her after a bit. She was sitting behind her husband's pit in the shade of a beach umbrella thrust deep into the ground, a bottle of wine in a tiny tub beside her chair. She was knitting.

"Sit down, my dear, sit down, Stephanie," she said. "Have some wine."

"Thanks, Julie," Stephanie said. "I just finished a vermouth. I'll wait."

"How does it go with our heroes?" Julie Delafont said. "I haven't looked at the chart for half an hour now."

"Munoz first, then Dennis, Caducci, Martin, a few minutes ago," Stephanie said. "I think Maurice is farther back."

"He was eighth," Julie said. "He knew the car was not going well this morning, and then too, of course, it isn't a factory car."

Stephanie lit a cigarette and stretched her legs straight in front of her. "The sun is good," she said.

"This is no sun," Julie said. "Wait until you get to Nassau."

"I shan't be there," Stephanie said.

Julie Delafont peered quickly at her across her knitting. "Dennis isn't running?" she said.

"Oh, yes, he's running," Stephanie said. "It's just that I'm not going."

They heard a shout, and a double screech of brakes hard on as a car came too fast into the pits. Both looked, and saw a flash of it. It was green, not blue, not red, so they paid no attention.

"I think I will have a little drink, if I may," Stephanie said. "I guess I'm getting jumpy. I'm getting so I hate all the noises. The only noise I like to hear any more is the pop of the champagne cork when they open the bottle for the winner, just that one pop and all the blessed silence, not a single damned engine running." She took a little sip of wine.

"Don't be thinking like that, don't run off down *that* alley, Stephanie," Julie Delafont said, "or you'll find yourself giving up the whole thing, and Dennis, too."

"That's just it," Stephanie said after a bit. "I am giving Dennis up, I'm going to give him up."

"I see," Julie said. "I must say you've surprised me." She spilled wine into her glass. "Tell me, how long has it been now, that you and Dennis have been lovers?"

"July a year ago," Stephanie said. "July, at Rheims."

"That isn't very long, is it," Julie said. "A pity, too. It's a sad thing, to fall out of love."

"Don't tease me, Julie," Stephanie said. "I haven't fallen out of love. I adore Dennis. There cannot be anything else like him in this entire world. But I'm going to leave him because I can't stand the life he has, that's all, I can't stand watching him make a bet with his life practically every week. Do you know how many times Dennis ran last year? Forty-one! Every single important event in the world except Indianapolis! Look, Julie, I know what it's like out there, I know what goes on out there, and I can't take it. I stalk around like a sleepwalker for two days before a race and I shake for two days afterward. Instead of getting easier as time passes, it gets harder. If I keep on, I'll ruin both our lives."

"My God," Julie said, "I think you're mad. Look. All this you are talking about, the racing, this is nonsense. The fact of the matter is that you love him, by which I mean, you like him, you admire him, you desire him. That is reasonable love, that is lasting love. You may not find it again. Therefore it doesn't matter *what* the man does, whether he is a garbage collector, a banker or the public hangman. Don't you see that?"

"No, I don't think I do," Stephanie said.

" 'The beauty of the young is God's apology for their stupidity,' " Julie said. "Look, Stephanie, the only men worth having are the ones who are passionate for the world, for their work in the world. These are the only good ones, and there are not nearly enough of them to go around. With a man like Dennis, or Maurice, it is possible to have a life, not an existence, a life, something that is not just cabbage soup and winter rain on the roof. My God, you don't give up a man you love because he will die. They will all die, and the most of them before us, we know that. What an idiocy! You are making me angry."

"I'm sorry if I am," Stephanie said. "But don't you see, what good am I, what use to Dennis, when I can't even keep him from seeing how frightened I am? Today, just before the start, he took one look at me and he knew. I'm sure he always knows. In time he'll hate me for it. Right now, I hate myself for it."

"The essence of the thing is so simple," Julie said. "It's impossible for me to understand how you miss seeing it. Look—you are afraid of only one thing, really. That he will die. Don't you think he's afraid, too? Every one of them is, it's the main reason they do these madnesses, to see the fear of dying rise up in themselves and then to push it down again. He is going to have to do this dying, not you. Give some thought to him. And for yourself—think only how dear he is, what he means to you, the kindnesses, the delights in his body, and every time he gets into a car, kiss him good-bye, that's all, kiss him good-bye!"

"*You* do that?" Stephanie whispered.

"Certainly I do that. I kiss him good-bye. I pat his dear face, I walk away saying to myself, ah, my Maurice, he was the dearest and best of all men who ever lived in this world! Sometimes I even think of how I will tell the children. I say good-bye to him. I tell myself calmly that he is dead. And then, every time so far at any rate, I am lucky. The noise, as you say, is over and Maurice is back with me. So I can kiss him again, and give him a drink, and wash the oil from him and take him in my arms again, and comfort him. What else is more satisfying? What else should we do, but meet our men as they come down from the mountain, and comfort them until they have to go back again? And when they go back, kiss them good-bye!"

Stephanie sat silent for a long time.

"I'm sorry, if I have disturbed you, Stephanie," Julie Delafont said finally. "If I was too rough, I am sorry. It's just that that's how it seems to me to be, that's how I have been so happy, all this time."

"No, no, you weren't too rough," Stephanie said.

"At any rate we have drunk up all the wine," Julie said. "And there's only a half-hour of this foolishness left. Let's walk down to the corner and watch these crazies for a few minutes and then we can come back and see the finish. I love to watch the finish. That idiot with the big flag, seeing how close he can stand without having his feet run over. I do hope I'm watching the day somebody gets him!" She giggled like a girl. She stuffed her knitting bag under the cushion of the chair and reached for Stephanie's hand.

They walked together behind the pits to the first corner. The sun was low now, butter-yellow on the drivers' faces as they came down the long straightaway and into the corner; the air was cooling, night was coming in. There were fourteen cars left. Caducci was out, Perdita in a Maserati was running fourth behind Munoz, Dennis, Marshall, Spohk. Dennis was within two car-lengths of Munoz, and had been hanging to him like that for more than 100 miles. Spohk was well back, driving magnificently, with his characteristic indifference to danger, but his car was not fast enough to bring him up to the leaders and everyone was watching the fantastic Munoz-Marshall duel. Their two cars ran as if tied together. Twenty-five times a lap each driver watched the other accept a chance to make a mistake—and none were made. A trifling error by Munoz could suffice to let Dennis pass him; one by Dennis and Munoz would run hopelessly far ahead. Almost anything would do: an imperfect gear-change, a brake application a split-second early. But they came around like a train.

"They're so incredibly good they make it look dull," Stephanie said.

"They'll finish that way," Julie Delafont said. "I think they're reconciled. Maurice, as you can see, he is not."

Maurice Delafont was lying seventh over-all, and second in his class to Stehrs, in a Gordini. Stehrs had been well ahead, but his car was slowing, and Delafont had him in sight now and was closing hard on him. He was pushing, delaying his braking to the rim of disaster, whipping the wheel madly back and forth as the car slid, spinning his back wheels as he bored out of the corner.

"Look, how excited," Julie Delafont said. "Like a damned wet-nose schoolboy. You would think he'd been driving for six months, instead of God knows how many donkey's years."

Excited or not, Delafont was hurrying, and every time he came around he had made a few more yards. A man standing behind Stephanie and Julie was timing the interval. "Delafont will catch him," he told his friends. "If he keeps on at this rate, he'll catch him with two laps to spare." Stephanie and Julie turned to look at the man; he held his watch up to show them the interval and they both had their backs to the circuit when they heard the rubber-shriek and the shouts. They snapped their heads around. Blue car and white car, the white one driving for the side of the road, its driver fighting to hold it out of the ditch, the blue one flipping end-for-end down the course, like a clown's toy; a man flew out, tumbled through the air; to the people standing at one side it seemed he would miss the telephone pole; no, he hit it high and fairly and face-on in a terrible embrace; just for a second the body stuck there; then it fell, backward, arms piteously outstretched. The white car had got around; there was nothing else in sight, nothing to be heard but the soft thud of the body hitting the ground, the quick sigh from the crowd. This much Stephanie was sure of, then Julie was gone, out in the road, tugging at the body, people pulling her away, a man tearing off a yellow sweater to wave it madly at the cars still coming. When she dared, Stephanie ran across. That was when Julie began to scream. She screamed rhythmically, methodically, her chest working like a bellows, in breath, out in a long bare-souled animal howl, in breath again. Her eyes protruded, she knew no one, the veins in her forehead purpled and she screamed. In the fifteen minutes it took for an ambulance to come she destroyed her voice.

Stephanie was helpless before the ambulance came, but afterward she could at least admit it and she left and walked alone back to the pits. Munoz had won, Dennis behind him. He was waiting for her, his face black with oil and rubber except for the egg-shaped patches around his eyes where the goggles had ridden. His shoulders sagged with fatigue.

"He's dead?" Dennis asked.

"He's dead," Stephanie said. "I was there. So was Julie. They've given her a tremendous dose of morphine or something."

"What a pity she had to see it," Dennis said. "What a miserable thing for her."

"I really thought she was losing her mind," Stephanie said. "I suppose it was only hysteria. Only! The odd thing was, we had been talking about it just a little before, the chances drivers take, and she said she was always reconciled to Maurice's death, every time he went out she gave him up over again, and felt only lucky when he came back to her. And then, when it happened, she went completely to pieces."

"That was because she saw it," Dennis said.

"No, I think she always knew she would," Stephanie said, "but she made up that other fiction, and for all those years they lived in it, and were happy."

"The poor sod," Dennis said. "One trip to the well too many. My God, the man was over fifty."

"Let's go home, Den," Stephanie said. He threw his kit into the little car behind the pits and they bumped off across the field to the roads, solid with traffic now in the gray twilight. Dennis ran alongside the road, cutting in and out with easy virtuosity. The hotel was eight miles distant.

"You said you were going to tell me something tonight, Steph," Dennis said.

"No, I'm not going to tell you anything, darling," Stephanie said. "I'm going to soak you in a tub, and give you tea-and-rum and take you to bed, those are the only plans I have for you."

"*Vive les* plans," Dennis said. "Dear God, *vive les* plans."

9 · Change of Plan

(This story was first published in *The Atlantic Monthly* in September, 1952. It was republished in the anthology, *The Best American Short Stories* in 1953 and it has since been republished at least a dozen times in collections published here and abroad.)

PIETRO LONETTI sat in his car, a little man, very erect, well back from the wheel. He looked confident and happy, and so he was. In about one hour and a half he intended to kill himself. The decision had calmed him; it had put an end to the torments of the five years that lay leaden behind him; it had restored the lilting serenity, the certainty that all was for the happy, happy best that he had, as a younger man, worn like a feather in his hair. Pietro Lonetti felt very well indeed.

He looked around. Most of these people were new to him. Some of them had still been driving sports cars when the war started. He knew Pierre Marten, in the Ferrari, an old competitor. He knew Lyon, of course, with his bull neck and wrestler's arms, and

Ignace Manelli. Manelli had one of the new Alfa-Romeos. But so many of the others were young and new. The boy next to Lonetti, for instance, in the blue Talbot. Maurice Lascelle, called "Popo." He had been a great hero in the French Resistance. He drove very hard, but with no style. The Englishman, Danton, in an old E.R.A. That pink skin, Lonetti thought, that bland blue eye. A thin old man of about twenty-nine summers. He looks a bit like Dick Seaman, but Seaman is a dozen years dead, burned in a Mercedes-Benz at Spa. Varzi, too, dead in a skid in the rain. Rosemeyer long dead, Christian Kautz dead, Ted Horn dead, Hepburn dead, Lonetti dead . . . the dour little man grinned to himself. Not yet, he said, not quite yet. Lonetti will die when he wants to. And not in bed, no matter what the damned doctors say. And after he has won this one. And in no accident.

The sixty-second gun boomed out and one engine fired, coughed, and settled down to an undulating roar as the driver gunned it up and down; another started, then two, three, another, two more, until the hot July air was pulsing with the sound of thirty open exhausts.

Lonetti hunched his shoulders a bit and stared at the fat man who was the starter. The fat man held the bright flag over his head as he counted off the seconds on his stop watch. He will be late, Lonetti thought. He loves himself and what he is doing and he will do it for as long as he can. In twenty years of watching starters, Lonetti had learned to read their little minds, he was sure of that. This one would hold the flag for a bit too long, and before he dropped it, he would lift it a bit, to get a wider, more spectacular swing. Lonetti would go on the lift and make a fifth of a second for himself. He ran the engine up. The fat starter's shoulders bulged, the flag imperceptibly lifted and started down. Lonetti let in the clutch, bore down on the gas and got away in a rush. He was a clear half-length ahead of the blue Talbot. It was enough. He grabbed the Maserati's crooked gearshift, banged it into second and wound the engine up tight, snatched third and ran it up to 7,000, slid through the first corner with the ease of a boy pulling a toy around the floor on a string and settled down into the first straight, three miles long. He stood on the throttle and locked his knee. There was 175 mph in the car under him and Lonetti wanted all of it.

It was a good French road, string-straight and lined with poplars that had watched two wars. The trees slid past in a smooth and solid wall and the road rushed hysterically under the bellowing Maserati, like something in a nightmare. It was a good road and Lonetti knew every pebble in it. He had carted plenty of silverware, plenty of francs, away from this circuit before the war. They had called the race something else, in those days. Now it was the "Grand Prix Robert Benoist." Benoist, another hero of the Resistance, like Lascelle. He had driven in Bugattis before the war. The Germans had killed him. Lonetti remembered him well, a big, pleasant man. He would win Benoist's race now, and a few of them would mutter about it: "Why did it have to be Lonetti. That louse . . ." Lonetti shrugged. He would not be around to hear them. He shot a quick look into the left-hand mirror. The Talbot was fifty yards behind him, the Alfa hard on its tail. Lonetti grinned. "Driving Lessons Given Here," he said to himself. A right-angle turn, one of the nasty ones, loomed ahead. Lonetti braked at the last possible tenth of a second, yards past the normal point. The engine screamed as he kicked it into second. He put the right wheel six inches from the grass and kept it there, to a hair, as the car cornered in an insanely fast four-wheel slide. He flicked it straight and roared at the hill ahead. He had doubled his lead on Lascelle and he screamed with laughter and pounded on the side of the car. They'll write about that one all right, he thought.

". . . at the second corner, Lonetti clearly demonstrated that his 51st winter had taken nothing from his legendary skill. He laid the elderly Maserati into the bend at an incredible rate of knots, causing grief to the novice Lascelle, who foolishly imitated him and lost vast yardage in the subsequent skid. *Il Maestro* slid the corner in his patented position and was obviously looking at 8,000 rpm as he urged his ancient mount up the hill, steering with one hand and beating happily on red tin with the other. . . ."

The red car left the ground at the top of the hill and sailed like a bird for fifty feet. It came down square and straight and Lonetti grabbed fourth gear and rocketed away. He felt wild exhilaration and he screamed again. There was a leggy blonde perched on a rock beside the road. She wore a green sweater, and she stood out from the hundreds around her like a wax candle burning on an ash heap. Lonetti gave her his big, big smile. That's for me, that's mine, he thought. She'll wave the next time around, and when they hang the roses on me I'll throw her a handful, and tonight . . . he swore under his breath. Tonight? Tonight you'll be shaking hands with Varzi. The hell with her and all of it, he thought. He settled down to drive. When he came around again the engine heat and fumes were beginning to bite into his throat and when he passed the blonde he didn't look.

". . . at the twentieth lap, Lonetti had increased his lead to 22 seconds, but the little man was obviously in distress. He was seen to be coughing continuously, and blood began to show on his sleeve as he drew it across his mouth. He held the comparatively slow Maserati in front by dint of black wizardry and a refusal to entertain any regard whatsoever for the welfare of the machinery. Manelli and Lascelle, in faster vehicles, were content only to stay in sight and pray earnestly that the Maserati would disintegrate under the punishment. . . ."

The brass-bright July sun was hot enough, but the shadeless grass beside the road looked cool to Pietro Lonetti, because the car was a moving furnace. There never was a cool one, Lonetti thought, they all roast you to death. Or gas you. The noxious smell of burning gasoline and half-burnt oil was sweet to him; it opened the door of his memory on all the good and happy things that had ever come his way; it meant more than the remembrance of violets in the hair of one's first girl, or the longed-for chimney smoke of one's boyhood, or the crystal scent of rain in autumn. The smell was the warp and woof of his life, but the stuff itself was killing him. He coughed, and felt the bleeding, and he leaned out to gulp clean air, but it was no use and he knew it.

Still, he had lasted the first hour and he would last the rest of it.

The faster cars had lapped the others now, and there were only signals from the pits to tell position. Lonetti didn't need signals. Until somebody passed him, he was first. He waved as he went by for the thirtieth time, and came up fast on the car ahead. He thought of passing him in the corner, but it was the E.R.A., Danton, the Englishman, and Lonetti backed off and let him go through the corner alone. He could take him at will on the long straight, and he would humiliate him there if he could, but he would not take a chance on crowding him in the corner. Lonetti was not notorious for his sportsmanship, and in the old days he would crowd any man in a corner if he felt like it, but he did not feel like it now. They said he hated Englishmen, and so he did, maybe, but he was not going to kill one on the road. He blasted past Danton in the straight, staring at him. I wonder if he was RAF in the war, he thought. He may have been. Leo may have seen his face that close in the sky over Libya and died for it. He may have been the one. Or he may have been the one who looked down his bombsight at Milan, there in '44. He seems mild to have burned three women alive. . . . Lonetti shook his head. That was a hundred years ago. That was an ancient pain; there had been worse ones since. It was all over anyway. He had cast up the accounts and written out the checks, and he would settle now for a little taste of the one good thing and then he would be happy to leave.

He flew on. He knew he would win. He was happy. He sat up straight, so proud of what he knew was being said of him that he could almost hear them talking. For twenty years Lonetti had been the standard by which other drivers were judged. There were many serious men who said that he had been born great, that he was the only authentic genius motor racing had ever produced, that his skill could not be explained in rational terms. Lonetti believed them. He knew that he could tell, for example, exactly how many pounds of a car's total weight rested on any single wheel at any time, cornering or straight, braking or accelerating. He believed that he could drive at 150 miles an hour through a slot an inch wider than the car. He had done it, so he believed it. Other men had to practice in cars, get used to them, feel out their peculiarities. Not Lonetti, *El Maestro*. They were all one to him, so long as they had four wheels, something to steer with, and a loud pedal that could be held flat on the floor.

He put it down hard now, to try to pass the two cars looming up ahead. One was Marten, a notorious road hog, the other was old Lyon. They were having a private race for the corner, and when Marten saw Lonetti coming up behind he moved over imperceptibly, blocked him off and let Lyon get around first. The three cars went around nose to tail in a hellish howling racket and slid into the straight like triplets. The others drew away there. Lonetti put the whole weight of his body on the throttle and shook the wheel in rage, but the revolution-counter needle would not go up where he wanted it: past the red danger line. He banged the gears into fourth and moved to the right-hand side of the road. The pits were only a couple of miles ahead.

He stopped the car where they waited for him and old Giorgio threw up the bonnet, the question in his eyes. "Plug," Lonetti croaked. He reached for the glass of water the kid had ready, drank it and turned to look over his shoulder, down the road, as Giorgio savagely swiveled out the plugs. Nobody could do it faster, but he couldn't do it in twenty seconds, and Lascelle and Manelli roared past him, sitting there nailed to the concrete. They were out of sight when the bonnet banged down and he was pushed off.

Pietro Lonetti had never been loved by other drivers, who did not always race as if immortality and the wealth of the Indies lay in winning. He gave them good cause now to hate him. He drove as if he were alone on the road. He passed them in bunches as they braked for the corners, slamming through the crowd of them flat out to stand viciously on the brake for a second and then drift through the corner in his own weird slide. He went into every corner with the nose of the car pointed dead wrong for the entrance but right for the exit, stealing yards and seconds from the lesser men who had to do it by the book. He went into one corner behind Marten, caught him in it and slid around him, staring arrogantly out at the six inches that lay between the two cars and instant death. He was coughing constantly now; the blood ran unheeded down his chin and he grinned wickedly at Marten as he left him. He had terrified the man, he knew it, and he ran away from him roaring with mirth and pounding the side of his car like a maniac blacksmith. Manelli he passed at the pits, his

Alfette blowing out a fog of blue smoke, and he could see the Talbot ahead. He had two laps in which to take it, and as he passed the stands he pointed ferociously ahead, his big white teeth stripped. Let no one miss this, he thought. We will see now how much resistance is in this hero, he thought. We will separate the men from the boys here. We will motor a little bit now.

Lascelle saw him coming and he tried everything he knew. On the straights he took every ounce of power the car had, and held his own, but it was either slow up for the corners or crash, and the insane Italian behind him crept closer with every bend in the road. Lascelle wanted to win. It was the first big race in which he had had any luck; it would make his reputation. Too, he had served under Robert Benoist, and the very idea of an Italian taking the cup away made him want to kill again. But every time he looked into the mirror Lonetti was a little closer to doing it.

At the beginning of the last lap, on the long straight in front of the stands, it finally happened. Foot by foot, the red Maserati pulled up beside him. Lonetti held the red car dead alongside and, when Lascelle looked over, the little man grinned wolfishly at him. There was blood all over his shirt. As they went past the stands, locked together, Lonetti bowed graciously to the people, and suddenly then, in horror, Lascelle knew why he had not pulled on past: he intended to amuse them with the spectacle of two cars running suicidally together into a corner that was, at that speed, but one car wide. He was going to make the kid quit, brake, and pull over. Lascelle knew, and everyone knew, that Lonetti had done this a hundred times in the past, and that in the end, and always, it had been the other man who had felt terror slam his foot down on the brake. Lascelle decided, suddenly, that he would be the one who did not quit. Live mouse, dead lion, he thought. He kept his foot down. After all, he just might live through it.

Pietro Lonetti was surprised, fifty yards from the corner, to find the Frenchman still with him, but he drove the bend as he had intended to, coming out of it slightly faster to clear the road, since he knew that otherwise nothing in the world could keep Lascelle from sliding into him. As it was, he felt the cars tick, nose to tail, as the blue Talbot moved behind him. It seemed to him that he heard the scream of the rubber, in two great howls, as the Talbot spun, and as he topped the hill he heard the crash and saw in his mirror the first orange burst of flame as the car exploded against the great trees beside the road.

He had it won, now. It was all over, they would give him the flag as he swept past, the crowds would scream his name, the journalists would pound their typewriters, he would take his victor's lap and at the end of it, as he had so long planned, he would fold his arms, proudly lift his head, and smash himself to death against the wall in the exit road, where everyone could see that it was no accident, and no one could come to harm by it. That had been his plan. That was why he was in the race. But suddenly now it didn't seem so much of a plan. It was empty. It was nothing.

Pietro Lonetti lifted his foot and let the red Maserati run along the side of the road at a bare 50 miles an hour. He felt as if he could get out and walk. He could see the separate blades of grass, each petal on the flowers along the ditch. He coughed and was surprised to taste the blood. His arms trembled and for the first time he felt the blisters on his palms. Everyone went past him. They roared by like a long freight train. He coasted into the pits. None of the din was for him. The photographers were elsewhere.

"Jesus and Mary!" Giorgio screamed at him. "What happened? What did you break? What let go?"

"Nothing let go," Lonetti said. "The car is fine. This is good iron. I took my foot off, that's all."

"Man, man, you threw it all away!" Giorgio said. "For what? For that kid, that dumb Frog? For what, for Christ's sake!"

Lonetti looked up at him. "Take off that steering wheel, Giorgio," he said. "Take it off, and lift me out of here. I want to go home."

10 · You Want to Buy a Brand-New 1903 Automobile?

THE CABINETMAKER who turns out replicas of antique furniture has been with us a long time, and so has his cousin, the outright faker who "manufactures" antiques, his tools a length of rusty chain, bird shot and a library of stains and polishes. There are men who will deliver Van Goghs and Manets to order; and, if you can't afford a Paul Revere tea service, something very like it isn't hard to come by. But up to now the antique-automobile collectors have been secure in the conviction that their *bijoux* couldn't be counterfeited. If a car looked like a 1903 Curved-Dash Oldsmobile, then it *was* a 1903 Curved-Dash Oldsmobile, or, at worst, a 1902. No more. There are now at least three firms soliciting orders for antiques-to-order. Any one of them will, for a price, deliver a replica of an antique automobile guaranteed to deceive even an expert—if he doesn't get too close. There are limitations, of course; modern engines are used, and only a few types of cars are available.

It was inevitable that someone would begin the commercial fabrication of antique automobiles. Demand has long since outrun supply, and the hobby, almost unknown before the Second World War, has grown astonishingly since. Enthusiasts belong to one or all of three big clubs, the Antique Automobile Club of America, the Veteran Motor Car Club of America, the Horseless Carriage Club, and there are flourishing special-interest clubs, too, the Rolls-Royce Owners Club, the Mercer Associates, the Classic Car Club, to name three. The clubs publish well-printed magazines full of news and technical information, they organize tours and competitive events, and they lobby for members' interests—the special antique-automobile license plates available in several states, for example.

The compulsion to own an old automobile and to spend hundreds of hours and perhaps thousands of dollars in restoring it to better-than-new condition is more complex than the drive that sends men to, say, stamp collecting. It's a love affair conducted in public, for one thing, with a consequent obvious factor of ego inflation.

"When I put my foot on the running board of something like an SJ Duesenberg," one collector said, "that minute I become a millionaire!"

Most collectors would agree with him—except for those few who are in fact millionaires! The pride of owning something that is unique, or nearly so, is strong among them. Nostalgia matters deeply too, the yearning for kinder, simpler times. James Melton, one of the country's pioneer collectors, and a major force in the field, stated the case in his book *Bright Wheels Rolling*. Talking of a 1911 Franklin limousine, attempting to recreate the world it moved in, he wrote, "Just at dusk on a crisp winter day, a light cover of new snow on the ground, and more still falling. Down Park Avenue in New York, or Commonwealth in Boston, or upper Michigan Boulevard in Chicago—a street like that. Thirty or thirty-five miles an hour, certainly no more. There you are, happy and comfortable on fine brocaded upholstery, seeing out by the light of cut-glass side lamps but knowing no one can see in, the musky scent of fresh roses in the big flower vase, the steady crackle of the tires on the snow, your progress serene, unhurried, your happy arrival as certain as anything can be in this world. *That* was living!"

The old-car collector is usually a sophisticated type, and he would not allow himself the cliché, "They don't make 'em like that any more!" but he harbors the conviction that some at least of the old cars are superior to anything within range of the normal pocketbook today, and this too is part of his *mystique*. He's right: well-maintained Silver Ghost Rolls-Royce automobiles have run for 500,000 miles.

To satisfy these fantasies, to indulge themselves in pleasures denied those who are not *cognoscenti*, the old-car collectors have scoured the countryside. In the Good Old Days, say 1932–39, fine antique automobiles were easy to locate and cheap to buy. Sometimes $50 would fetch a good specimen, and a garageman in Michigan actually *paid* a customer to haul away a T-head Mercer Raceabout, the rarest of all U.S.-built automobiles. Demand and inflation have changed all that. A Duesenberg double-cowl phaeton that cost $750 in 1940 is valued at $9000 today and the owner won't consider selling it. The Mercer that was hauled away as junk is worth all of $5000, and it is not for sale, either. "New" finds are rare. The last "new" Mercer Raceabout, for example (there are fewer than thirty extant), was found in 1949 in a village in Alberta. It had stood unprotected in an orchard for seven years. It might have tempted a junkman to a reluctant offer of $25, but its owner wanted $1500—and I had to pay him $1250.

The best sources, the back-road rural repair shop and the dim, dusty garage, were mined out years ago. Collectors have bought survey maps and worked over promising areas lane by lane. They have circularized postmasters in hundreds of rural communities and they have subsidized traveling salesmen, coaching them carefully in the fine art of obtaining detailed information about an automobile while appearing to have absolutely no interest in it. Year by year the pickings have grown thinner. Still, as the occasional big winner keeps the flame burning in the roulette-player's heart, so does an occasional discovery convince the antique car fanatic that there is hope for him. Gardner King, a Connecticut collector, recently found a Thomas Flyer, duplicate of the 1908 New York–Paris race winner. Body and upholstery were long gone, but the engine and chassis were sound, if well rusted, needing no more than a year or eighteen months of work. The new owner, fortunately, is an expert mechanic. If he were not, he could take the Thomas to a professional restorer. One of the best of these does business on rigid terms: Minimum time, one year; minimum price, $6,000.

Not all old automobiles are valuable. A 1916 Dodge, for example, is practically worthless, while a Stutz of the same year is a prize, and from such simple classifications the matter spirals upward into esoterica that only an expert can sort out, such as the comparative value of otherwise identical Springfield-built and Derby-built Rolls-Royce cars. (Incidentally, the abbreviation "Rolls" is a vulgarism.) Old automobiles are divided into three basic categories: Antique, Veteran and Classic, the corresponding years being about 1900–1914; 1914–1928; 1926–1935. Factors of age and rarity aside, excellence of condition, which usually means restoration, is paramount in determining value. Some restored automobiles have been taken apart literally to the last cotter pin; plated parts redone in heavy nickel; chassis as well as body repainted in twenty coats of hand-rubbed lacquer, and the interior upholstered in a fashion that only a few craftsmen know. A collector on whom the passion truly sits will spend the price of a European vacation in a search for a full set of brass lamps, and the seller may have his soul for six new tires of the correct period. (Firestone has brought out of storage many old "nonskid" molds and tires made in them are reasonably priced and completely authentic.)

When a dedicated old-car owner brings his machine to a *concours d'élégance,* the judges may be reduced to squirming around on the ground beneath it, trying to soil a handkerchief with a spot of dust or a drop of oil that he has somehow missed. A few years ago a white Rolls-Royce touring car regularly won its class, and frequently won best in show in Eastern competition. Its bonnet (hood) had been left in unpainted aluminum, as was the vogue when the car was built, and it glistened like new silver in the sun. To maintain its sheen, it was buffed every thirty days with jewelers' rouge, and never touched with an ungloved hand. No one considered the owner an eccentric. An eccentric might be a man who, having driven his car to a meet and parked it, would scrub out the treads of the tires with a new toothbrush. Most people think an ordinary old scrubbing brush good enough.

Few automobiles produced today seem likely to be much sought after twenty years from now, so the replica-makers may be pioneering a lucrative field. In time it may be worth while to forge an entire automobile from the wheels up. I once heard a collector say he would bid $20,000 for a certain famous "missing" Bugatti if it ever appeared on the market, and if he made the remark in the hearing of certain enterprising European mechanics I think that the car might miraculously be found.

11 · "Knock Down the Wall, *s'il Vous Plait*"

Ettore Bugatti was in my view the most interesting man who ever had anything to do with the manufacture of automobiles. I am prejudiced, beyond doubt. Henry Ford made more money than Bugatti, by a number of hundreds of millions of dollars, and he was a mover and a shaker. Ferdinand Porsche was technically more brilliant. Henry Royce was a more stable and a sterner personality. Marc Birkigt may have been a sounder designer. W. O. Bentley was more single-minded. H. F. S. Morgan may have been a greater eccentric.

But Bugatti's personality was uniquely multifaceted and his cars are as likely to know immortality as any mechanical device man has made. Today, twenty years after the last automobile of his design was made, men in every civilized country in the world are passionately involved in preserving them, and more: in running them on the road and even in racing them. A world-wide club, The Bugatti Owners Club, has for a quarter of a century published a magazine concerned exclusively with Bugatti automobiles, and the only book of its kind in the world is *The Bugatti*

Book, a 375-page, 376-illustration volume which lists the ownership and past history of every known surviving Bugatti—fewer than 500—together with technical data on each of the seventy-odd different models Bugatti made.

Bugatti was an Italian who worked in France during most of his life. He made only 9,500 automobiles in all. He died a French citizen in 1947. He came of a family of notably artistic bent and his own early training was as an artist. He built his first automobile when he was in his late teens and he designed and built motor cars steadily from then until the end of his sixty-six years of life.

Bugatti's cars were quite unlike any others. In the first place, they were much ahead of their time. For example, in 1936 a Bugatti passenger model ran 136 miles in one hour. The record stood for twenty years! Secondly, his cars differed widely one from the other. Bugatti made tiny cars, chain- and shaft-driven; he made big ones, one, the Type 41, or Bugatti Royale, or Golden Bug, so big that it was driven by an engine approximately twice as big as a big Cadillac engine, and costing $20,000 for the bare chassis, without a body. He made superb racing cars, including the Type 35, the most successful racing automobile of all time, winner of 1,045 races in two years, winner of more races than all other makes of automobile put together. He built fast, luxurious sedan-limousines and he built two-seater sports cars, the Types 57S and 57SC, so beautiful and so fast that surviving examples still running attract attention for their modernity of line and command respect for their speed and roadability in competition with the best of contemporary motor cars.

Bugatti was interested in many things other than cars: in food and wine and horses and art and dogs and exotic poultry and boats, notably, but the automobile was his primary concern. He made his cars in a small kitchen-clean factory in Molsheim, Bas-Rhin, and he made his factory the center of what amounted to a little duchy. His chateau was on the grounds, so was his distillery, his stables and riding hall, his art museum, his powerhouse, his private track, his kennels. His guests and clients stayed at his hotel in town. He was an autocrat. He alone governed, roaming his establishment on bicycles of his own design and manufacture, dressed in clothes of bright color that had been cut to please him, and no one else.

He was his own man, and to the degree that a personage of less than royal blood could, he lived as he pleased. Indeed it is not on record that he thought of himself as less than kings, and it is held that he once refused to sell an automobile to a reigning Balkan monarch, King Zog of Albania, because he didn't like the man's table manners.

Ettore Bugatti was in truth a unique individual, but much nonsense has been written about him, much that has been said seriously should be classified as hyperbole, and legend has often been recorded as fact. He was an innovator, certainly a mind of great force, a purposeful character; his was a superb mechanical talent. (But it must be said that his cars, for all the wonder of them, are less than sheer, ultimate perfection: they have strange little flaws, some of them, minor but actual nonetheless, and they are certainly the most difficult cars in the world to work on.) Bugatti was a theoretician who was also a practical executive, a doer. He doesn't seem to have been the kind of man who would build a cabin cruiser in the basement and then wonder how to get it out, but he was, and he did.

When Bugatti conceived the huge Type 41, the world was rocking along in a boom, much as it is now; anything could be sold, and price meant little. Bugatti laid down a series of thirty Type 41's and was perfectly sure he could sell them at a $20,000 chassis price. The market crash of 1929 and the subsequent depression changed the picture. He sold seven Royales, and that was it. He had engines for the other twenty-three built or building. What to do? He decided to put them into *automotrices,* four engines to each.

The *automotrice* was a railcar, a self-powered passenger carrier notably useful for light-load and short-haul work. The idea was not Bugatti's. The French national railways had railcars before Bugatti made one, but in his opinion they were trucks, nothing. The Bugatti *automotrice* would be an *automotrice de pur sang,* strictly No. 1 grade. He rang the bell and issued the order: the factory was to drop everything and run up a railcar. The draughtsmen were put on a rush basis and materials were ordered.

Since the Molsheim factory had not previously built anything bigger than a 20-foot Type 41, the question of where the work would be done was paramount. Bugatti ordered a big shed built. Most railway cars are built on tracks, but *Le Patron* had said nothing about tracks, so the thing was laid out on the bare floor.

Bugatti personally supervised the work, and even the racing department personnel, the Molsheim elite, were put on the project. Being a Bugatti, it was quite unlike any other railcar. The engines were mounted in the center, two on each side; an aisle between them allowed passengers to move from one end of the car to the other. Instead of sitting the *chauffeur* in front, Bugatti put him in a cupola on the roof, directly over the engines. Here he had a superior view of the track ahead, and could as well, if he liked, admire the countryside and keep an eye out for anything creeping up behind, although Bugatti did not intend that anything would creep up behind his *automotrice:* he designed it for 120 miles an hour, even though the executives of the *Chemin de Fer de L'Etat* thought that 70 was very fast. This placement of the crew offered another advantage: brave passengers could sit in the front seats and wonder what was keeping the thing on the rails when it hit the curves.

Bugatti specified wheels built on a Michelin patent, with a rubber cushion between hub and rim, and since he designed the car around 1932, when his devotion to cable-operated brakes was still untouched by argument about the superior efficiency of hydraulics, he put cable brakes on the *automotrice,* as though he had never heard of M. Westinghouse and his air gimmick. They worked well, too: the car could be stopped in 300 yards from 62 miles an hour.

Except for wheels and *bogies,* or trucks, all the main components were straight Bugatti: even the seats were the steel-tube spring-cushioned kind later used in the Type 57's. The sheet-metal skin was done to coach-builders' standards, and the bumpers at each end, commonly black-painted castings, were machine-turned steel. Finished, *automotrice* No. 1 was a lovely thing to look upon—but unfortunately the nearest rail, at the Molsheim station, was a mile and more away, a concrete wall surrounded the entire factory area, and the gate wasn't wide enough to take the car. What to do? *Le Patron* issued a series of orders, the first of which was to chop a hole in the wall on the side leading to the road from the Strasbourg-Selestat highway to the Molsheim railroad station.

The road would have to be closed, naturally. This was a matter of a phone call to the local *gendarmerie*. Ettore Bugatti was more than Molsheim's first citizen; he was indeed *Le Patron,* the boss, the chief in a medieval sense. The population of Molsheim was about three thousand people and Bugatti employed one thousand of them, and knew the names, and much of the history, of many. His solution to the problem of moving the *automotrice* to the station was the same as the Pharoahs' solution to the problem of building the Pyramids: manpower. He suggested that all hands rally round one night at eight o'clock. No one objected, or felt put upon. Bugatti's people liked him. He would have been hurt if they had not.

It was a scene to be remembered, that moving night. The wall had been breached, log-rollers were laid under the *automotrice* and in the light of hundreds of torches and flashlights it was drawn out of the shed. It came slowly and reluctantly. It moved majestically through the torn wall, and with much shouting and a good deal of laughter it was turned on the road and faced toward the station. Moving it was a slow process, necessarily. It would have been easier with the wheels under it—had they not been flanged, so that the sharp edges would have dug into the road, ruined it, and worse, offered so much resistance that even a thousand strong men would have had trouble keeping it under way. As it was, the whole night was required for the job. Fortunately the road was level for the most part. A crane was used for the final step: putting the car on the tracks. There simply wasn't room for enough men to get a grip on it.

René Dreyfus, former champion of France and a team driver for the Bugatti factory, rode with Jean, Bugatti's older son, in the first test runs. He tells the tale: "We scared ourselves half to death. Used to going fast only in automobiles and aircraft, our positions high in the cupola seemed terribly strange. It was hard to believe that we were in control of the monster. For a perceptible fraction of time, entering each bend, the body of the car on which we were looking down continued straight on, for all the world as if it were going off the rails into the countryside; then the flanges of the wheels would bite, the trucks would take hold, and the front end would seem to snap into the proper course. I will always remember Jean, sitting there with his hand on the polished steel throttle lever, shouting to me, 'Shall I shut off?'

"The *automotrice* was quick: it would get to 60 miles an hour in a little over 90 seconds, and to 75 in 2 minutes 12 seconds. It would do 124 miles an hour carrying only crew, and 93 with 107 people aboard. In 1935 a Bugatti *automotrice* did the 504 kilometres between Strasbourg and Paris in three hours and a half, and set records that were to stand for more than twenty years. On a demonstration run for railway officials, Jean blasted through a station so fast—around 120—that he broke glass in the waiting-room windows, and, naturally, terrified the men standing there to watch. The car had superb handling characteristics, once we understood it, and it could be taken safely through switch points three times faster than regulation maximum speed for ordinary trains. Bugatti made a good many railcars after the first one had proved itself, but the rest of them went to the station on rails, and the narrow little road outside the factory was left to the automobiles it had been designed for.

"Even so, its use was not always conventional. I remember a cold Sunday morning on which it was used for adhesion tests on Dunlop tires. The tires were supposed to be superior in the wet, but unfortunately the road was dry. The factory fire engine was brought out, a hose line laid to a nearby brook and the road thoroughly flooded. A Type 51 Grand Prix car was run out and warmed up and I began the tests. The car would stay on the road in the sharpest bend at about 90 miles an hour. I had a very pleasant time, with nothing to do but drift through the bend a few times, wait for the mechanics to change the tires and then do it again. I'm not sure that the Dunlop people who rode with me, watching the Tapley meter, had such a good time. The car had an extra fuel tank in place of the second seat, and they sat on that, not a very comfortable place, high in the wind with no screen in front of them and only a fuel filler cap to hang to.

"Odd improvised projects like that were commonplace at Molsheim, and for me at least were more recreation than anything else. It would not have occurred to me, for example, to wonder if I would be paid for trying to make a G.P. car slide off a wet road. It was part of one's life, that was all, a bit of the strange golden time when it sometimes seemed to me that we were not citizens of France at all, but of a tiny state called Molsheim. In the ordinary way of things, money didn't matter much, it was not important to get rich, what mattered was accomplishment and living well in the sense of taking everything one could out of life. Meo Costantini, the veteran Bugatti team driver who was for years manager of the racing department, never took a *sou* in salary. Ettore Bugatti himself lived like a rich man, but he was never wealthy. He *used* money, and kept little of it.

"There were times, to be sure, when this attitude, charming though it might be, and useful though it might be as a guide to *living* life instead of enduring it, was a bit awkward. Still, there were ways around. When I had not been paid for a while, and needed money, it would not occur to me to *ask* for it, and of course it would be unthinkable to approach M. Bugatti. If one were not paid, it meant only one thing: there *wasn't* any money just then. So I would go to see M. Pracht, the treasurer, and we would have a bright little conversation, moving around the subject for a while and then getting down to cases. In the course of the next day or two I would pick up a chassis, or two chassis, and take them to Robert Benoist, a former team driver who had a Bugatti agency in Paris. I would sell them to Benoist and be in funds again.

"If M. Bugatti did not often reward his employees with money, he had other means. Like the head of any state, he instituted a supreme decoration, a sort of Bugatti Victoria Cross. This he conferred rarely, and it was much coveted: a wrist watch made by Mido to Bugatti's own design. It was very thin, very elegant, and the case was formed in the familiar horseshoe shape of the Bugatti radiator. When a driver had made a notable win against heavy odds he might be given a Bugatti wrist watch. Even a customer might be given one, if he were a notably *good* customer, say one who had bought eight or nine cars and made no complaint if some little thing went wrong with a couple of them. One was summoned to *Le Patron*'s presence, perhaps in his chateau on the grounds, and there, with all due ceremony, the plush-lined box would be presented. It was a great honor, and no one would have equated a watch from M. Bugatti's own hands with mere money.

"I no longer have my watch. I left it in France when I came to America to run in the 1940 Indianapolis race. The war intervened, I enlisted in the American army, and my watch was lost to me during the Nazi occupation. I very much wish I might have it back, or, failing that, another like it, as a reminder of an era we will never know again, as a memento of a man who took what he wanted from life, and in the grand manner.

"I like to think of Ettore Bugatti when, told that the *automotrice* was finished, he must have said, 'Knock down the wall, please, and ask eight or nine hundred of the men if they would be good enough to push the car down to the station for me tomorrow night.' "

12 · The Chevrolet Brothers and Durant

LOUIS CHEVROLET is remembered as a man who designed a wine pump and an automobile. The wine pump didn't amount to much and he made little money from it. The automobile, the Chevrolet, became one of the legends of the century, a fountain from which billions of dollars flowed, but not much of it went Louis' way. He was a racing driver, too, Louis, and so were his brothers, Gaston and Arthur.

The Chevrolets were Swiss who moved to Burgundy in France from La Chaux de Fonds when Louis was an infant. As a young man he ran a bicycle shop, he invented his wine pump and he came to America in 1900 to represent a French manufacturer. He lived in Brooklyn and he worked as a mechanic for a foreign-car dealer, E. Rand Hollander. Gaston and Arthur had come across the Atlantic with him, hot with pride and energy, full of hope. France was the world capital of what was called automobilism in those days, and the three Chevrolets all wanted the same thing: a wheel, a ride in somebody's racing car. Hollander introduced Louis to Alfred Reeves, a race promoter who was looking for new boys to throw into the pit against the great Berner Eli Oldfield, a converted bicycle racer who'd been beating everybody with Henry Ford's "999," handlebar steering and all. Louis was a hungry tiger and he went. He beat Barney Oldfield three times in 1905, once in a 10-mile race at Brunot's Island, Pittsburgh, once at Hartford, Connecticut, once at Morris Park, New York. Walter Christie, inventor of the front-wheel-drive Christie racing machine, was in the Morris Park field. Louis drove a 90 FIAT in those races.

He made the FIAT team for the Vanderbilt Cup race of 1905, and he wrecked the first car assigned to him, a 110 FIAT, smashing it into a telephone pole. He took another car for the race itself, a 90, and was in eighth place at 150 miles when he hit a second telephone pole. He was a heavy-footed driver, Louis, and so were his brothers. In the opinion of Peter Helck, whose view of the period is authoritative, all the Chevrolets were rough on the machinery.

The Chevrolet driving style attracted a man who moved in much the same fashion in his own field: William Crapo Durant. Durant, a promoter who operated on the principle that $1000 was the smallest unit of U.S. currency, thought it would be pleasant to have a Chevrolet for a chauffeur. In 1908, when this notion occurred to him, Durant was head of General Motors, a company he had organized. He had been head of his own insurance agency when he was twenty-one, and a millionaire carriage builder before he was out of his thirties. Promoters behind the Buick car being made in Flint, Michigan, had asked Durant to come in and take over. He gladly did so. He raised Buick capital from $75,000 to $1,500,000. He sold $500,000 worth of stock himself, in one day. Price of the stock quadrupled in four years, and the Buick plant couldn't keep up with orders. Everybody seemed in line for a killing except David Dunbar Buick himself, an inventor of fabulously diverse talent who was said, when he died a poor man, to have made at least fifty fortunes for others!

Durant decided to organize a really impressive holding company and call it International Motors, including in it Reo, Ford, Buick and Maxwell-Briscoe. Ford and Ransom Olds wanted too much money, so the deal collapsed, but Durant and Briscoe went ahead. They asked J. P. Morgan & Co. for $500,000. The Morgan lawyer didn't like Durant's attitude (almost *nobody* liked Durant's attitude) and besides that he didn't see any future in horseless carriages. He recommended refusal. The decision was to cost the House of Morgan about $200,000,000. Durant went ahead without Morgan and organized General Motors with a capital of $2,000. Twelve days later he made it $12,500,000. Sixty days later he bought Oldsmobile for $17,279 in cash and some GM stock and was on his way. He told the Oldsmobile engineers what kind of car to make. In fact, he showed them: he had the body taken off his Buick and sawed into four equal parts. Then he ordered the sections moved apart from each other. "Make a bigger Buick," he said, "put an Oldsmobile radiator and hood on it, and raise the price $250."

This, then, was the tycoon who in 1908 offered to audition Louis and Arthur Chevrolet for the post of chauffeur. He took them to the dirt track behind the Buick works and got into a car himself. Louis won and was somewhat surprised when Durant announced that the chauffeur's job was Arthur's. Louis had been faster, yes, but Arthur had taken fewer chances! However, there was a consolation: the Buick company raced its cars, as every contemporary manufacturer of any prominence did, and Louis found himself in the big leagues.

He began to run on the one-mile dirt tracks, and he won a fair share of the events he entered. Journalists of the time usually ranked him just after Oldfield, Earle Kiser and Jay Webb, the top drivers of the day. He ran a Cleveland in the Twenty-Four-Hour race at Brighton Beach in 1908, and again in the same race in 1909 and 1910, placing fourth both times and sharing the wheel with Arthur in 1910. He ran in the 1908 Vanderbilt Cup race, and won the Cobe Trophy at Crown Point, Indiana, in June, 1909 on a stock 30-horsepower Buick, doing 396 miles at 49.3 miles an hour. He led during 9 of the 17 laps. He won a 10-mile race at Indianapolis in 1909, again for the Buick team. At Lowell, Massachusetts, in September of 1909 he won the Yorick Trophy for 158 miles by a full 20 minutes. Trying for the Lowell Trophy on the same circuit he broke the Buick's frame after making the fastest lap of the day. In the same month he won his class at the Riverhead, L.I., Motor Derby, doing 113 miles at 70 mph, which was really fast for the time. He led the 1909 Vanderbilt until a cylinder head cracked on the fourth lap, and in the 1910 running he led for 7 laps and then had total steering failure while in fourth place. He wasn't hurt, but his riding mechanic was instantly killed. Arthur was running in the Buick team that year, too. Louis won a 2-mile event at the Atlanta, Georgia, Motordrome in 1909, and a 200-miler as well, averaging 72 mph in a Buick.

Meanwhile, back at the foundry, Durant was making automobiles and big decisions. In 1909 he bought Cadillac. Henry M. Leland, who owned the firm, was a man who knew his mind. His first price was $3,500,000, take it or leave it in ten days. Durant didn't get around to it for some months, when he was told that the price had gone up to $4,125,000, take it or leave it, ten days. Durant procrastinated again and when he went around with the $4,125,000 he was told that the market was up again: $4,500,000, take it or leave it, ten days. Durant wasted little time in bringing Mr. Leland the extra $375,000.

He tried to buy Ford for $8,000,000 (cash; Henry Ford wouldn't even discuss anything else, and as a matter of fact suggested *gold* cash) but couldn't raise it, the far-seeing New York bankers being of the opinion that this represented a ridiculous overvaluation of the Ford assets. He did acquire about two dozen automobile and accessory companies, though, grabbing them off like a mad squirrel harvesting nuts in a blizzard. Among them was something called the Heany Lamp Company, which cost $7,000,000 in GM stock. Heany was one of Durant's mistakes. John Heany had a patent on tungsten incandescent lights which would have most seriously embarrassed General Electric. But GE went to court and had the patent declared void. Durant's $7,000,000 had bought nothing. It was too heavy a blow, and the GM board of directors began to bay. They thought Durant needed $7,000,000. In truth, the company was short $12,000,000 and nobody would lend it.

Finally a New York syndicate agreed to help. In these days of the Securities Exchange Commission and the other such instruments of enlightenment with which Franklin Roosevelt prevented American capitalism from cannibalizing itself, it's hard to believe what bankers of the happy 1900–1914 period could and would do once they smelled blood. The banks agreed to loan GM $15,000,000 at 6 per cent per year interest. Of this the firm actually received $12,000,000. The other $3,000,000, by agreement, never left the vaults. Then, as payment for having arranged the loan, the banks took $4,169,000 in GM preferred stock and $2,000,000 in common. All in all, the syndicate stood to make a 75 per cent profit on the deal, plus $900,000 a year interest. The final condition of the loan was that Durant resign, which he did on November 15, 1910.

Durant had not left General Motors in a destitute condition, and he used some of his capital to buy the Flint Wagon Works. Here he set up the Little Wagon Company. (This was not a synonym for "Small Cart," the president being named William H. Little, once general manager of Buick.) Louis Chevrolet, naturally loyal to the man who'd given him his chance, proposed to design a small car, a *voiturette* such as Ettore Bugatti had first shown the world in the Bébé Peugeot. Durant thought it was a good idea, providing the car were strengthened to cope with American rural-road conditions, and Louis went ahead.

The first car the Little company made was a four-cylinder model priced at $700. In 1911 the Chevrolet company appeared with a fairly big five-passenger touring car designed by Louis Chevrolet and priced at $2,150. It was a notable success, and 2,999 units were sold. Louis was a principal in the Chevrolet company, and Arthur and Gaston were also involved, on lesser elevations. During the next two years, Chevrolet sold 16,000 cars and made a profit of $1,300,000. New models poured out, such successes as the Royal Mail roadster, at one time as much a part of a doctor's outfit as his stethoscope; the Amesbury Special, the "490" and the Baby Grand. But Louis wasn't convinced that the company's future was very bright, and in 1913, after a minor dispute with Durant, he dropped out. Durant bought up his interest in 1914 and Louis went off on his own.

The Monroe racing car was of Louis' design, and it won at

Indianapolis in 1920, Gaston Chevrolet at the wheel, beating full teams of Ballot and Duesenberg machines. Louis had designed the Frontenac, too, and the Frontenac was big for a while, and the brothers must have thought, now and then, that the "Fronty" would be the golden egg. Race-car oriented, no business men, they couldn't know that they'd left the golden egg back in Flint. Frontenacs ran seventh and ninth at Indianapolis in 1919, Louis and Gaston driving and Arthur in the pits. They won at Sheepshead Bay, an important circuit of the time, in July and September of 1919, a 110-mile race at 110 mph, 150 at 109 mph, Gaston driving both times. On the same day in July, the 4th, that saw Gaston win at Sheepshead, Louis won at the Tacoma board track in a Frontenac, 80 miles at 100 mph. They had a good car and it had run fast from the beginning, but it wasn't going anywhere. Louis won at the Uniontown Board Speedway, 112 miles at 102, as early as December, 1916. On the two-mile boards at Chicago in 1918, Louis did 100 miles at 108. Now and again he drove something else—a Stutz, for example, on the boards at Cincinnati in May, 1917: 250 miles at 103.2.

Frontenac cylinder heads turned the Model T Ford into quite a fast machine for its time, and for a while "Fronty Ford" was something one heard much about, and that looked like money to Louis, too, but the appearance of the Model A Ford killed it.

Chevrolet and Durant were prospering. Durant steadily built the company, planning and scheming for one day, one hour. He set up Chevrolet in Delaware, he affiliated with the Du Ponts. He began to buy General Motors stock in big bundles. It was easy. The stockholders were angry because the banks controlling the company had seen the profits run to $58,000,000 in three years, but, true to the code of the "insiders," hadn't declared a dime in dividends! On September 16, 1920, Durant walked into the GM annual meeting, lackeys laden with bundles of proxies staggering behind him, and said quietly, "Gentlemen, *I* control this company."

He did, too. He ran it in a big way. He paid Walter Chrysler $500,000 a year to run Buick, a salary that represented a $494,000 raise in two years for Chrysler. He brought in Delco and Hyatt

Roller Bearing and Kettering and Sloan and Fisher Body and Frigidaire. But he couldn't stop expanding, juggling. He finally got too far out on the wire, the company's accountants guessed about $30,000,000 too far out, and the GM doors shut behind him again. This time there was no Chevrolet on which to ride back in. He started to make the Durant automobile but it didn't work. He was bankrupt in 1936 for almost a million. He had assets of $250.

In the same year that saw Durant out of General Motors for the last time, Gaston Chevrolet was killed driving a Monroe at the Los Angeles Speedway. Louis had stopped driving in 1923, and Arthur even before that. Arthur had never really liked it, and he doesn't often show in the record: 1910 Vanderbilt Cup, Marquette-Buick, out at 88 miles with a broken chain; 1910 Grand Prix, Savannah, out at 130 miles with a broken crankshaft while running eleventh.

Louis tried boat racing in 1925, and won at the Miami Regatta. He worked for Stutz for a while and then in 1929 he and Arthur organized the Chevrolet Brothers Aircraft Company, intending to make airplane engines. It didn't turn out well, the brothers quarrelled and there was recourse to law. Louis won, but it was a case of winner take very little. In 1934 he went back to work for Chevrolet, stayed until 1938 when the illness which was to cause his death forced his retirement. He had a small pension from GM. He died in 1941. During the Second World War, Arthur Chevrolet worked for Higgins in New Orleans as a master mechanic. In April, 1946, when he was 61, he hanged himself.

Durant lived longest of the four. He died in 1947. He was running a chain of bowling alleys and a supermarket in Asbury Park in New Jersey. Not just a bowling alley, a chain. Not just a grocery store, a supermarket. Characteristically, he was in early on a couple of things that were booming. He was thinking big, and all he needed, probably, was a little more time. But he was eighty-six, and his time had run out.

13 · The Wonders of Steam

FEW THINGS MECHANICAL are so firmly embedded in American folklore as the steam automobile, and particularly the Stanley Steamer. The last Stanley was made in 1925, and the peak year of the car's popularity was probably 1902, but the indestructible legends live on: the Stanley brothers, the famous "Mr. F. E." and "Mr. F. O." (they were identical twins) had a standing offer of a free car for anyone who could hold the throttle open for sixty seconds; no one knew what the top speed of a Stanley really was; the owner of a Stanley had to have a steam locomotive engineer's license to drive it; the possibility of a boiler explosion in a Stanley was terrible to contemplate, and so on.

None of these things is true, and the facts are more interesting by far. A Stanley Steamer engine had only fifteen moving parts, and a strong man could pick it up in one hand, yet it could drive a heavy automobile with a silence and a smoothness that no other motive power could duplicate. The top speed of the passenger models of Stanley was around 60 miles an hour, but a racing model crashed while doing a claimed 197 at Ormond Beach in Florida in 1907! A boiler rupture in a Stanley was a rarity, and only an inconvenience when it did happen: the steam was made in coiled tubes inside the boiler casing, and an "explosion" was impossible.

More than one hundred American firms made steam automobiles. One by one they dropped out of the race to put the country on wheels, and the internal combustion engine won the day. Why?

The gasoline-powered engine is indisputably ill suited to the task of driving an automobile. Compared with the steam engine, its disadvantages are ludicrous: in the first place, it cannot even start itself, but must be started by a separate power source. It must be fitted with a complicated carburetor or an even more complicated fuel-injection system; and, once inside the cylinders, the fuel charge must be fired by a precisely timed ignition system of battery, coil, distributor, spark plugs. Because it produces no torque, or power, until it is turning rapidly, it must be fitted with a clutch and a gear-change mechanism before it can be relied on to move an automobile. It has a standard gear-change mechanism, there's a shift lever to push about; if it has an automatic transmission, it will be so complicated that only five factories in America can build it, and even so it will not produce genuinely smooth, imperceptible speed changes.

Most gasoline engines are cooled by water with consequent cooling-system leaks, winter freeze-ups and so on. The gasoline engine's fuel requirements are fussy and the stuff is expensive. The engine itself is so complex that only a specialist can do basic maintenance work on it, and its tolerances are so critical, its stresses so high that it rapidly wears itself out. It's easy to see why the steam-car men laughed at the very idea of gasoline-engine supremacy when the upstart device came along. Even electric car devotees were scornful for a time. (Incidentally there is reason to think that the electric automobile may be coming back; several designs are in being as this is written.)

Did "the interests" run the steam automobile into the ground? That was a common belief in the 1920's and one still hears it: the gasoline-car builders sabotaged the steamer by means foul and devious—or the petroleum producers ganged up on it. It's true that gasoline-engine people put out some rough stories about the steamer ("Would you like to see your little children blown sky high?") but they weren't fatal. And the oil men had little to lose. In those early days, before vast investments had been made in refining plants, they were as happy to sell kerosene as gasoline, and they sold more of it.

No, the steamer wasn't sabotaged. It was done to death by the stubbornness and lack of foresight of some of its makers, and by two or three minor technical shortcomings. If the builders had been just a bit more progressive, if the technicians of the day could have come up with just a few basic improvements, the gasoline engine might be a museum curiosity today.

It's easy to forget now, but the steam engine had a tremendous head start in the race. It was man's first important prime mover. Windmills and waterwheels aside, the first mechanical device man set to spinning was run by steam. It was an aeolipile made by Hero of Alexandria, a physicist before the Christian era. It was a reaction engine, like a lawn sprinkler. Nicholas Joseph Cugnot, a French artilleryman, built the first self-powered vehicle ever to move upon a public road, and it ran by steam. (It ran first in 1765; last, about ten years ago, when it was taken out of a Paris museum for a trial.) Huge buses, some carrying as many as twenty-two passengers, were in use in Britain in 1801.

There were steam carriages in America before 1896, when F. E. Stanley built his first car, but they were slow and cumbersome. The first Stanley was a good automobile. The Messrs. F. E. and F. O. Stanley ran a prosperous photographic plate business in Newton, Massachusetts, and in 1896 Mr. F. E. saw a European automobile on exhibition and remarked drily that he believed he could make a better one himself, and, as a matter of fact, he guessed he would. The Stanleys were fifty-three years old at the time, shrewd, saving, close-mouthed men, Yankees among Yankees. They built their car, sold it, built two more, sold them, and in 1899 built two hundred and sold them all. They were the first successful automobile manufacturers in history. Their cars were light, good looking in their way, well designed and capable of startling performance for the day. In 1899 one of them climbed the 12 per cent ten-mile grade to the top of Mount Washington, the first automobile ever to see the top. Demands for Stanley Steamers poured in, and so did offers to buy the company. Mr. F. E. and Mr. F. O. weren't interested in selling, but to amuse themselves they put a price of $250,000 on the company and were startled when the Locomobile Company laid the money on the line and asked for the keys to the plant.

The brothers spent the next year in designing a new steam car and in 1900 they were back in business—and in court, defending a suit brought by Locomobile, the contract of sale naturally having specified that the Stanleys were not to make their car any more. The twins didn't contest the suit, for that would have cost money and they had an earned reputation as "close." They simply redesigned their redesign, this time so completely that no infringement was evident. Locomobile gave up, Mr. F. E. and Mr. F. O. bought back their company for a fraction of the price they'd received for it and began to build steamers again.

In their best years the Stanleys produced about a thousand cars annually. They did business on their own terms. Buyers paid cash. No guarantee of any kind was given or implied. Mr. F. E. and Mr. F. O. were fair and honest men, and they considered a request for a guarantee a slur on their integrity. If something went wrong with a car due to material failure or design error, they'd fix it at no cost—but they wouldn't promise. They painted their cars black, for choice. They would have no truck with yearly model changes, and they never enjoyed spending money for advertising. *They* knew that their car was the best thing of its kind in the world, and they saw no reason to boast in print about it.

Mr. F. E. did unbend in one direction. He liked racing, and in the early days occasionally drove a car on the track. Later, and for high-speed work (at one time the Stanley held five world records) Mr. Fred Marriott usually had the helm. Mr. Marriott, the chief factory mechanic, was a big man, rugged enough to survive one of the most spectacular crashes in automobile racing history.

In 1907 he took a racing Stanley to Florida to try some record runs. The car was very light. The body looked something like an upside-down boat: it was flat on the bottom and the decked-over top was gently curved. It was sharp-ended fore and aft. The engine was the standard Stanley high-speed model, the one used in the car catalogued as The Gentleman's Speedy Roadster. The boiler was running at 1300 pounds of pressure to the square inch, as against the normal 600. Mr. Marriott took a flying start and was doing an incredible 190 miles an hour when he crossed the start of the measured mile. A few yards beyond that point, with the speedometer showing 197 and climbing, the car struck a small bump. With the front end inclined, the airfoil shape of the body, flat below, curved on top like an airplane's wing, asserted itself and the car simply took off and began to climb. It was airborne for over 100 feet and when it hit the beach it smashed itself to pieces. The boiler was picked up nearly a mile away. Mr. Marriott, happily, survived, although terribly injured. The Stanley brothers, horrified at Marriott's narrow escape, vowed never to race their cars again, and never did.

They went on producing passenger models, and some of them were very fast. To try to beat a Stanley Gentleman's Speedy Roadster a gasoline enthusiast needed to spend $8,000 or $10,000 for a Renault or a Lancia—and then he might lose. A Gentleman's Roadster won a 150-mile Florida race by more than 4 *minutes*. The Stanley Fast Touring car cost only $1,000, the 12-passenger Mountain Wagon $2,500.

The Stanley brothers retired in 1917, and from then until its demise in 1925 the company was in other hands. Useful improvements were made on the cars: they had condensers which enabled the boiler water to be used over and over again, thus increasing the distance the car could run on a tankful, and the open-flame pilot light under the boiler had been replaced by an electrically ignited unit. One of the things that had mitigated against a wider acceptance of the steam car had been the open pilot light: ferry boats and public garages wouldn't accept steamers until the pilots had been turned off, which meant that the boilers would cool and the car wouldn't run until the water had been heated again. It might take twenty minutes or more to fire up an early Stanley from dead cold. And while the main controls of the car—steering wheel, throttle and brake—were simple enough, the auxiliary water- and steam- and air-control valves were not, and some Stanleys had thirteen of them!

The hard core of Steamer devotees were men who didn't mind the fuss of firing up their cars, watching the water level in the boiler and paying attention to various pumps and valves; they didn't mind the rather stark basic design of the cars and they weren't put off by the fact that a brand-new Stanley might look just like one five years old. No inconvenience outweighed for them the endearing qualities of the Steamer: for example, the way it would sit stolidly in its garage of a bitter winter night, a faint glow from the pilot light showing on the floor, hissing softly once in a while as it kept itself and the whole garage cosily warm. And once on the road, the steam man was king. His car ghosted along in an indescribably smooth, steady rush, responsive and quick. A steep grade might stall a gasoline-engined car, but it meant nothing to him. He could, if he wanted, stop in the middle of a steep hill, hold the car stationary without using the brake by letting a wisp of steam into the cylinders, and accelerate away.

But for most people, these things weren't enough. The advent of the electric self-starter in 1912 cost the steamers a lot of customers, people who had been afraid to risk their wrists on a hand-cranked gasoline automobile. And while the steamers were incredibly fast over short distances, their limited steam-making ability brought them up short if high speed was sustained for too long a time. The boilers of the day were simply too slow.

By 1926 the Stanley automobile was out of production. Futile attempts to revive it were made during the years 1934–36. Mr. F. E. had died in a road accident, driving one of his own cars in 1918, and Mr. F. O. died of a heart ailment in 1940.

Next to Stanley, the greatest name in steam automobiles is that of Abner Doble, who made his first car in 1914. Abner Doble is a brilliant engineer—he still lives—and is certainly the world's foremost steam-automobile expert. His cars were built to the most exacting standards of quality, and were tremendously advanced in design. For example, in 1923 Doble was selling automobiles that required no more firing-up procedure than the turning of a key on the dashboard. Forty-five seconds later there would be 750 pounds of steam pressure in the boiler! Even today, the best gasoline-engined car should not be driven away from cold in much less time. By 1926 Doble had so improved his condensing system that his cars would run seven times as far as an early Stanley on a tankful of water: 750 miles on 30 gallons. They would do 95 miles an hour.

But they were expensive, and few were made. They cost about $8,500 because of Doble's insistence on the most advanced engineering practice, plus the best obtainable material, from chrome-nickel steel for the chassis to African ebony for the steering wheel rim. The Doble did not survive 1929, but joined the great White Steamer, which had been one of the very best, and the Toledo, the National, the Eclipse and the rest in oblivion.

A few years ago Abner Doble designed a wholly new steam automobile, and a West Coast industrialist seriously considered its production. But the cost would have been great, and the chances of public acceptance slight. There are a few steamers on the road today, many of the old ones run on festive occasions, and every so often a die-hard steam enthusiast, or someone newly infected with the bug, will throw away his gasoline engine and drop a steam engine and a boiler into his car. If you meet one of these hybrids at a traffic light, you'll know it: he'll run away from you.

Beyond doubt, superbly efficient steam cars could be built today. They would be cheap to make—remember the Stanley engine's fifteen moving parts—cheap to run, incredibly long lived. They would conserve our dwindling oil resources: a steam engine uses little lubricating oil. They would transform our big cities: no exhaust sound would come from them, and almost no smoke. Some day we may have them, for the atomic-powered car, if it ever comes to pass, will be, like the atomic submarines, driven by steam.

14 · Miss Jellinek's Namesake

THE DAIMLER-BENZ Aktiengesellschaft makes, among many other things, a line of automobiles named after Mercedes Jellinek, daughter of the man who was Austro-Hungarian consul in Nice—in 1900. Probably no other automobile company currently functioning offers such a range of product: the Mercedes-Benz 300SL, one of the two or three fastest cars in the world, stands at one end of the line, and at the other is a four-cylinder sedan, the 180D, that will deliver about 36 miles to the gallon of No. 2 diesel fuel.

Between are ranked various other carriages, and in point of fact a gentleman could outfit himself with an entire *scuderia* of automobiles without going to another make: a 300SL for fast touring, a 300D for a luxurious town carriage, a 190SL roadster for short trips in which tremendous speed is not required, and a 180D for a hack. Cost? Well, if you *must* consider it, $30,330.

The Daimler-Benz company is unique among automobile firms in many more ways than one. It is the oldest company in present production: the first car built by Karl Benz, one of the two founders, ran in 1885. It can be argued that Karl Benz and Gottlieb

Daimler *invented* the automobile. And in the course of more than half a century of racing, Mercedes-Benz automobiles have built up an incomparable record of success. The company believes that racing is the best and cheapest form of advertising, and when Mercedes-Benz automobiles have been raced they have nearly always been close to unbeatable. In 1938, for example, Mercedes-Benz cars won eight races out of twelve, and finished 1-2-3 in four of them! In 1955 Mercedes-Benz entered eleven races and won all of them!

Automobiles, or something very much like automobiles, had been run long before Gottlieb Daimler and Karl Benz appeared on the scene. Steam-powered vehicles had run successfully in the eighteenth century, and by the early 1800's regular steam-coach service was available in England. The gasoline-powered engine was unknown. The four-stroke principle on which it operates was discovered by a Frenchman, Beau de Rochas, and engines were built on this principle by Etienne Lenoir and the Austrian Siegfried Marcus. Marcus exhibited an automobile in Vienna in 1873 and is held by some authorities to have been the inventor in fact. But Marcus was concerned with many other lines of research; the automobile did not interest him and he dropped it.

Karl Benz' first car, which he built wholly from scratch, never having even seen one, had three points in common with nearly all present-day automobiles: it had electric ignition, a differential gear and water cooling. Daimler's car, which ran a year after Benz, was notable for an ingenious system of ignition: a platinum tube, kept hot by a tiny Bunsen burner, conveyed heat into the combustion chamber which in turn set off the gasoline vapor. Incidentally, Daimler, who died in 1900, never met Benz, and their two companies produced independently until 1926. In 1900, Emile Jellinek, a very rich investor in Daimler's firm, had suggested that the cars would sell better in France under a French name, and so they were named after his daughter, Mercedes.

Benz died in 1929, a very old man full of honors. He had lived long enough to see the Mercedes-Benz automobile well established indeed. It was more than established: it was one of the standards of the world. From the point of view of excellence in engineering and construction, Mercedes-Benz compares only with Rolls-Royce. In the purpose for which their cars are made, the two firms have little in common. Rolls-Royce has for decades concentrated on the production of luxurious limousines and town carriages, while Mercedes has made high-performance and sports cars and small sedans for the most part. Before the First World War, Rolls-Royce too made a few sports racing cars, but afterward the paths of the two firms diverged. The French Grand Prix of 1914, run for 466 miles over a 23-mile course near Lyons, showed for the first time the pattern of racing that was to bring Mercedes-Benz decades of world dominance.

Up to 1914 automobile racing was pretty much an individual's game. A driver went out, ran as fast as he could, won if possible. Little attempt at unified direction was ever made. Mercedes changed all that. Three months before the 1914 race, the Germans showed up with seven drivers, seven cars, a crew of mechanics and a manager. Every morning at five o'clock on the dot the manager blew a whistle, the drivers got into their cars and went out on the circuit. Until one o'clock they practiced. Every corner was taken over and over again at varying speeds and attitudes. At one o'clock the party came in for lunch and a discussion. At two they went out again, and at seven they came in, had dinner and went to bed. This went on for a week. A month later they were back again, with obviously different cars. As new discoveries about the course were made, the cars were sent back to the factory for alteration.

The French expected to win easily with either the Delage or Peugeot teams. For one thing, their cars had four-wheel brakes, which the Germans had not, and four-wheel brakes were held to be worth a minute per lap. Nevertheless, the Mercedes cars won the race going away, first, second and third places. They crossed the line in that order, the French crowd watching in stony silence. A month later the two countries were at war.

The Mercedes-Benz racing pattern has always been the same: long periods of design and test and preparation during which the firm fields no competition cars; a sudden reappearance with new and devastating equipment run with Prussian discipline and an obsessive attention to detail; then retirement again.

In 1934 the Nazi regime offered Mercedes a grant of $100,000 a year to subsidize the firm's racing program. (A competing firm, Auto-Union was similarly helped, and in later years the amount of money was much increased.) The Nazi notion was propaganda pure and simple, and it worked very well indeed. For five years, until the advent of the Second World War, the big white Mercedes-Benz and Auto-Union cars mopped up everything in sight all over Europe. They even came to the United States, in 1937. These were astonishing automobiles. Mercedes-Benz began with a car that weighed a little more than 1700 pounds and developed 400 horsepower. By 1936 the engine was putting out 600 horsepower, with road-holding and braking power to match, and in 1937 it was 650 horsepower. These cars would do 200 miles per hour. In addition, the Mercedes pit crews, operating under the iron hand of the legendary Alfred Neubauer, team manager, could put fuel and oil into a car, change four wheels, wipe the windshield, give the driver a drink, and have it back on the course in under 30 seconds. Only the big Auto-Union cars, with their huge sixteen-cylinder rear-mounted engines, could compete with Mercedes, and Mercedes went right on winning races until August 20, 1939, with the Second World War a couple of weeks away.

Some of the prewar race cars were renovated and run, as a kind of rehearsal, in two 1951 races in the Argentine, and in 1952 the 300SL hardtop coupe with gull-wing doors swinging from the roof won the Twenty-Four-Hour sports-car race at Le Mans, France. By 1954 Mercedes-Benz was ready with another Grand Prix racing car, the model W196, weighing 1540 pounds —much less than an MG—and producing 300 horsepower. It won five races that year, was second in two, third in three—in other words, it was close to unbeatable. It continued to mop up in 1955, and in that year Stirling Moss won the Mille Miglia, Italy's 1,000-mile open-road race, in a 300SLR at the incredible average of 97.9 miles per hour, a figure that may represent the all-time record for the course. That year, Mercedes-Benz won the sports-car championship of the world, the racing-car championship, and the touring-car championship—all there was to win, and retired from racing once more.

At the moment the firm is still in retirement. It will probably not field a racing car for some time to come, and many observers believe that, when it does, the car will be powered by a gas-turbine engine.

Best-known passenger-carrying Mercedes-Benz is the six-cylinder 300SL roadster, an $11,000 item that is one of the two or three fastest production cars in the world: on the quickest rear-axle ratio catalogued, it will do 166 mph. Specially set up at the factory, 300SL's have done 180 mph.

The 190SL, available as both convertible and hardtop, is a smaller, more tranquil sports car, capable of around 110 miles an hour and demanding less skill in handling than the 300SL, which can be extended only by a highly competent driver. The 190SL runs in cost from $5000 to $5400.

Mercedes-Benz sells a line of what might be called standard sedans, the 180, 190, and 219, the first two available with diesel engines as models 180D and 190D. Much of Daimler-Benz' non-automobile business is concentrated in diesels: buses, trucks, marine and industrial engines, and the small passenger-car diesel engines reflect the firm's experience. They deliver an astonishing economy; 32 to 46 miles to the gallon of No. 2 diesel fuel. Except for a peculiar starting procedure and a typical diesel "shake" when the engine is shut off, one would not know that they are diesels. The engine is started on a glow plug: the starting-key is held in until a dashboard indicator shows that the glow plug in the combustion chamber has been brought to red heat; it is then turned farther and the engine starts—but always. Turning the key off will not stop the engine. The fuel supply must be cut off, and the 19-to-1 compression ratio will then cause a short shake as the engine comes to rest. The Mercedes-Benz diesels are so sturdily built and so economical that a number of New York taxi drivers run them, and a New York fleet owner is contemplating buying 200.

The 180D has a top speed on the road of about 80 miles an hour, although it takes a little run to get to it, and it will go all day at 70, and, driven with a modicum of skill, it will put up very high average speeds.

Finding diesel fuel is not a problem. All truck stops have it, and once you've started looking, it's surprising how many gas stations turn out to have one pump carrying a little "diesel" tag. I did run into two attendants who practically had to be shown the engine before they'd start the pump. Both of them had at one time squirted a tankful of No. 2 into the regular, gasoline-burning 180 sedans, with a consequent *bruhaha* involving draining the tank, cleaning the fuel lines and so on.

When diesel fuel was 20 cents a gallon and less, the 180 and 190D would have been even more attractive propositions than they are now, when it's around 32 cents; but still it's a great pleasure to sit there and cruise for a couple of hours with the needle barely showing movement.

Mercedes used to make big limousines, but they never had the distinction of Rolls-Royce or Daimler (England) or Packard town carriages. They were heavy and lumpy-looking, notably including the big 7.7-liter "Grosser Mercedes" model which was made especially for Hitler and his gang. These were very big cars, nearly all of them fitted with armor-plate bodies and window glass. Seventeen of them were made, and a few have survived, including a convertible touring car which was for a long time exhibited out of Chicago as Hitler's personal car. He had probably ridden in it, at that. He visited the factory when the Grosser Mercedes were being built, and at one time specified that a toilet should be put under the front seat. For some reason it wasn't done. The Mercedes workers used to refer to the Grosser Mercedes as "the Volkswagen" but not very loudly.

Currently Mercedes-Benz offers one luxury car, the 300D at $10,000. It's a convertible sedan with automatic transmission. A smaller sedan, the 220S, costs about $6000 less and is altogether de luxe by U.S. standards: full of such touches as a heating system for the driver and a separate one for the front-seat passenger, hot-air vents to demist the side windows, *und so weiter.*

Typical of Mercedes-Benz thoroughness is the mounting of the famous three-pointed star radiator ornament. To prevent juvenile delinquents and careless garage attendants from breaking the thing off, it's set on a strong spring. Bat it around as much as you like, it will always snap erect again, and to take it off requires a screwdriver, a little time and considerable enterprise.

Because of the solidity of Mercedes-Benz cars and the care with which they are built—the factory maintains a very high ratio of inspectors to workers—they have notable longevity; and their performance ability, plus the fabulous racing history with which they're associated, has given them glamour. Consequently they are in great favor with antique- and class-car devotees. The famous models S, SS, SSK and SSKL and the 540K command high prices on the world market, and one, the SSKL, almost never appears. The S series, among the finest sports cars ever built, was designed by the great Dr. Ferdinand Porsche. They were six-cylinder supercharged cars, lithe and lean. Usually the distance from radiator to windshield was as great as that from windshield to taillight. The first S stood for "Sports." Next came "Super-Sport," "Super-Sport-Kurz [Short]" and "Super-Sport-Kurz-Leicht [Light]." The SSK, as the name indicates, had a shorter chassis than its predecessors; the SSKL, produced only to special order, was extremely light, its chassis a lacework of drilled-out holes. Only a few more than three hundred of the S series were made, and David Scott-Moncrieff's definitive book, *Three-Pointed Star,* lists only nineteen surviving.

The 500K and 540K models (in this case the K stands for "Kompressor," or supercharger) were made in the 1930's and are big and heavy eight-cylinder automobiles. Some of the most impressive coachwork ever built was laid on 540K chassis, the two- and four-passenger convertibles being particularly attractive. The 540K was not really fast, being capable of something over 100, but its manner of acceleration was impressive. As was the case with the S series, the Mercedes-Benz supercharger was arranged to blow through the carburetor rather than draw from it, a commoner practice. Therefore its use produced a tremendous piercing scream as the pressure air was forced through the carburetor. Further, it was a "demand" supercharger, brought into use only for fifteen or twenty seconds at a time in order to build up speed or increase power for a hill. (It raised the horsepower from 155 to 180). It was usual for a passenger hearing it for the first time to try to bail out of the automobile, and motorists being passed often made things easier for the 540K driver by mistaking the sound for a siren's blast.

The S and SS cars were the best of all, according to at least one authoritative opinion: that of Edward L. Mayer of London, who has owned 115 Mercedes automobiles!

Among the rarest of Mercedes models, so rare that even the factory would very much like to find one of each, are the SSKL's and the cars made under license in America by Steinway of Long Island. That's right, the piano maker.

15 · The Small-Car Revolution

DESPITE THE DIN of discovery that has accompanied the unveiling of Detroit's new scaled-down automobiles, the small car is no new thing. In 1910 the remarkably gifted Ettore Bugatti designed for Peugeot the first true miniature motor car, the Bébé Peugeot, and it in turn inspired the famed Austin 7, which appeared in this country as the Bantam in the 1930's. Postwar, the little Crosley moved briefly among us, and, in a size or two larger, we had the Hudson Jet and the small Willys, all of them notably ahead of the times.

Perceptive minds long ago noted the need for small cars. In 1924 Kettering of General Motors said: "The wanton consumption of horsepower in propelling heavy motor vehicles portends disaster. Investigations have shown that the average automobile carries on its everyday travels the equivalent of only one and a half persons. The streets of our large cities are absurdly congested with these great empty vehicles. The wise automobile manufacturer reads, along the road of progress, signs that point the way to a smaller, lighter, less expensive car."

General Motors Corporation

Above: The burly Louis Chevrolet, race driver and inventor. He should have been one of the richest men in the world.

Left: Tazio Nuvolari, probably the greatest driver of all time. He had brilliant technique coupled with a fiercely competitive attitude.

Wide World Photos

Left: Alfonso, Marquis de Portago, whose friends believed that he regretted not having been born three or four hundred years sooner.
D. M. Bartley

Stirling Moss, *below*, a Briton, the greatest living racing driver, has won almost every important race in the world.
MG Car Company

Wide World Photos

Above: Juan Manuel Fangio of Argentina, five times champion of thc world, adjusting his goggles on the circuit.

Below: The Cunningham team at Le Mans, 1953: William Spear, Briggs Cunningham, Gordon Benett, Phil Walters, John Fitch.

Wide World Photos

Arnold Studios

Before the First World War, match races between auto and airplane were not uncommon. This one was unusual: the pilot was a woman, Ruth Low. The driver was Gaston Chevrolet. He lost.

Wide World Photos

An unusual view of a Stanley Steamer, showing the asbestos-lagged boiler. The engine was mounted on the rear axle.

Victor Chelminski

The most successful racing automobile of all time: the Type 35 Bugatti. This one, owned by the author, is equipped for use on the road.

Jesse L. Alexander

The sponge-rubber braces in this Ferrari cockpit hold the driver's legs against the lateral "G" forces set up in bends and corners.

George Moffett

Above: Perhaps the noblest "gentleman's carriage" ever built: the Type 41 Bugatti. This one was Bugatti's personal car.

Below: The Duesenberg was the most costly American-production automobile. In '32 its price ranged from $14,750 to $17,750.

James E. Potter

Kettering was right, but the cycle had further to run than he thought. When he spoke, the American automobile was nearly ten years from its dollar peak (the SJ model Duesenberg at $21,-750) and 35 years from its apogee in sheer size (the 1959 Chryslers and Cadillacs). The significance of the automobile as a status symbol, the most important factor in its physical growth, probably began with the full-page Duesenberg advertisements carrying but one line of copy ("He drives a Duesenberg") and portraying a tycoon standing on the deck of his sailing yacht, or at ease in his manor house listening to a pipe organ of cathedral dimension.

By 1949 it was clear that American acceptance of the small car was inevitable, and I remember saying as much to a friend at General Motors in that year. His skepticism was firmly rooted in the conviction that the domestic buyer wanted bigness for its own sake.

Armed forces personnel serving in the European theaters comprised the first significant segment of the population to be exposed to the small car, and its impact on them was heavy. By 1939 the American automobile had been standardized; the great days of diversification were long gone, and there were only slight points of significant difference between one make and another. Advertising had persuaded us that there *was* no other kind of automobile. Very few motor cars were imported, and they were nearly all expensive limousines such as the Rolls-Royce or high-performance sports cars such as the Bugatti.

Thus the GI's discovery that Europe had many small, fast motorcars of novel design notably impressed him. He remarked that a small car could be comfortable; that it could be lively in traffic, and that the handling of it could produce a sensuous pleasure akin to skiing or riding. A few GI's brought cars home with them. Others, returning to find a shortage of the Detroit product, sought out the foreign-car dealerships beginning to open on the East and West coasts. Old-line importers such as J. S. Inskip of New York, for decades purveyor of Rolls-Royce cars, began to take on such makes as the British MG, a classic sports car, and new dealers appeared, notably M. E. Hoffman, who popularized Jaguar, Mercedes-Benz, Porsche and FIAT. Hoffman began business with one used car and four employees; ten years later he grossed $38,000,000 in twelve months.

A phenomenon noted almost immediately by the dealers was the preponderance of professional people among the purchasers of foreign cars. Clearly their appeal to the egghead was strong, and it was this fact that inclined observers to the belief that a noteworthy trend was in the making. The role of the intellectual in forming the American market place has often been disparaged, but not by the knowing; the first cracks in the dam unloosing floods of such commodities as Scandinavian modern furniture, high-fidelity phonographs and Ivy League men's wear were dug by East Coast nonconformists. Today, with the foreign car firmly established, it's still true that more professional people buy them than buy domestic cars, and even such traditionally conservative segments of the professional population as physicians conform, *vide* the staff parking lot of almost any big hospital.

The re-establishment of road racing counted heavily in the small car's comeback, too. Since the 1920's automobile racing in this country had been in the hands of promoters, and a unique type of single-seat automobile, useless for anything but racing, had been evolved. Americans learned that road racing in fast two-seater cars was the classic form of the sport, reaching back more than half a century. Many of the early purchasers of MG's raced them; and, when their skill outreached the MG's exciting but limited performance, they moved on to faster cars. By 1957 the *Wall Street Journal* could report that automobile racing was the biggest U.S. spectator sport, attracting 8,000,000 more devotees than baseball. Those who could race did so; others could at least participate vicariously through the purchase of a small imported car that might be blood brother to a racing model.

Thus the imported car acquired standing as a status symbol, and when the well-to-do began to buy them as second cars their place was secured.

Meanwhile American publishers began to bring out motoring periodicals in emulation of the magazines that have been a fixture on the European scene for decades. Staffed by young men, most of them newly exposed to the *mystique* of the sports car, and enthusiastic about performance rather than "styling," they were critical of the Detroit product and they exerted an influence out of proportion to their circulation totals. The sales of imported cars continued to rise: in 1954, 32,403; 1955, 58,460; 1956, 98,171. By 1957 the ubiquitous Volkswagen was outselling the Studebaker, Lincoln, Imperial, Nash, Hudson and Packard, and it is significant that four of those cars are no longer being made. American Motors, first U.S. company to commit itself to the small, or "compact" car, was astonishing the industry with production and profits. In 1958 the blow fell: for the first time in fifty years the rest of the world produced more automobiles than we did, and we imported more units than we sold abroad. All who ran now could read: the days of the really big, chrome-festooned wheeled scow were numbered.

As one looked back, the straws in the wind had been many, the most telling of them probably the Edsel failure. Beneficiary of the most extensive pre-release publicity campaign of the decade, the Edsel had proved almost unsaleable. Charles Kreisler of New York, a Park Avenue dealer whose acumen is legendary in the trade, had accepted the Edsel franchise for all of Manhattan. "For three or four days thousands of people paraded through my showrooms," Kreisler said, "but almost none of them were buyers. Within a week I was certain the Edsel would not sell, and, as soon as I could, I dropped the Edsel franchise and took on the Rambler."

Nevertheless, the public-policy statements of Detroit executives reflected an apparently unyielding hostility to the idea of a small car even as late as 1958, when Edward H. Cole of Chevrolet said that the demand for small cars was "flattening off" and that the American industry would never, in his opinion, produce one. The propaganda line was started by Ernest Breech of Ford, who doubted that the American people would be willing to accept the "lower standard of living" reflected in the small car.

Still, the engineering staffs had long considered the possibility. Ford had made up a small rear-engined car in the 1930's, and the Big Three regularly purchased, tested and stripped every foreign car on the world market. So when the decision was taken to make a "compact" car (the term had come to mean something bigger than a VW but smaller than the smallest Ford), the technical people were ready. It was time: there were more than 1,000,000 foreign cars on U.S. roads, 300,000 of them Volkswagens; and the import dealers, having passed 300,000, were confidently talking about 500,000-unit years.

Ford and Chrysler decided to make "standard" cars. Chevrolet, under the leadership of the previously skeptical Mr. Cole (perhaps he hadn't really been so skeptical, but only marking time) weighted its decision more heavily with the novelty factor that has certainly contributed much to the success of the imported cars. Chevrolet elected to use an air-cooled engine and to place it in the rear, after Volkswagen and Porsche practice. The engine is a "flat" six: three cylinders opposed to three.

The advantages of a rear-mounted engine in a small car are considerable: no drive-shaft tunnel intrudes on passenger space; with no exhaust pipe running the length of the car, ground clearance is improved; engine weight on the driving wheels makes for superior traction in snow and ice.

Against the rear engine are the facts that luggage must be carried in front, where the wheel wells restrict available space, that station wagons and other variations on the standard model are harder to make, and that the car may have a tendency to oversteer. Oversteering is a phenomenon that makes a car appear to turn more sharply in a bend than the angle of the front wheels would seem to warrant, and is caused, among other things, by extra weight in the rear.

Ford publicists were quick to exploit the oversteering potential of Chevrolet's new Corvair, illustrating their contention with pictures of the erratic flight of an arrow carrying its head where the feathers should be. The argument was, of course, specious, if only because an automobile does not fly in free air but is guided over the ground by the friction of its wheels.

The Ford people further argued that only very small cars, carrying light engines, could safely put them in the rear. Examples from the past contradict this, too. The Czechoslovakian Tatra is an old make and carries a big V-8 engine in the rear. One of the most successful racing cars of all time was the German sixteen-cylinder Auto-Union, a rear-engine car. (Granted only first-rank virtuosi could drive it at its limit.) The present-day Porsche, a delightfully stable car, is rear-engined; and, while early models oversteered notably, minor modifications soon cured the trouble.

The Corvair actually handles very well indeed, and while oversteering can be demonstrated in it, the phenomenon appears only in violent cornering at high speeds, circumstances the average driver never experiences. Corvair overcomes the passenger-compartment heating problem, a difficulty inherent in air-cooled-engine cars, by offering an efficient gasoline-burning heater.

It is significant that Chevrolet engineers, talking privately among themselves, have expressed over-all contentment with the Corvair, and surprise at the few "bugs," common to all new mechanical devices, that it has shown so far. It is an inch shorter and 3½ inches lower than the Ford Falcon—but 20 inches *longer* than the Volkswagen. This 1½-foot extra length is the mark of the compact over the small car.

The Ford Falcon is the result of a conservative approach. Its engine offers 90 horsepower—10 more than the Corvair, 10 less than the Chrysler Valiant. Ford engineers are confident that it will show 30 miles to the gallon under careful usage, although few drivers will reach that figure if they exploit the car's performance potential. In styling it shows its relationship to the rest of the Ford line: appealing but not radical. It handles like a Ford, offering a combination of liveliness and good road manners.

Chrysler's Valiant has the shortest wheelbase of the three, if only by 1½ inches, and weighs the most by 300 pounds. It also has the most powerful engine, 100 horsepower, and is probably a genuine 100-mile-an-hour automobile. In keeping with Chrysler policy of the past few years, the Valiant has been designed for an air of novelty and excitement and luxury, and so effectively that when it was first shown to automobile writers late in September, 1959, they applauded spontaneously, an unusual reaction indeed.

There is no reason to doubt that the new American "compact"

cars will succeed in their assault on the market. They'll sell well, and so will the compact 1960 versions of Buick, Pontiac, Oldsmobile and so on, to be followed, if one can believe rumor, by small Cadillacs, Chryslers and Continentals. And if present plans mature, truly small, not "compact," cars may be offered by the Big Three in 1962 at prices brutally competitive with the cheapest foreign makes.

However, the best opinion seems to be that the Valiant, Falcon and Corvair will not destroy or even seriously injure the present imported-car market. Most dealers take the view that the new cars are not competitive with the imported models, but rather with U.S. big cars; that they will not satisfy the customers' wish for the *cachet* that goes with driving an imported model, and that Detroit wage levels will not allow production standards competitive with the best foreign cars. Indeed, some dealers believe that the new cars will, by drawing attention to the desirability of small machines, *increase* the appeal of the imported models. They cite the amazing climb of the $2000-class Rambler to crowd Plymouth for third place in national sales. If figures mean anything, Rambler's notable increase in sales has taken nothing from the imports. The rapidly growing popularity of the Studebaker Lark, one of only four U.S. makes to show a sales increase in 1959 over 1958, is another case in point. The Lark, available as sedan, station wagon or convertible, is in the $2200–$2500 range.

Imported cars come in fantastic variety. In price they range from $1110 to $22,500. In speed, from 50 miles an hour to 160. In gas mileage, from 55 miles to the gallon to 7 or 8. You can buy a car with an engine of one cylinder, two, three, four, six, eight or twelve. You can have the engine in the front or the rear, air- or water-cooled, front-wheel drive or rear. Many Volkswagens have been sold on the merits of the car's air-cooled engine. It has no water to boil off in summer or freeze in winter. The Swedish SAAB, the French Citroën, the German DKW all have front-wheel drive, which makes for roominess (no drive-shaft hump and tunnel) and in small cars gives remarkable sure-footedness on the road.

Because we are a nation of shoppers, always on the lookout for the new and different, the points in which small foreign cars differ from our own appeal to Americans. But most of us approach a small car with three big questions: (1) Wouldn't it be dangerous in an accident? (2) Can anything that small be comfortable? (3) Where can I get parts?

We have been brought up to believe that size and weight in an automobile mean safety. It's an article of faith with most laymen that only a heavy car can really hold the road and that weight of metal offers protection in an accident. Neither of these beliefs has much connection with reality. Springing and weight distribution govern road-holding. Racing cars weighing 850 to 1500 pounds will stick to the road with incredible tenacity at speeds up to 150 miles an hour, while some passenger automobiles weighing two tons are so dangerous that knowledgeable professionals won't drive them 75 miles an hour on anything but a dead-straight road and are uncomfortable even then.

Weight as a protective factor in collision is equally meaningless. It must be, since accidents killed about 40,000 Americans last year, most of them riding in heavy cars. Given a choice between hitting a solid, immovable object at 30 miles an hour in a 50-ton tank or a small automobile, the wise man would take the automobile. Its metal structure would crumple under the impact, decelerating the car comparatively slowly. The utterly rigid armor plate of the tank would stop it instantly, and the driver, unless he were strapped to the seat, would fly into the metal interior at almost the full 30 miles an hour. The driver of the car might live —as a man occasionally lives when he jumps or falls from a high building and lands on the yielding metal top of a parked car. People die in automobile accidents by being thrown against the interior surfaces of the car or by being hurled out of it to the ground. In a small proportion of accidents the body metal of a car may prevent injury, but in these cases the size of the car itself is of no significance.

In "pre-crash safety," which covers ease of steering, road holding, braking power and so on, most small cars are safer than the big ones. True, most of them do not have blistering acceleration, "to get you out of a jam," but this lack is a safety factor in itself, because it acts as a brake on the driver's judgment. In nine cases out of ten, the driver who needs terrific acceleration in the 30–60 mph range needs it because overconfidence in the amount of power at his disposal has caused him to take a foolish chance. In the past few years, while the power of automobile engines has mounted steadily, state highway patrol officers have noted an alarming increase in high-speed head-on collisions on straight stretches of two-lane road. They blame these accidents on driver overconfidence in engine power. Another danger has been pointed out by John Fitch, well-known American race driver: when the full power of a big American car is unleashed in a panic application, the automatic transmission usually drops into a lower ("passing") gear, and this often produces rear-wheel spin with consequent loss of traction and of control that is impaired or lost entirely.

Are small cars comfortable? For front-seat passengers, yes. For back-seat passengers, not entirely, because leg room is restricted in most of them. This is not as important a factor as it sounds, however, because the average passenger car load in the United States is 1.5 people. In "ride" the small car may have a slight edge, although most Americans require some time in which to become accustomed to it. Leading European designers believe that a "taut" suspension, requiring the passenger's body to make fairly abrupt but short accommodating movements, is less fatiguing than a soft suspension which requires long, slow muscle adjustments. I would rather drive five hundred miles a day in a small car like the Renault Dauphine or the SAAB than in a softly sprung big car. The Rolls-Royce, acknowledged leader of the world's luxury cars, offers a ride surprisingly firm by American standards. Taxi drivers believe that tightly sprung cabs like the Checker are much less fatiguing than cabs built on standard passenger-car chassis. (The Checker company now markets a family sedan priced around $2500 and designed to stand up under ten years of hard service.)

Availability of spare parts was a problem when the small car first appeared in this country. Today the major importing firms maintain heavy stocks of spares. Most importers set up special schools for the training of their dealers' mechanics, see to it that they have any needed special tools. There is nothing exotic about the smaller foreign cars, and any competent mechanic can do straightforward maintenance work on them.

A reversion to the shopping methods of twenty-five years ago seems to characterize foreign-car buyers. In recent years the typical American buyer has chosen his car on the basis of size, color, upholstery and sheer power. American manufacturers minimized mechanical features or concealed them in synthetic terminology: "Turboglide," "Firedome." Dealing at first with sports car admirers who were technically knowledgeable, foreign-car dealers emphasized the nuts-and-bolts features of their cars. Since they still have a comparatively small range of optional equipment, they have continued the practice. In dealing with women they emphasize ease of handling and convenience. To men they talk about gas economy, road adhesion, braking power, and they urge the potential customers to drive the car. Once he has relearned the use of a manual gearshift (some small cars now have automatic clutches, and automatic transmissions are coming) he usually decides that the small car is not, as he had feared, too slow.

Best-liked foreign car is the Volkswagen. Amazingly, the Volkswagen is still being made on the design laid down nearly twenty-five years ago by the famous Dr. Ferdinand Porsche. Year-to-year changes have been slight, and the factory will not admit that radical redesign is even envisioned at this point. The air-cooled, rear-mounted engine is remarkably long-lived, often runs for 100-000 miles without major attention. The VW is a big seller in one hundred countries, functions just as well in the tropics as in the sub-Arctic. One very rarely hears a VW owner complain about the car.

Comparatively a newcomer, the Renault Dauphine is crowding the VW hard, has outsold it in some areas. Renault is one of the oldest automobile manufacturing firms in the world, and Renaults were famous before the turn of the century. The Renault's four-cylinder engine is rear-mounted, water-cooled, produces a top speed around 70 miles an hour. The Renault has a semiflexible steering wheel, a padded dashboard.

The Morris Minor 1000, made in Britain, is based on a design by a racing-car specialist and is notable for remarkable road adhesion and for cornering power. It has two highly desirable design features rarely found in a small car: rack-and-pinion steering and torsion-bar suspension.

Another British importation, the Hillman Minx, is sold through a dealership of six hundred firms. It has a lively engine, and test drivers have been impressed by its brakes, which appear to be highly fade-resistant. The Hillman has an "American" design look, particularly in the convertible.

The Austin A-40 was one of the first British cars to attempt penetration of the U.S. market and the current model sells well. It's a notable gas miser and some owners report 35 miles to the gallon day in and day out.

Until quite recently, most Italian cars available in this country were very expensive. The Ferrari, the Maserati, the Lancia are among the fastest cars in the world, and among the most expensive, too. FIAT is selling heavily. Four cars are offered, two economy models, a medium sedan and a sports car. The small cars are the FIATS 500 and 600 (engine size in cubic centimeters), the sedan is the 1100 and the sports car the 1200. The 1100 is comparable to Volkswagen and Renault and delivers a comfortable ride together with the superior handling characteristics demanded by the racing-minded Italian consumer. The FIAT Multipla, competitive with the VW Microbus, is a remarkably roomy six-passenger carryall.

General Motors imports two small cars: the Vauxhall Victor and the Open Rekord. Both these cars, and the Taunus, made by Ford's German subsidiary, are American-looking, scaled-down Detroit designs carrying more chrome than is usual in Europe. In workmanship, economy and performance they are equal to the independent importations. They are about $200 more expensive, the higher prices reflecting additional weight and size. For example, the Vauxhall is 751 pounds heavier and 9 inches longer than the Renault Dauphine.

Chrysler retails the French Simca, an independent make of sprightly performance and good economy, and Ford offers cars built by its British subsidiary, the Anglia, Consul, Prefect and Zephyr.

Not all imported cars come from Europe. The Japanese are sending one, the Toyopet Crown, into the West Coast market, and the Datsun is sold in the East as well. Both are well-built, sturdy cars designed for the American consumer. As camera buyers have known for some time, the prewar notion that the Japanese could produce only shoddy industrial goods has no validity today.

Among the *newest* cars in the world is the Swedish SAAB, built by jet aircraft manufacturers. Free from the burden of old dies and tools to carry over, the SAAB designers started from scratch to produce an economical, safe, high-performance car. The SAAB has front-wheel drive, a wind-tunnel body, a three-cylinder, two-stroke engine with only seven moving parts. Exceptionally sure-footed, the SAAB has done very well in competitive events, is really impressive on snow and ice.

The Citroën ID19 is another front-wheel-drive car, product of a company that has made more automobiles on the f.w.d. design than any other in the world. The ID19 is a motor car of very advanced design, and some testers believe that it offers the best ride over rough surfaced roads obtainable in the world today without regard to cost.

Another car of unique quality is the Volvo, from Sweden. The Volvo is probably the fastest of all the smaller cars, it is among the most rugged, and it can honestly claim the most efficient passenger-car engine currently made: it produces more horsepower per cubic inch of size than any American-built engine up to and including the Cadillac.

The DKW is a German car similar in design to the SAAB in that it has a three-cylinder, two-stroke engine driving the front wheels. An intensive drive to popularize it is currently underway. Like most German-made cars, the DKW is exceptionally sturdy.

A compact car that is not often seen but offers remarkable utility is the Mercedes-Benz diesel. At around $4000 this is the most expensive of all economy cars, but its longevity and maintenance figures are so good that the handful of New York taxi drivers who have bought it are ecstatic about the machine. Some of them claim to have run this diesel engine 100,000 miles at a maintenance cost of less than five dollars! As we have mentioned, it will produce up to 46 miles to the gallon, and the diesel fuel it burns costs about 32 cents a gallon. (It will run equally well on No. 2 fuel oil, at 10 cents a gallon, siphoned out of your furnace tank, but if you are tempted by this economy and get caught at it, Uncle Sam will deal with you as a tax dodger, which is to say, severely.)

Under the standard small cars come what the Germans call *Kleinwagen:* subminiature cars, or cabin scooters, or bubble cars. These are the real babies: one- or two-cylinder engines, top speeds around 50 miles an hour, limited passenger space. Some of them, like the FIAT 500, are simply tiny standard automobiles; others, like the Heinkel, Isetta, Janus, are best described as cabin scooters. Used in the city only, they have a lot to recommend them in low initial cost, fantastic gas mileage, ability to park almost anywhere. Some *Kleinwagen* owners estimate they save $50 a month, but the cars are certainly too small ever to sell even a fraction of the American market.

Some authorities believe that the stream of small foreign cars may reach its peak at around 500,000. Detroit executives frankly hope so, believe that the production of domestic small cars may wean buyers back. Best guess is that Americans will continue to buy all the small foreign cars Europe can send, plus as many as Detroit wants to build. George Romney of American Motors, whose current standing as a prophet is the best in the industry, believes that by 1966 small cars will account for 50 per cent of all American sales. That means, minimally, 2,500,000 units. If Romney is right, we are watching the beginning of a revolution in American taste. History is on Romney's side. The automobile was invented in Europe, and nearly every major change in it was originated in Europe and was brought to this country, after a time lag of ten years or so, for economical mass production. Ten years from now the American small car may well be the world's standard.

16 · The Desirable Bastards

For years automobile connoisseurs have dreamed of the happy results that must attend the mating of the best in American and Continental practice. The typical European sports car has a lovely Italianate body, sleek, low, chrome-free, running a small, fussy, fast-turning and hard-to-service engine. The typical American high-performance car has a big, immensely powerful, slow-turning engine, that can be fixed in any crossroads garage, driving a grotesquely oversize, barge-like, chrome-curlecued body. Why not take the European body and stick the American engine into it?

A lot of one-shot automobiles were turned out to this formula, some by major firms, some by individuals. The Nash Rambler Palm Beach, the Chrysler K-300, the Dart, the Norseman were some of them. Individually made, their cost was fantastic, a minimum of around $40,000.

Some of those who drove them thought they were almost worth it. They were beautiful, they were exotic, and they were fast. What more is there? Only handling and history. The thoroughly experienced driver, wedded to firm suspension and quick steering, found them a bit insecure, and the traditionalist found them socially unacceptable: he wanted a car that had behind it decades of elegance, or of race-winning, or of style-setting.

Still, the idea of engine-swapping was no new thing. The British had been doing it for years, and the Allard, one of the most successful racing sports cars of the postwar period, was usually delivered in this country without an engine, so that the purchaser could drop in a Cadillac or a Chrysler as he chose. Engine-swapping had been done even on a wholly domestic basis: when the Loewy-designed Studebaker appeared, a good many of the *cognoscenti,* enchanted by its lines, were prevented from buying only by the lack of horsepower in the Studebaker engine. The legendary East Coast racing mechanic, Bill Frick, began to drop Cadillac engines into Studebakers. He called the result a Studillac and he sold seventy-five before he tired of making them. They were quick, good-looking automobiles, the Studillacs, and even today you occasionally see one running away from some over-ambitious contemporary.

The idea of the transatlantic bastard car had occurred to people in Europe, too; and, after the Paris Automobile Show of 1951, the French Compagnie Facel-Metallon, builders of bodies for the Simca Sport and the Ford Comète began to consider making a new high-performance car. Before the war, France had produced many such: Bugatti, Talbot, Hotchkiss, Delage, Delahaye. Some of these were still being made, in very small quantity, but they were prewar in conception and design. The Facel-Metallon people wanted something that would be new from the tires up.

By March, 1953, a test car was in being, and in November there was a second. Both of them ran 110,000 kilometers in France, Switzerland and Belgium. The final design was shown to the press in July, 1954, exhibited at the Paris Show in October, and the first production car was delivered in March, 1955. It was called the Facel-Vega.

The Facel-Vega is a genuine high-performance automobile *de grande luxe.* It uses a big Chrysler V-8 engine and transmission, but the chassis is special, a welded arrangement of 4-inch tubes and in the coupe model the car is short, at 104 inches only a bit longer than a Nash Rambler. There's a bigger four-door sedan.

In the old tradition of the custom-made automobile, unhappily almost gone now, the Facel-Vega offers numerous options to the buyer: Chrysler automatic transmission or the magnificent Pont-a-Mousson four-speed manual gearbox, with synchromesh on all gears, reverse included, as an option on the option. Disk brakes, power steering, right-hand drive are all available, and the interior can be finished in any leather or any fabric available on the world market. An enormous stack of fitted luggage is tagged at $350 extra.

A two-seater in the European tradition, the Facel-Vega coupe makes no concessions to three-abreast seating. The two front bucket seats are separated by the necessarily high transmission tunnel, which carries controls for the lights, windshield wipers and windows, the latter electrically raised and lowered. Part of the impression of luxury the Facel-Vega makes derives from the dashboard, a tremendous, door-to-door expanse of walnut paneling.

With 360 horsepower available at 5200 revolutions per minute, the Facel-Vega is fast: using a 3.31 axle ratio, the makers claim 0 to 60 mph in 7.5 seconds, a fabulously quick reading, and a top speed of 130. An alternative 2.93 rear end will produce 150 miles an hour, in theory at any rate. Most owners value the car's comfort and agility over its top-speed potential, but it's nice to know that the quickness is available. At 150 mph the Facel-Vega joins the legendary likes of the Ferrari Super as one of the fastest passenger automobiles in existence. And at $9500 the cost is around half while the exclusivity is not much less. There will never be many Facel-Vegas around, even though the French diplomatic service is to be equipped with them. That's a pity. In a really well-ordered world there'd be one for everybody who wanted it, one for everybody who wanted to know the joy of sliding along a string-straight moonlit road in utter silence, power underfoot to run away from anything, a month's luggage nested under the deck, someone pretty and amenable in the other seat, and Mexico dead ahead!

Cousin to the Facel-Vega is the Dual-Ghia, a Chrysler-based Italo-American high-performance car. The Dual-Ghia originated in Detroit when Eugene Casaroll, head of Dual Motors, a subsidiary of the Automobile Shippers firm known as a sponsor of Indianapolis Five-Hundred cars, fell victim to the wish for a fast, unique automobile. He made a couple of tentative stabs at it and then asked the Detroit representative of the Italian coachbuilder Ghia, Paul Farago, to give the matter some thought. Farago thought for a while, then bought two Dodge D-500 chassis and took them to Italy.

The D-500 Dodge had created a considerable stir when it appeared in 1956. It would accelerate from 0 to 60 miles an hour in 9.6 seconds and in another 40 seconds arrive at 115 mph—and all this with a total weight of over two tons.

In Italy Farago had his two D-500 chassis cut up and reworked in the interests of a lower center of gravity. Ghia designed a typically handsome convertible body, unusual but restrained, and the completed car weighed 200 pounds less than the D-500 Dodge. It was consequently a little faster in acceleration and in getting to top speed, 123 mph. Moving the 230-horsepower engine six inches rearward in the chassis materially improved the car's handling qualities over the parent Dodge. The Dual-Ghia was available with power brakes and steering and automatic transmission at about $7500 and a production run of one hundred was planned. The car went on the market in the middle of 1957. By March of 1958 the last one had been sold and none has been made since. Hoagy Carmichael had one, Dan Topping, Gussie Moran were owners. Gilbert Kahn of the famous New York financial family had one, liked it so much that he said he was sure he could sell six of them to his friends. Frank Sinatra got one and so did Peter Lawford and Eddie Fisher.

Unlike the Facel-Vega, available only as a hardtop, the Dual-Ghia is a convertible. It offers American big-engine performance, American big-scale comfort (there's room for three in back) with Italian styling. Retaining Dodge suspension, it's not a competitive sports car, but it certainly is a high-performance automobile of unusual grace and beauty.

Out of production now, the Dual-Ghia may appear again. The new one would be different in at least two ways: it would be a hardtop, and it would probably cost around $10,000.

For the thinking man who wants something a little bigger than the Dual-Ghia or the Facel-Vega—say, rather more than twice as big—there's the Cadillac Eldorado Brougham. The six-page publicity release announcing the car said nothing about it, but the 1959 Brougham is being shipped, chassis and shell, to Italy to the famous Farina coach works for finishing. The styling, although executed by Farina, is basically Fisher, and few onlookers, not noticing Farina's signature plate on the car, would take it to be anything but standard Detroit.

The Brougham is a limited-production car and is unique even in its own category in that there are no mechanical options. There is no need for options. The American public wants nothing to do with a stick shift, understands nothing about alternative axle ratios, and everything else is standard: air conditioning and air suspension, automatic dimmer, power front *quarter* windows, power seats and electric door locks and power rear-deck lid. The customer can, however, have anything he likes in the way of interior options.

The Brougham is an all-out attempt at a series-produced luxury automobile of the first category. It is an enormously comfortable prestige-building carriage, with remarkable suspension characteristics, marvellously good power steering—and the most brutally snobbish horn note in the world. It is full of novelties, such as a rear-quarter window that slides out of sight when the door is opened, in the interests of easier entrance. The Brougham is 225 inches long and at $13,075 costs a little less than the small, or economy model, Rolls-Royce.

That's the field at the moment: Chrysler, Dodge, Cadillac engines; Facel, Ghia, Farina coachwork. If you can't be made happy by a choice out of this group you are fussy indeed. However, there is hope for you. Buy a couple of whatever chassis you like, take them to Italy, wander around Turin until you hear the unmistakable sound of hand-held hammers basing aluminum, and then go in and talk to the man. Eventually you'll find one who'll listen to you, if you've remembered *the* important thing, which is: Bring money.

17 · The Duesenberg Man

MANY AMERICANS have never seen a Duesenberg automobile, the most luxurious and expensive this country has known (they sold for $14,750 to $25,000), but in the little town of Weston, Connecticut, they're almost commonplace. Duesenbergs rumble into Weston from far places: Chicago, Montreal, Buenos Aires, New Delhi. They turn off the main road at a mail box marked "A. J. Hoe." Here, in a cramped six-car garage, Arthur James Hoe, forty-five, master mechanic, has made a career out of working almost exclusively on Duesenberg automobiles. His services are not cheap, and he prefers to work unhampered by the owner's opinions, but during the last fourteen years some 225 Duesenbergs, more than half the total built before the company dissolved in 1937, have been in his shop. Hoe works on other kinds of high-performance cars, of course, but his main interest is the Duesenberg, and he is the world's ranking authority on the car.

Just before the Second World War, a Duesenberg in reasonably good condition could be bought for $1000 or so. Today the cars rarely come on the market at all and when they do the price asked ranges from $3500 to $10,000. To restore a thoroughly beat-up Duesenberg to like-new condition Hoe charges around

$6000, will not expect the car to come back for any kind of repair for at least five years. He runs a flourishing parts business by mail, often diagnoses ailing cars over the telephone, and is so well known in sports-car circles for his rigid ethical standards that strangers have commissioned him to find, buy, restore and deliver cars to them. He makes no charge for what he calls "learning time" on a car, and guarantees his work unconditionally. When he finishes a Duesenberg, it will deliver its rated 320 horsepower, if it's the big Model SJ, and it will be as fast as it was the day it was built.

A design engineer for Sperry Gyroscope during the Second World War, Hoe was asked, after VJ Day, to fix a car for a friend. He took a leave of absence from Sperry to do the job. When it was finished, another came in. He didn't resign from his engineering job, he just never went back to it. Hoe knows the history of every car that comes in: a roadster that belonged to Clark Gable, another that was Gary Cooper's, Jimmy Walker's town car, Dolores Del Rio's limousine. They are unique: it's unlikely that we will ever build $25,000 cars again.

18 · "He Never Stole a Whole Automobile"*

"Some years ago I went to work for a garage owner who called himself 'Honest Eddie.' On my second day there I asked another mechanic why the boss was called 'Honest Eddie.'

" 'I guess because they never caught him stealing a whole automobile,' the fellow said.

"I worked for Honest Eddie for two years and I never saw him steal an entire automobile either. I saw him steal everything from taillight bulbs to engines out of cars in for repair, but I must admit I never knew him to steal the whole package. Being caught would have spoiled the racket for him. It's a good racket, the auto-repair racket. The take must run into hundreds of millions of dollars a year.

"How does it work? Like taking candy from a baby, mostly. The racket is almost foolproof because the average American is sure that he's a great natural mechanic. This, and his refusal to admit ignorance, makes him the perfect sucker. I've watched such

* This chapter is in the first person because it is based on material given me verbally by a veteran mechanic who wished to remain anonymous.

boneheads taken by crooked mechanics so sure of themselves, and the chump, that they used double talk.

" 'The portoflan opening on the coil was completely plugged up,' the mechanic would say. 'Once they get that way there's nothing you can do with them, they'll short out every time. So I put in a new one.'

"The chump needed a new coil like he needed pneumonia, of course. What happened to the old one? It got a quick wipe off with a clean rag and was sold next day as a factory-rebuilt unit.

"How many garages and repair shops will cheat? About three out of five, I would say, on a national average. Four out of five in big metropolitan centers. Of small country-town shops, probably only one in five, not because they are any more honest but because their customers live closer to them and are able to hurt them by talking about their work. Different standards apply to the city slicker, of course. If a Cadillac or an Imperial pulls into a country shop missing on one cylinder because of a loose plug lead, the chances are about 8 to 1 that the owner will be stuck for a carburetor cleaning job at least.

"I guess I must have showed a little surprise the first time I saw that particular switch because after the car had gone on its way (it was a big Buick) old Honest Eddie explained things to me.

" 'Sure the chump didn't *need* it,' he said, 'but it didn't *hurt* him any, and, who knows, maybe we did him a good turn at that; maybe that pot was about to gum up anyway. He's probably lucky he came in here, and he could sure afford it. That was a fifty-cent cigar he had in his face.'

"Honest Eddie looked thoughtfully down the road. I knew what he was thinking. He was kicking himself for not having stuck another $2.70 on the bill.

"Carburetor cleaning is one of the best chiselers' gimmicks. The modern four-barrel carburetor looks so complicated to the average car owner that you could tell him it had two hundred moving parts and he'd almost believe you. All he really knows about the carburetor is that it is a gadget with a lot of adjustments, all of which are important to the running of the engine. He's afraid to touch it himself, and if he's told that it needs only cleaning, at

$3.00 or so, he's delighted that it's nothing worse. Carburetor cleaning has another advantage: it can be done right under the chump's own eyes and still look good. Any carburetor, unless it's brand new, will yield enough gum and dirt to color the cleaning solvent. In Honest Eddie's shop we never took even that chance, though. The can we used for cleaning carbs had a teaspoonful of nice black dirt in the bottom. It was very impressive.

"In the next few years carburetors will be gradually replaced by fuel-injection systems, most of which are so complex they make a carburetor look as simple as a paper clip. A mechanic who can't steal the price of a winter vacation out of four fuel-injection jobs is a dope.

"New spark plugs are easy, too. Most drivers don't know what spark plugs should look like, and a good hustler can wave a perfect plug under your nose and say, 'See that gray glop all over the points? Completely fouled up. They're all like that.' So you buy a new set. Your old ones are sandblasted, the porcelain shined up, they're repackaged in the little boxes your new set came out of and everything is set for another sucker. (Incidentally, a fouled plug is coated with black, oily looking carbon. A grayish or brownish coating is normal and harmless.)

"The electrical system of a car is a total mystery to nine out of ten owners. Condensers, coils, cut-outs, generators—you'll believe anything you're told. The only 'evidence' you have is the performance of the car after it's been 'fixed.' A $10 engine tune-up may make a notable difference in the way your car runs, and that $10 charge is legitimate. But you may be stuck with $26.50 *on top* of the legitimate $10 and not a cent of it will contribute to your car's performance.

"A list of the parts of your car that can be used as a basis for cheating would fill pages. Even the smallest items can be used. For example, practically every car that came into Honest Eddie's shop was stuck for a couple of light bulbs. Even if everything else was on the level, and it rarely was, the light bulb bit went through. We liked to wait until the customer called for his car to work the bulb switch because if that was done right it was worth an extra half dollar. Before he showed up we loosened the bulbs in their fittings. When the chump got behind the wheel we'd ask him to switch on the headlights, "just for a last check on the adjustment." The headlights were always OK, but a side light, taillight, back-up light, or something else, was always out. You put in a new bulb, held up the perfectly good old one for him to see that it was burned out, smiled and took your tip. It's a small swindle, the bulb switch, but I think Honest Eddie used to work it for about $250 a year, and what's wrong with that? It's all money.

"Windshield wiper blades are a soft touch, too. And with automatic transmissions and power steering on so many cars today, it's worth while to steal transmission fluid as well as hydraulic brake fluid. Take a little, leave a little is the governing principle. You just stick a syringe into the reservoir and pump the stuff out. Again, it's not a big deal, but it adds up. And the risk is zero.

"There's very little risk in anything a crooked mechanic does, until he starts switching engines, and few shops will go that far because of the danger involved in monkeying around with serial numbers. After all, if you drive into a garage and the mechanic on duty tells you that the funny clicking sound you complain of shows you need a valve job, and you nod wisely, like a dope, where's the risk? You'll get a valve job, maybe even a good one. Of course you don't need it, but you're getting what you order, and what you pay for, and what's the beef? If you don't know that the clicking noise is just one miserable little tappet out of adjustment, that's too bad. I have parlayed noisy tappets into more than valve jobs. I can remember selling new crankshafts, a set of new pistons, a complete set of bearings, and all many more times than once.

"Is it possible to get a car repaired and not be overcharged a month's rent? Of course. But you have to work at it. You have to remember a few rules.

"1. First, don't go to a strange shop if you can help it. Find a friend who knows a good shop, or thinks he does, and have him call the foreman and say he's sending you around. This may help. If you pick a shop on the basis of advertisements, be careful. Watch out for the ads that read, 'My friends say I must be out of my mind, charging so little for the kind of work we do. I'm starving to death all right, but I'm getting my kicks, too.' You bet he is. Stay away from him. You should starve like he's starving.

"2. Take the car around yourself, don't send it with anyone, and particularly not with your wife. Many mechanics just can't help themselves when they see a sick car come in with a girl at the wheel. They get a rush of larceny to the head. After all, the poor little thing probably doesn't know a widget from a waffle iron, so why not take her? The temptation is almost irresistible.

"3. Don't talk much, and if you do talk, try to make sense. The man who tells the mechanic, 'There's something wrong with the motor,' is asking for the business and will get it unless the shop is honest. The man who says, 'It breaks down around fifty miles an hour' has a better chance because he sounds as if he might know something about engines. But don't diagnose the car yourself unless you really know what you're talking about. A friend of mine, a high type, once ran a garage, and when a noisy fat-faced citizen brought in a car, announced what was wrong with it, and said he'd pay $265 to have it fixed, and not a dime more, my friend looked it over and agreed. That's what he charged, too—for a quarter's worth of bolts and the fifteen minutes it took to install them.

"4. If you can stay with the car, do so. In a strange town and a strange shop, *always* stay with it. If the boss mechanic says the work will take three hours and there's a nice air-conditioned bar around the corner, thank him, but buy a Coke out of the machine and study the nude girls on the calendars. Many small-town garages have specimens running back for years. Meanwhile your mere presence may prevent larceny.

"5. Don't underwrite a blanket overhaul. Insist on seeing a written work sheet. Go over the work you want done, item by item. If you want to ask for labor charges in advance, you can in most cases, because all the regular repair operations have been standardized for every make of car in the country. Of course if some unusual difficulty is found, the charge will go up, but at least you can know in advance approximately what it will be. As for material, if the mechanic says, 'You probably need new brake-linings,' tell him, 'Save the old ones for me; I want to take them back where I bought them.' This one remark may help him to decide that you don't need a new set after all. It may not, too: he may have a spare set of beat-up linings around the shop.

"6. When you find a good shop, act like a human being. Pay your bills promptly. Don't try to chisel. (A lot of people do, and they're one of the reasons some garage men cheat.) Don't take advantage of a friendly shop by borrowing tools or hanging around talking with mechanics who should be helping the boss pay off the overhead by doing a little work. Be considerate. Don't wake the poor man at midnight to ask him if he thinks it's too cold for your car to stand out with plain water in the cooling system. Remember, a good shop staffed by good mechanics can keep your car running like a watch for years beyond its ordinary life span.

"The man in the back row there says he owns a foreign car and what about him? Well, friend, all I can tell you is that when an import came into the old shop, Honest Eddie himself always took over, and that meant that the bite would be anything from two to three times normal. Of course some foreign cars are mighty tough to work on (although many are easier than American cars) and a mechanic who can and will do the job is justified in asking top money for it. Did you ever look under the hood of a Mercedes-Benz 300SL, or any model Ferrari, any Bugatti? On the other hand, plenty of imported cars are straightforward enough but require special procedures and special tools. Most of the time the foreign car owner has to find an expert in his own make. Otherwise the rules are the same for him as for everybody else—but he has to be twice as crafty!"

19 · Slump and Be Happy

A milestone in the evolutionary history of *Homo sapiens* was passed some time back, quietly, almost without notice, when a Ford Motor Company engineer said that the shape of the seats in a new model were meant to conform to "the modern slump."

Heretofore there have been only two schools of thought in the design of motor-car seats: the American and the European. The European masters have favored a seat back with a soft, indented center surrounded by a firm, shoulder-gripping roll meant to brace the upper arms and shoulders. The Americans have remained true to the horse-drawn carriage maker's concept of a flat surface, upholstered to uniform tension throughout. Both have assumed the passenger to be an upright biped built around a straight, vertical spine, and therefore best catered to by a straight seat back.

But modern man does *not* have a straight spine, and all credit to the courageous Ford technicians for abandoning the pretense. The seat backs of the new car they talked about did not rise in an unbroken vertical line: six inches or so from the top they bent sharply forward. The round-shouldered, hollow-chested rider thus could know comfort denied his brothers in lesser vehicles. He would not need to press his shoulders into the seat back under the delusion that they belong there, nor would he have to sway in midair, his modern slump unsupported anywhere.

Now that ground has been broken, need we stop with automobile seat back? Will not the manufacturers of household furnishings, theater seats and the like have the courage to junk their comparatively puny inventories and come proudly if belatedly into line?

And who will be the first among the cutters and tailors of clothing for men to face up to reality? (The iron-handed esthetes who dictate women's wear need no urging; yearly the *haute couture* announces the shape of women to come, now hipless, now bereft of bosom, now shapeless altogether. They conceded the modern slump in the early 1920's.) What is needed now is comparable courage among purveyors to men. I look forward to the day when every three-pane fitting mirror in America will mount a sign: "Our suits are designed for men who stand *naturally*. Do *not* force your shoulders back. Slump!" Unimagined benefits will follow. Pitilessly delineated fore and aft in the all-seeing mirror, the average man pulls in his sagging abdomen, puffs his chest, forces back his brittle shoulders and holds himself so, at whatever cost, while the fitter measures and marks and pins. Naturally, when the suit is delivered and he slips into his true stance, the modern slump, the garment fits like a hand-me-down. Think of the pain, the heartache, the economic waste that would be avoided if he would stand before the fitting mirror as he stands waiting for the bus: shoulders slumped forward, chest caved in, abdomen drooping, all his weight hanging on one hip. Fitted thus, his new gray flannel would become him like something built for Lucius Beebe or William Powell the Elder.

Euphemism is horrid, disaster lies in the denial of truth, and Darwin was right. Let a deluded rear guard of gymnasts and physical education fanatics fight on, if they will, but as for you and me, let us slip our hands trustingly into the firm grasp of such as Mr. Ford's anonymous *mahatma*. They have proved that they know the True Way. Are they not even now planning for the day when the leg will be a mere vestigial appendage? Certainly. Where is the clutch pedal of yesteryear? Designs for accelerator and power-brake controls built into the steering wheel lie safely vaulted in Detroit. *Que sera . . .*

20 · Somebody Wants to Kill You

HUNCHED in a foxhole in the middle of the night, waiting for word to pull out on a night patrol, to go looking for men who want nothing so much as to kill him, an infantryman is entitled to feel fear, and he'd be stupid if he didn't.

When you get behind the wheel of your car and pull out of the driveway, what do you feel—anything at all?

Last year 38,300 Americans were killed stone-dead in automobile accidents. That's more than our total losses in the Korean War. Since we began to drive in the 1890's we've killed more than 1,000,000 people. That's more than we've lost in all our wars since 1776.

A soldier on patrol has better than a ten-to-one chance to come back to his own lines unhurt. There is one chance in two—50-50—that the car you're driving today will be involved in an accident sometime during its useful life. The chances that *you* will be in it at the time are one in four.

The soldier on patrol has at least the comfort of knowing that if he's killed or injured it will be because he was trying to accomplish something worthwhile. *Your* accident will be needless, preventable, and probably 90 per cent your own fault. In addition you will probably involve someone else in it.

Somebody wants to kill you. He may miss. He may only cripple you for life or put you in the hospital for six months. And he may get you.

Who wants to kill you? You want to kill yourself, obviously. If you didn't, you'd do something about it.

You can blame the automobile manufacturers if you want. It's true that they don't make cars as safe as they can.

You can blame the police and the courts. The roads are full of licensed drivers who aren't competent to handle a pony cart, and it's true that many a $25 fine covers an offense that should get a man forbidden to drive for a year—or life.

You can blame reckless drivers, men, women and children who think that mere possession of a 200-horsepower automobile automatically makes them expert. The roads are full of them.

But there's no point in this buck passing, because all of these people are you.

Nobody's making you buy unsafe cars, and your only excuse is that you haven't bothered to find out what a *safe* car looks like. You elect the politicians, you insure unsafe automobiles with a telephone call to your broker, you pay the premiums, you let your local policemen and your local judges do as they please, and if you say you never did a reckless or a stupid thing on the road in your life, I'm sorry, but you're strictly a liar.

So, let's face it, you're trying to kill yourself. Maybe you're not as obvious about it as the Louisiana farmer who kissed his children good-bye on Christmas Eve and then drove straight into an oak tree at 90 miles an hour, but still you're trying to kill yourself.

Keep trying, and you'll probably make it. The percentages are working for you.

If the idea of spending your last two minutes on earth sitting in your car and wondering how the steering post got six inches into your chest appeals to you, stop here. You're hopeless, and for you we can only pray it will be quick.

One of the earliest fatal nonracing accidents of which we have a complete record took place in England in 1899. The driver of a primitive, nameless *voiture* let it build up too much speed downhill, burned out the brakes in panic applications, failed to make the turn at the bottom and wrapped everything around a tree. This accident originated the newspaper cliché: "The driver apparently lost control of the machine." The last accident of the same sort occurred yesterday, any yesterday, within a hundred miles of where you're sitting.

That 1899 motor car, wood framed, rumbling along on wagon wheels, was not a notably safe conveyance. Give it one thing, though: it wouldn't exceed 15 miles an hour on the flat. And excuse the driver to this extent: like all pioneer motorists, he was essentially a researcher. He had a lot to learn. You can't justify yourself in the same fashion. It's all been learned for you. It's all written down somewhere. All you have to do is read it.

Sixty years have gone by, and about 1,500,000 human beings from a day to a century old have been spread bloodily on the world's highways since 1899. Let's be generous with ourselves, admit that we learn slowly, and claim that we required fifty years to learn how to handle the automobile. It's time that results were showing, isn't it? Last year 35,000 Americans were killed on the roads. This year, 38,500. Who'll bid 50,000? Do I hear 75,000? Do we need a century to learn? Are we all insane? Imagine yourself a flying saucer pilot, orbiting the planet earth and busily monitoring our radio. Would you report: "The earth people cannot be considered intelligent beings in the correct sense of that word. Their irrationality is particularly evident in their unremitting slaughter of each other. They kill each other by the millions over differing political beliefs, in warfare, and even in the pursuit of pleasure. Wherever the automobile is available it is held to be man's most useful possession, next to the dwelling itself. It is a primary source of pleasure and recreation. Yet it kills a shocking percentage of all those who attempt to use it.

"The earth people unceasingly bemoan all these deaths, claiming that they are needlessly inflicted on the victims. Yet they tolerate them, and this paradox can be explained only in terms of low intelligence and chronic neurosis."

You wouldn't write that? Why not? What *would* you write?

21 · You Can Have What You Want

An insurance company once printed an advertisement entitled "Driver's view of an accident about to happen" or something similar. The picture was a blank white square. Exactly. That's about what registers on a driver's mind just before the last crunch. An associate of mine found himself looking at such a picture recently. He was waiting at a traffic light in Central Park in New York. He was driving a car that was comparatively new to him. It was borrowed, and he'd had it for about nine hours and maybe two hundred miles. It was a brand-new, four-passenger convertible coupe with a rated horsepower of 340, and it was just out of the shop. The light changed, he stepped on the gas, he set himself for a curve coming up. That's all he remembers. The car hit a tree in the exact center of the front bumper. After a while the firemen came with their axes and their compound levers and sliced at the wreckage until they could get the driver and his passenger out. They weren't terribly hurt: both had broken jaws, the driver's thigh was badly fractured. The spare tire on the car could be salvaged, but little else was worth bothering with. Of course, they had gone barely 150 yards. If they'd had a chance to work up speed, it might have been a *serious* accident.

Was this a safe car? We'll never know. The car had been turned into junk, and the driver can't testify. In effect, he wasn't there. He doesn't know what happened. He's just glad that a little stainless steel wire in his jaw, a few pins in his leg, and six months of convalescence made him almost as good as new.

Is *your* car safe? No, it isn't. I don't care *what* you're driving, it isn't even reasonably safe. Some cars are safer than others, that's all, and the chances of your having one of the comparatively good ones are thousands to one against it.

Why isn't yours a safe automobile? In the first place, because it's likely to hit some other object, stationary or moving. (Don't laugh, you may well live to see automobiles that cannot hit other objects. We'll get to that.) Second, and most important, when it *does* hit something, a dangerous thing happens: *it* stops and you don't. Fifty thousand words may not suffice to explain this phenomenon clearly, but ten minutes and a little effort will make it very clear indeed. Wrap an old blanket around the front bumper of your automobile. Then point it at some suitable barrier: a parked car is best, or a stout fence, a wall, whatever. Run at this barrier at 5 miles an hour, a speed just enough to lift your speedometer needle off its peg. Whack! Interesting, wasn't it? Did you feel your chest reaching hungrily for the steering wheel? Did you notice how your head, which is an upside-down pendulum weighing about ten pounds, suggested shyly that it would like to throw itself off your neck and through the windshield? Now supposing you had run this little test at 60 miles an hour instead of 5. Nothing extraordinary about that: people all around you are doing it every day, people who are convinced that they're just as bright, just as sensible, and just as much entitled to live as you are. They kill themselves that way.

Mencken was probably right. The ignorance of the average American is inexplicable. Drive a small car, any small car, and as sure as you're sitting in it someone will say, "Don't you worry about what would happen if someone hit you? It's so *small*."

Given a choice, would you rather run 35 miles an hour into the First National Bank Building, right where the vault lies, in an unpadded Sherman tank or a Volkswagen? You take the tank, sucker. I'll take the Volkswagen, and I'll be standing around while they're looking for something with which to scrape you off the inside of the nice, safe tank. The front of the Volkswagen, soft sheet metal, as we have seen, will crumple and decelerate me at a rate that I can at least live through. The proof plate of your Sherman won't give you a millimeter. You'll fly out of your seat at the full 35 miles an hour into hard, cold metal, and may God bless you and keep you.

Every red-blooded, right-thinking American boy grows up believing that a big car is a safe car. He might as well believe that the moon is made of blue cheese. But Daddy thinks so, and Daddy knows, doesn't he? No, junior, he doesn't. The old man has a paid-up membership in a tribe of fairly dense fellows, as witness the rate at which they keep getting their names in the papers:

Toll the bell for Mr. J. R. B., twenty-nine, New York, who "failed to make a curve" as the small-town newspapers so often say, skidded, rolled and was thrown out of the car, coming to rest ninety feet from it, dead.

Consider Mr. J. D. D., fifty years of age, dead in Pennsylvania when his car skidded across the road, turned sideways and let an oncoming truck hit it in the middle of the driver's door. Dead.

Ponder the case of Mr. B., thirty-three, Wyoming, who was going a shade too fast when he saw a slow-moving car ahead of him. Mr. B. stamped on the brake pedal, skidded, lost control, hit a tree, went through the windshield. Dead, of course.

Were these gentlemen, good and worthy souls all, driving safe automobiles? No, they were not. Would they be alive today if they *had* been driving safe automobiles? Yes, probably, even though each of them did a foolish thing and died for doing it.

Is there any such thing as a really safe automobile? Certainly not. An automobile is inherently unsafe, and so is an airplane, a bathtub and a 12-gauge shotgun. But most of us, boarding an airplane, give some passing thought to the fact that it's inherently unsafe. We buy flight insurance; we do not argue with the stewardess who tells us to fasten our seat belts; we put out our cigarettes when the *no smoking* sign flicks on. Even an eighteen-year-old boy, whose judgment inclines him to be afraid of practically nothing, will hang on to something when he steps into a tub of soapy water; only a moron will treat a shotgun, loaded or unloaded, with anything but full respect. But our attitude toward our automobiles is different, weirdly and unreasonably different. An automobile is for fun, for transportation, for convenience, for prideful possession. If airplanes, bathtubs or shotguns killed 38,000 people a year the Congress of the United States in its sovereign majesty would surround their use with a wall of legislative restriction. It would be difficult indeed to buy them—if their use was countenanced at all. But anyone with the price can buy an automobile and a half-blind idiot eighty-nine years old can be officially licensed to operate one with no difficulty at all.

An exaggerated analogy? Certainly—but not by much. For an automobile is a wickedly, malevolently dangerous thing. I *like* automobiles, and for years I have rarely owned fewer than six of them at a time; the history and function of the automobile have fascinated me all my life; for recreation I would rather drive a fast automobile on a good road than do almost anything else. Nonetheless I argue that no other possession a man can own is so likely to turn and strike him dead—together with half the members of his family and a couple of total strangers. The combination of a fast automobile and a bad driver is demonstrably the biggest hazard in contemporary civilian life—and the least understood.

It's time we did something about it, because if we don't it will be done for us. The straws are in the wind: as this is written, Congress, noting that we now make at least five automobiles of over 300 horsepower, has begun to ask the manufacturers if engine units of such power are really necessary; the suggestion that a national, federally enforced speed limit may be desirable has been bruited about. If the *total* number of persons killed and injured continues to increase year by year—and it will—the fact that the *rate* of fatality per driven mile decreases or remains constant will not prevent federal intervention. (It will come, and no stone-age nonsense about states' rights will stop it.) Skepticism is footless in this connection. Alcohol didn't kill 40,000 people a year, but it was outlawed anyway. No one is suggesting that the automobile be outlawed—it is the main prop under our economy, and we would have the living standard of a backward Balkan principality without it—but conditions of its *use* can be governed, and if the present trend continues, its use *will* be governed as sure as Ford.

What to do? That's easy. You'll have to learn to drive. You don't know how now. Oh, very well, perhaps *you* do. But the next five hundred people you might meet on the highway—*they* don't know how.

Second, you'll have to persuade Detroit that you want a safe automobile to drive and ride in. In order to accomplish this, you'll have to inform yourself a bit. You'll have to learn what a safe automobile looks like.

Do these two things and you'll live longer. And you won't have to drive a car that is automatically governed to 45 miles an hour. I know, I know: the governor is impractical because it would prevent the necessary use of surplus power in an emergency. Not at all. A mechanical breakthrough device that would allow full use of maximum power is easily fitted to any governor. Also easily fitted is a lock-on switch that lights a bright blue light on the rear of your car and leaves it on. The first police officer who sees you stops you and asks for a convincing explanation. Three unsatisfactory blue lights and your license is gone. Too tough a policy to be feasible? Not at all. Drive 45 miles an hour in a 35 mile zone in Connecticut today and your license is gone for thirty days, no argument, no discussion, no fixing, you're grounded. The idea is no new one. Royal Air Force fighter planes in the Second World War were equipped with a throttle stop restricting speed. It could be broken through in emergency so that the engine could be run at maximum, but the broken stop had to be explained when the pilot returned to base. Racing automobiles carry a tachometer, the engine-revolution counter used instead of a speedometer, fitted with two pointers. One registers speed of the engine for the driver; the second hand follows the first—and sticks at the highest reading reached. The driver can't set it back and the reading must be explained to the team manager.

You *can* have a safe automobile. All you have to do is to make enough noise about it. The machinery exists. Even the psychological apparatus exists. For years Detroit has fostered the myth that the American automobile is designed by the public. What the public wants, the public gets, the tale goes. "We put chrome on cars because the public wants it; we make them bigger because the public wants them bigger." This is demonstrable nonsense because for years now the American public has had no choice at all in essentials. Within a given price range there is almost no basic difference among American automobiles. They are marketed on the time-tried system that has made this economy the most materially successful in the history of the world: Dream up a new model, sell it, next year dream up another and persuade the customer that continued possession of his old one marks him as unsuccessful, reactionary or both. I have no quarrel here with enforced or artificial obsolescence. As a system of economy it works and it works very well with what I conceive to be notable benefits to everybody in the game from top to bottom. But I dislike seeing it fraudulently labeled, as Detroit does fraudulently label it in proclaiming that the buying public dictates every change that's made in automobile manufacture. However, call it what you will, the machinery is there, and if enough people were suddenly to announce that they *know* what a safe car looks like and that they want one, please, Detroit would have no recourse but to produce it—or attempt to reverse the trend by a massive propaganda effort.

Will you know what to do with a safe car if and when you can have one? Which is more important, the driver or the car? The driver is more important. A bad driver can take the safest car it's possible to build today and run it into the front of a Greyhound bus. Let us consider the driver, then. Let us ponder what lousy drivers we really are.

In considering this interesting question, we must break up and throw away a few cherished illusions. Most Americans believe that we are the best drivers in the world, just as they believe that we are the most literate people in the world. It comes as a blow to discover that we are not the most literate people in the world, despite our incredible production of printed matter, we aren't even in the first five. So it is with driving. We aren't the best by any means. The most expert automobile drivers are, of course, the professional racing drivers. The Championship of the World is determined on a rigid mathematical point system. No American has ever been Champion of the World. Any questions?

Man for man, the Italians are the most expert drivers in the world. Give the average Italian an automobile of one-third the horsepower of the one you're driving and he'll run away and hide from you. For sheer skill and dash, the Italians are supreme. The English are better than we are, too. The percentage of really good drivers per capita is probably higher in England than anywhere else. The British take driving seriously. They work at it. An American who had the Italian's mechanical skill at the wheel plus the Briton's knowledge and judgment would be a pretty good driver. Does this mean that the Italians and the British are *safe* drivers? No. The Italian accident rate is shocking, and the House of Commons regularly resounds to bitter oratory about the needless death of Englishmen on the roads.

But factors not present in the American equation intrude here. Most of Italy has no speed limit, and British roads, narrow, curving, neglected, are terribly dangerous in themselves. Part responsibility for the wicked Italian accident rate must be assigned to the mixed-traffic hazard: a heavy percentage of pedestrians, cyclists, horse-cart and scooter travel.

Considering these hazards, the Italian motorist drives with skill as well as *brio*. He knows the abilities of his car intimately: its steering characteristics, even such *esoterica,* vital to survival, as its oversteer or understeer tendencies, its braking power, its accelerative rate. The Italian never merely sits in a car and steers it. He *drives* it, dominates it, every minute.

The Briton drives much more sedately, as a rule, but he enjoys the benefits of yet another characteristic: He thinks of Motoring in just that way, with a capital *M.* He considers Motoring more than just a means of transport. It is to him a separate pursuit, a special recreation, a sport. Only in England could a publisher bring out a book titled *Car Driving As an Art* and anticipate selling a profitable number of copies. The British support dozens of automobile periodicals, the two leading examples are weeklies much bigger than *Time,* and every big British newspaper carries a full-time automobile expert on its staff. Combined, the Italian and British attitudes toward driving represent what the American attitude had better come to be, if we are not to be regulated out of all countenance: an effort to acquire reasonable manual skill in the handling of a dangerous and complex vehicle, plus an understanding of the theoretical physics of its behavior, and a concern with the moral and legal aspects of its use.

If only a few tens of thousands of Americans learned to drive in that fashion, and if they had available to them reasonably safe automobiles, then the present apparently irreversible trends toward a continually increasing number of citizens slaughtered and a federal regulative effort could both be arrested.

A measure of the malevolent danger of the automobile lies in the fact that most people injured or killed in automobiles were traveling at speeds under 45 miles an hour when the roof fell in. (It's important, but I hesitate to set it down because surely everybody who can read knows that *most accidents take place on straight, dry roads in clear weather.*) Forty-five miles an hour isn't fast, but it's fast enough. The spectacular, high-speed accidents are more certain, but the killing automobile's solid core of accomplishment lies in the 30–45 mile-per-hour bracket. Even that modest rate of speed isn't necessary. Fifteen miles an hour can be fatal. Every year 6,000 or 7,000 people are seriously injured in this novel fashion: sitting in a stationary car, or one moving very slowly, they are hit from behind by another automobile doing 10 or 15 miles an hour. The sudden acceleration moves their bodies forward, but the flexibility of their necks lets their heads stay behind. The consequent whipping action of their necks causes injuries ranging in severity from muscle strain to broken vertebrae. This doesn't happen to racing drivers because the backs of their seats are built up to head height. Is there any reason that the seats of passenger cars could not be so extended? None that I know, except that it would cost a little money and might prevent backseat passengers from seeing through the windshield. The auto manufacturers might say that the customers wouldn't stand for the increased cost. I don't know. I don't know how to equate injury with money. In 1955 the cost of automobile accidents was $10,300,000,000. If a pulled neck muscle is worth $27.50, how much for a broken neck? I do know that it's smart, pulling up to a stop light, to keep a bright eye in the mirror, and if you see someone sailing up too fast, to slide down in the seat until your head is supported. There are lots of little things like that you can do to stretch your life expectancy, but is it unreasonable to expect, spending $3000 or $4000 for an automobile, that the thing will protect you just a bit by itself?

Of course this wheeled wonder, the automobile, our servant, our mistress, our pastel-toned executioner, has been growing in safety down the decades. Surely it has. And in time it will be as nearly perfectly safe as a mechanical contrivance can be. But must 10,000,000 people go to the hospital, and the morgue, while we wait?

How *much* safer is it, anyway? In 1912 I wasn't driving automobiles because I hadn't been born but I owned a 1912 automobile a few years ago and drove it a useful number of miles and so, without relying on the dubious testimony of contemporary authorities, I can form an estimate of the changes of the past forty-five years. This car was a Mercer Raceabout—and, by the way, I wish I knew where another one could be found for sale today. The Mercer Raceabout was a two-passenger car, the passengers in bucket seats. It had a big engine, gas lamps, wooden-spoked wheels, a big round gasoline tank behind the seats and a little cubbyhole compartment on the tail which would hold a few tools, your extra straw hat and two road maps. It cost $2500 and was much esteemed by the bloods of the day because it was guaranteed to do 75 miles an hour and was famous on the racecourses of the time. It had four speeds forward and one reverse, the big hand brakes worked on the rear wheels only and the foot brake worked—which is stretching the word considerably—on the transmission. The spark advance-and-retard mechanism had to be set manually by a lever on the steering wheel and it was easiest to shift gears by double clutching: two full depressions of the clutch for each movement of the gear lever. The steering was very stiff and very "quick"—little more than one full revolution of the steering wheel would turn the road wheels from full right to full left lock. The driver of a Mercer was a busy man. The car was a handful.

Mechanically the Mercer was an unsafe automobile. At speeds over 45 miles per hour the brakes had very little effect. The driver and his passenger were wholly exposed, so much so that each of them rode with one foot outside the body of the car, resting in a brass stirrup. One mechanical advantage over modern cars it did have: the very quick steering made for marvelously precise handling in an emergency. But over-all I considered it remarkably safe transport because its very disadvantages required constant attention to the business at hand. The driver was fully occupied: in curving or hilly country he had constantly to be changing gears, braking alternately with the hand and foot brakes; because the least motion of the steering wheel would change the direction of the car, he could never let his attention wander from the road. For another thing, the car was an extremely valuable antique, and the idea of its being touched, however lightly, by another car or a stationary object was almost horrifying. Consequently one drove defensively the whole time. In essence, the car itself was unsafe, but it forced its driver to use safe methods.

The ideally safe combination would be an automobile carrying as much built-in safety as imaginative engineering can devise, handled by a driver who treated it exactly as if it were a 1912 Mercer Raceabout: rare, valuable, underbraked, underpowered, its metal structure "a mass of fatigued stresses" to be guarded against all undue strain.

Is such a combination feasible? Certainly.

22 · A Solid Acre of Horse

All understanding of the mortal danger of the automobile to its warm-blooded cargo lies in the grasp of but one fact: when the automobile either stops or changes direction with violence the people in it either (*a*) do *not* stop or (*b*) do *not* change direction. In one of these two ways, and in almost no others, do they get killed or injured.

When an automobile traveling at 60 miles an hour hits a tree that has spent 40 years anchoring itself to the ground, the automobile's rate of movement is arrested from 60 miles an hour to zero miles an hour in perhaps six inches or a foot. The rate of movement of the passengers in the car is also arrested from 60 miles an hour to zero—in anything from six inches to 150 feet. People have lived through the latter kind of stop: a man thrown from an open car to fly through the air like a bird to the top of a fortuitously placed haystack, for example. You cannot count on it.

The *rate* of stopping is not *per se* dangerous, any more than speed is *per se* dangerous. Air Force experimenters have lived through brutally abrupt stops from three-figure speeds with no more damage than black eyes induced by the pressure of blood. It is possible, and not merely theoretically possible, so to protect a man that he could with safety sit calmly in a car as it was slammed into a brick wall at 60 miles an hour, but he would be so padded and tied down that he would be physically uncomfortable.

But without such protection, the following pattern inevitably repeats itself: The automobile stops, the passenger continues on, not at the full 60 miles per hour, but close enough, until he strikes something that is sufficiently unyielding to stop him: the dashboard, the steering wheel, the roof, or, after he has pushed a hole in the windshield with his face, the same tree that stopped the car. The impact kills him. Or, if the car does not hit anything, but instead abruptly changes direction, as in a roll or violent skid, the passenger, unable to accommodate himself, continues onward in the original line of travel, and at almost the original rate of speed until, again, he encounters something that will stop him. Often, in these cases, he goes out the door, which has usually accommodatingly opened itself for him, and flies or slides or rolls along until he comes to another car, a tree, a building or whatever. Or he may be brought to a halt by simple friction of the ground on his body, in which he will be lucky but very much the worse for wear. These are the two most-favored killing systems of the automobile.

Of course you may be sitting in your automobile listening to the radio and wishing your wife would hurry up with the marketing when a ten-ton tractor and trailer, lamentably out of brakes halfway down a hill, comes in the rear of the car and goes out the front, leaving you fatally inconvenienced behind it. A crashing airplane may land on the cloth top of your convertible, poorly stressed to receive it, or a loose cornice stone may drop off a building, but such mishaps are merely Fate's little jokes and we cannot concern ourselves with them here. As a rule, you may count upon it that when you have your accident the consequent injuries will come to you because the car stopped quicker than you could, or changed direction quicker than you could. That is the whole heart of the problem, and the solution lies here: the sudden stop or change in direction must be prevented, or, failing that, the consequences must be ameliorated.

To begin at the beginning, the car is sitting on the dealer's floor, and you are about to buy it. It is an important purchase. This device, this vehicle, can march very largely in your life for the next year or two. It offers, in the fullest measure available to most of us, the essential liberty to move freely about as an individual. It will give you great pleasure. It may contribute to your livelihood. Used merely as conveyance, as beast of burden, it will ease your life. It will serve, if you care for such things—and who does not?—as a public indication of your financial standing in the community, and even, if you like, as a badge of what you may regard as your social position. Weighed in these scales, your automobile is a useful, happy possession.

You sit behind the wheel, start the engine, move the car down the street, and you are at one with the enviable, handsome, smiling men and women of the ever-present automobile advertisements. The manufacturers spend from $20 to $140 of the price of every car they make for advertising, and it is money well spent; it must be if it makes you feel so good. You are completely in control of this machine. It is docile, willing, magically competent. Steady! By the time you get home you may have incubated such affection for this thing that you'll pat it on the fender as if it were a pet dog. But this is not a pet dog, or any kind of pet. This is a tiger. Some day it may turn on you, in a tenth-second's careless flick, and snick your head off. Maybe it wants to. Some cars do, some cars don't. Maybe it's not a tiger at all. Maybe it's a polar bear.

Roman Proske, one of the ablest animal trainers of all time, a man who spent his life with big cats and has the waffled body that proves it, thought of the polar bear as the most dangerous of all animals. Proske would happily work a cageful of mixed lions and tigers, confident that he knew what was in their fuzzy feline minds, and that he could, accidents barred, protect himself. Lions and tigers can be anticipated. The polar bear is different. He has no temperament. He will strike you dead as quickly when he is happy and well fed as he will when he is sunk in black anger.

To the keen, tempered senses of the professional automobile driver, some cars are tigers and some are polar bears. None are house cats. Only the amateur, out of whose fat-headed ranks the automobile snatches its million-odd victims a year, thinks they are.

The polar bear tendency in some cars is well shown by their automatic transmissions. A good automatic transmission will allow the car to stand still—*although in gear*. If inadvertent pressure is put on the accelerator—a child can do it—the car will squash a man against the garage wall. This kind of accident is becoming common. Push-button windows are hideously dangerous to children: a window can lift them by the chin and strangle them, and it has happened.

A few weeks ago I talked with a professional racing driver, a man crowding fifty and still running. Like nearly every professional, he has been hurt. He did two years in a hospital as a result of one accident alone. He believes he holds the altitude record for one track: competent observers estimated that the car threw him seventy-five feet into the air. When I met him he was testing a product for an oil company, driving thousands of miles a week over ordinary roads under carefully regulated conditions. The car he was using was a brand-new sedan of one of the six leading American makes. It was in flawless mechanical condition, and was being checked daily by a crew of high-priced mechanics to keep it in that condition. I asked the man how he liked the car.

"Well, I'll tell you," he said, "and you can tell anybody you like: If I were offered a thousand dollars a week for two weeks to run high-speed tests on that pig, I'd be scared to death. Does that answer your question, or do you want me to tell you what's really wrong with it?"

"Tell me," I said.

"It's all engine and no chassis. They must have hairpins in there for springs. You run it over a bump and it wallows down the road, one leg in the air, and then it comes down, you know, and then the weight shifts and it starts for the ditch. You can't even drive it fast on a *straight* road, and not be in danger of losing it all the time. The steering I don't even want to talk about. I wouldn't let my wife drive a dog like that down to the store. I don't see how they can sell it at all, much less by the tens of thousands the way they do."

Properly to evaluate testimony like this—and you can get a paraphrase of it from any professional—you must remember that this is a man who will get into a racing car and scream into a slippery dirt turn with twenty other cars tightly packed around him, probably at least some of them so close he could touch them, and still feel that he is comparatively safe. Scared, yes. All racing drivers are scared. But not too scared to do it. But for $1000 a week he won't go fast in a car that may be the very one you were belting along the Pennsylvania Turnpike at 80 last week. Who's crazy? You don't seriously think *he* is, do you?

In reading the reports of racing drivers and professional testers, the pussycat-tiger-polar-bear analogy comes constantly to mind. They always discuss the car as a living thing. They speak of its engine power, its braking power, the response, the "feel" of its steering. They discuss its tendency to oversteer or understeer. All cars do one or the other. An oversteering car acts, in a bend, as if it wanted to sharpen the corner, that is, go tighter into the bend. To control a severely oversteering car the steering wheel may have to be turned to the right in the middle of a left-hand bend. An understeering car, on the other hand, acts as if it wants to go straight, and to control it, more-than-normal leftward movement of the steering wheel must be used in the same left-hand bend. Oversteering and understeering have put many a good man and many a pretty girl under the grass for good, and yet it's a rare driver who can tell you what the terms mean, much less tell you whether his own car understeers or oversteers. But good drivers know the feeling because this is the beginning of the border-line country in which the car begins to tell you, to show you, that it has notions of its own, that it is thinking about taking control away from you and reserving it to itself for a little while—not for long, just for long enough to kill you. The pussycat is turning into the tiger.

Another cliché of the testers involves the word "warning." An automobile is a good automobile to the degree that it warns you of its intention to skid. Some cars will tell you in advance, as some horses will lay back their ears, lift their heads, or give some other sign that they intend to misbehave. A decently disposed automobile, like a proper dog, will growl at least once before it bites. If you take it into a bend too fast, perhaps it will roll markedly toward the side it intends to jump to, just before the rear wheels break loose. Maybe the squeak of its tires will rise to a certain level. But in some fashion or other it will tell you. A bad car won't. The English used to make a car called the Invicta which was a notorious beast. It gave no indication at all of incipient skid, and it was so malevolent and crafty that it often outguessed even good drivers. Bad drivers it could kill like typhoid. Early models of the contemporary Porsche, one of the world's truly great automobiles, used to do the same thing. The early Porsche was a violent oversteerer, and it could fling itself into a ditch before the average driver could blink an eye. A redesign of the car's independent rear axle setup cured it.

Once in a skid, the discipline of a car asserts itself. A good car will respond to the controls, and come quickly and easily out of the slide. A bad one will take the bit in its teeth and run. Driving a good car, you can deliberately provoke a skid, be out of it and down the road before you can really recall what you did to correct it. You merely twitched the wheel a trifle, fed a drop more gas, or whatever, and the automobile remembered its manners. In a bad car you can sit there trying everything in the book and you'll still get the telephone pole in your lap.

Sometimes, in those circumstances, things seem to take a long time happening. I remember a skid on hard-packed snow in a 1934 Packard roadster a few years ago. I lost the car in a slight rear-wheel slide to the left, overcorrected and set up a slide to the right, and that was the last one. I sat there for what seemed like a very long time, fiddling with the accelerator to try to get a little wheel grip, wondering if it might even be smart to try to spin the car all the way around, and trying to think of something else to do, before it half buried itself in a snowbank. I don't think that was really a mean automobile because in the ordinary way of things, on decent terrain, it gave no trouble, but it was clumsy and if it had been a horse you'd have called it stupid. It was "unforgiving"—another testers' cliché. A "forgiving" car will accept maltreatment or stupidity a few times without turning on the driver and smiting him hip and thigh. The automobile differs from other living things in that it doesn't mind a bit being hurt, it couldn't care less about being killed—if in the process it can hurt or kill you.

Pussycat? You can go down the street today and buy an American automobile the engine of which delivers 405 horsepower. Let's concede the Detroit argument that cars are big and heavy today, and that most of them carry power-eating accessories: power steering, power brakes, air conditioning, powered seats and windows, and so on. Very well. Let's say that these devices, plus frictional losses, transmission losses, and so on, take 150 horsepower from the 405 the engine delivered, bare, on the dynamometer. That still leaves 255. Sit there at the wheel and look through the windshield. There it is: an acre or so of solid horses, twitching and bulging its muscles. If you had the reins in one hand and a big whip in the other, would you, full of confidence, shake the reins, yell "giddap!" and slash the nearest horse with the whip?

You would? I don't think you're going to get well, friend.

23 · The Somewhat Safe Automobile—I

IF THE AUTOMOBILE you buy today isn't as safe as it should be, who's to blame? You, in the last analysis. You don't get in there and fight for what you ought to have.

It can be argued that the amorphous complex of men and machinery we call "Detroit" is to blame. A year or so ago a California brain surgeon, Dr. C. Hunter Sheldon, writing in the *Journal of the American Medical Association,* threw the challenge direct: He said that three-quarters of all traffic fatalities were due to faulty design of automobile interiors. He said that the auto makers knew very well what had to be done to make cars safer, but that they were not applying their knowledge and that few new ideas, as a result, were being put into use.

Said Dr. Sheldon: "The reason is very simple. The automobile industry states that it cannot make the necessary changes, because of production cost, until such time as the public demands them and makes known that it will accept such changes costwise.

"The public would gladly insist upon changes, but it is completely unaware of what changes to demand. . . ."

Dr. Sheldon's *cri de coeur* was no doubt sincere. As a practicing brain surgeon on the West Coast he has surely had under his hands some interesting examples of the destruction that high-speed accidents can produce on the human skull. And one segment of his indictment, at least, is mother truth: "The public . . . is completely unaware of what changes to demand."

Here Dr. Sheldon is probing one of the root structures of all Detroit mythology: the notion that the U.S. public gets exactly the kind of automobiles it wants. That this is total nonsense we have seen a few chapters back; the U.S. car buyer has no basic choice at all. He can have degrees of luxury, and what else? One of the reasons for the postwar boom in imported automobiles was the amazed discovery by U.S. armed service personnel in Europe that there *were* different kinds of automobiles, that the kind of machine they had previously thought to be the world's standard, the American car, wasn't universal at all. They discovered cars of from one to twelve cylinders, as we have remarked, diesel-engined cars, air-cooled engines, engines in the rear, four-wheel independent suspension, front-wheel drive and so on. They discovered that there were cars that would turn inside an American car, stop short of it in braking tests, out-accelerate it with half the engine capacity. Since the war we have seen European makers offer cars with fuel-injection engines, with air-oil suspension systems, and carrying tires that can't be made to squeal in corners, can hardly be made to skid, and will wear twice as long as comparable standard covers.

When the spent runners staggered into the barricades with tidings like these, the reaction of the abysmally ignorant U.S. public was quick. The hardest car to buy in this country today is not the Cadillac, it's the Volkswagen, most dealers in which are optimistic if they tell you they can get delivery in less than six months. The Volkswagen is an ugly looking little beetle which has no virtues except that it's small, handy, beautifully sprung and will get more than 30 miles to the gallon out of its four-cylinder, air-cooled, rear-mounted engine. The boats can't bring them from Germany fast enough, despite the fact that there has been virtually no Volkswagen advertising.

So it is with safety features. If the buyer doesn't know about them, he can't very well "demand" them of Detroit. The fact that it's difficult for a layman to know something that is probably obvious to a design engineer does not, of course, ultimately excuse him. When airplane pilots began to use safety belts to hold themselves down in the event of crashes at the modest landing-speed of say 60 miles per hour, I suppose really intelligent people might have considered their utility in automobiles, and no doubt a few did, but most of us, intent on Junior's dreadful grades in alegbra, or the inventory crisis at the widget works, may be excused for hoping to hear of such things from our betters. After all, this country is founded on the premise that the people, given the facts, will reason correctly from them.

They will, too. The magazine *Popular Science* polled its readers in an attempt to discover if they really were, as some authorities have suggested, feather-headed in such a life-and-death matter as the safe automobile. Distinctly, they were not. Readers were asked to name features they would like to have in their automobiles, and a list was offered: Crash padding on the dash, lighted glove compartment, two-tone paint job, shock-absorbing bumpers, car radio, electric clock, recessed rear-view mirror, airplane-type frame, nylon upholstery, airplane-type doors, electric window lifts, chromium trim, safety belts, collapsible steering column, whitewall tires, high back in front seat, padded steering wheel.

The vote was illuminating: *All* the safety items outweighed *all* the luxury items, as below:

	per cent
Crash padding on dash	97
Shock-absorbing bumpers	91
Safety belts	88
Pop-out windshield	87
Collapsible steering column	83
Airplane-type doors	81
Recessed rear-view mirror	78
Airplane-type frame	77

	per cent
Higher back on front seat	59
Padded steering wheel	58
Car radio	43
Air conditioning	33
Nylon upholstery	22
Two-tone paint job	17
Lighted glove compartment	15
Built-in ash trays	14
Electric clock	13
Electric window lifts	12
Chromium trim	11
Whitewall tires	10

The *Popular Science* poll was an impressive demonstration of good sense, and no other interpretation of it is possible. After all, if we don't know any better than to *want* to kill ourselves at the rate of 40,000 a year, then there is no hope; we had best open our veins and leave the land to the digger wasp or the Japanese beetle.

Of all the devices listed, the safety belt is the most valuable in the present circumstances. Probably the most important single feature of a safe automobile is its suspension system, for the suspension system, taken all in all, determines the car's road adhesion; and road adhesion, which means that the car will go where its driver wants it to go, is vital. But until the complex and basic things are done to make our cars truly safe, the seat belt will be supreme, for it can cover up a lot of mistakes, design mistakes and driver mistakes as well. Most of the evidence is in now, and the fact of the matter is that you are unnecessarily risking your life if you drive down to the corner drugstore without a proper seat belt in your car. *And* fastened. A man was killed recently in a mild little 35-mile-an-hour city-traffic accident because he was making so short a trip he didn't bother to fasten his belt. He actually *was* on his way to the drugstore. He didn't make it, being rendered dead by a collision.

There are any number of statistics available on the utility of seat belts. Some authorities believe that they would reduce the U.S. fatality total by 70 per cent if they were universally used. The Indiana State Police, for instance (this department has done much pioneer work with belts) studied 130 fatal accidents in a 90-day period. There were 220 automobiles involved, 153 people were killed. The Indiana troopers believe that if all 153 people had been wearing belts 69 per cent of them would surely have lived and another 12 per cent might have.

Before going any further into the matter, I would like to state my personal belief that any parent who drives a child under the age of 12 in a family car not equipped with belts is perilously close to criminal negligence. An adult may get his hands in front of his face, brace himself against a seat, duck for the floor, or whatever, all pretty hopeless moves but at least offering a thin chance; a child simply flies through the air like a bird.

If you want to be stubborn about the seat-belt question it will be necessary for you to submit with what grace you can summon to the injection of a few statistics. They are illuminating statistics and their absorption will not tax you if you can read without moving your lips. They derive from work done by the Cornell Aeronautical Laboratory in Buffalo, New York, Cornell University at Ithaca, and the Cornell Medical College in New York City. This group has done basic work in the growing effort to persuade us all to live a little longer.

The problem of living through an automobile accident, as we have noted before, is one of deceleration, the business of somehow stopping oneself before the crash hurls one face first into something like a telephone pole. (If you care, the face is highly vulnerable in accidents. Fifty per cent of the people injured in car accidents do not look the same afterward.) In assessing the deceleration problem, the Cornell people have used the *G* terminology made familiar by aircraft test pilots, establishing the value of one *G* for their purpose as the force equal to the subject's weight. The *G* force in serious accidents can range from 2 to 15 units. Therefore, a head-on collision which produced a force of 3 *G*'s—many head-ons produce much more—would require a man weighing 150 pounds to apply 450 pounds of restrictive effort on himself to hold himself in his seat. In other words, when he sees the accident coming, he must brace himself against something, the dashboard let us say, with sufficient strength to hold 450 pounds being slammed into him from the rear. You may be one of the few men strong enough to do this. It's easy to find out if you are. Assume a hands-and-knees stance on the floor and have your wife pile 450 pounds of furniture, old magazines or sacked garden fertilizer on you.

You made it all right? Bully for you. Now in a really severe accident, 15 *G*'s may be registered. Do you wish to try for 15, represented by a weight of 2250 pounds?

The doleful conclusions inevitably to be drawn from these facts impelled the Cornell physicists to decide that seat belts should be able to stand up to a loading of 3000 pounds, enough to hold a 200-pound man in a 15-*G* incident. Anything above 15 *G*'s is likely to collapse the structure of the automobile to the point where the accident must be classified as one of the rare nonsurvivable types.

Other pertinent data of interest to those who did not do well in the 450 pounds of furniture test: One belt per person, easily adjustable in length, with a foolproof buckle. The belt to be not less than two inches wide nor more than four, worn across the hips —not the abdomen—at a 45 degree angle, and fastened to the *frame* of the car. Common methods of fastening belt attachments to the floor of the car may be all right when the car is new; but, as it ages, it rusts, particularly in northern states which use calcium chloride to control road icing. The thin steel sheets that form most car floors will ultimately rust so thoroughly that you can jerk a seat-belt fastening through it with no more effort than it takes to pull the skin off a rice pudding.

Some people fasten seat belts to the seats. This produces an interesting effect in a crash. Since most seats are pinned so lightly to the floor that a hard sneeze will almost unglue them, the passenger who is belted to his seat is in effect the filling in a sandwich that is about to be stepped upon and will suffer the same squishy fate.

Arguments more noisy than forceful were used against the seat belt when the device first began to be seriously considered in 1950. Reactionaries in the automotive industry took up their proper role in the scheme of things, which is to serve as the devil's advocates, and argued that passengers being thrown forward against the restraint of the belts would probably be injured more severely than they would be if unrestrained. It was argued that belts were unnecessary and unproven and so on, but this opposition was soon blown away. The Ford company was boldest in embarking on a safety policy and deserves great credit. There is real danger in such a step for a major Detroit company. Any such policy decision can, in propaganda terms, be "turned around." It would be easy, for example, to argue that a company offering safety belts must feel that its cars were basically unsafe. When the old Rickenbacker automobile came out with four-wheel brakes it was severely, perhaps mortally hurt by the contention that brakes on the front wheels would dangerously interfere with steering. But nobody cared to argue that Fords, Mercurys, Lincolns were flimsy automobiles, and now you can, if you wish, get a seat belt for any automobile.

Only the so-called lap belts have so far been made available in U.S.-built cars. However, the lap belt, fastened across the pelvic region, is certainly useful. It restrains the whole body from flying forward, it keeps the wearer in the automobile—some 20 per cent of fatalities occur *after* the occupant is thrown from the automobile—and it holds the driver at the wheel, helping him to maintain control. Lap belts also can prevent passengers from knocking into each other. They do not, however, prevent "jackknifing," the deadly whipping forward of the upper part of the body on the hinge of the hips. For this, only a shoulder harness will do. Shoulder-harness belts are available as standard equipment only in the Swedish SAAB. I used to have a car—it was a Sunbeam-Talbot—fitted with a primitive but effective shoulder-and-hip harness combined, but my wife usually refused to wear it on the ground that it would mark the shoulder area of her coat, muss her corsage if she happened to be wearing one, and so on. I once lost my temper over this—to me—unfounded reluctance and forced her to put it on by saying, "Oh, well, it doesn't matter; Dr. Gold [our family dentist] will no doubt be able to identify you if I should happen to lose the car on this ice." Common honesty compels me to report that my wife did not speak to me for some time after this sally, however.

The real trouble with the shoulder harness is that most versions of it restrict movement to an intolerable degree. One cannot reach the glove compartment, for example. Some shoulder rigs are dangerous: they may not allow you to reach the hand brake, they may prevent you from ducking under the cowl if you start to skid into the tail end of a ten-ton truckload of sewer pipe. In most circumstances they will save your life, though. Fighter aircraft pilots are the men who know the most about them. In the words of one British report on the standard Sutton Harness, ". . . instances are recorded of aircraft literally fragmenting on impact with the ground but the pilot escaping unscathed. . . ."

There is at least one very fine shoulder-harness rig. It is called the Pacific Harness Safety Reel. A reel of steel cable controlled by a clutch is fastened to the car. The cable is fastened to the shoulder harness over the back of the seat. If the user wishes to lean forward as much as 18 inches, he can do so by moving his body slowly. But in a quick movement, such as that of even a 10-mile-an-hour crash, the reel will give him one-half inch of movement and then lock solid. Men using this rig have unhooked it and stepped out of automobiles that had been smashed into worthless piles of junk, "rolled into a ball" as the professionals say. Incidentally, one group of professional drivers do *not* believe in seat belts. These are the men who drive single-seat, open racing cars. Most, but not all of these men believe that they are better off being thrown out of their cars than restrained in them. Racing automobiles are stark-bodied, full of sharp metal projections, and the driver may well be safer thrown free, although I have seen them killed in the process, and I know one who came through a 140-mile-an-hour crash with only a skinned knuckle and credited his belt.

Yes, Virginia, you can believe there is a Santa Claus if he brings you a seat belt for Christmas. You *need* it, honey.

24 · The Fairly Safe Automobile—II

THE BELT is not the whole answer. Remember, we are considering here only a narrow segment of the problem; we are talking about those things that can be done to make automobiles of contemporary design tolerably safe. Belts, then, and what else?

Dashboard padding. The proper kind of dashboard padding is a tremendous safety factor in the transportation of children, in particular, because a belted child will jackknife faster than an adult, and the child's height will usually bring its head into contact with the dashboard, either full face going down or the top of the head hitting, whereas an adult is more likely to hit the windshield, rear-view mirror or sunshade. The instinctive arms-up attitude of an adult who sees an impending crash will work better on a padded dash, too. (But remember, you're not likely to have any warning at all. Generally, the first warning the victim has of an accident comes in the instant when he is flung from his seat.)

A flexible or breakaway steering wheel. The steering wheel should soak up a considerable amount of the driver's forward movement, thus helping to decelerate him at a rate he can survive.

Doors that will stay shut, not spring open in a crash.

Padded sun visors and a padded or otherwise protected rear-view mirror.

This is a minimum safety package, and is offered just that way, as a package, by Ford. A good deal of research effort went into it.

Ford engineers went to elaborate lengths to verify Cornell's belief that the four primary causes of death and injury in automobile accidents were (1) passenger ejection; passenger striking: (2) windshield, (3) instrument panel, (4) steering post. Everything held up, including Cornell's statement that automobile doors sprung open in 44 per cent of all accidents. Life-size dummies, wired to record location and severity of impact in every part of the body—they cost $4500 apiece—simulated passengers in the staged crashes that were run at the Ford proving grounds. (A distressing number of nice automobiles were turned into junk during the course of the experiments.)

Interest was growing in other areas. Early in 1956, for example, the New York City Fire Department, one of the best in the world, announced that it was embarking on a seat-belt installation program for its vehicles. Although fire equipment rarely runs over 45 miles an hour, it usually runs in heavy traffic, and often against traffic. New York began its program by protecting the three most-exposed men on hook-and-ladder rigs: the driver, the tillerman (he steers the back wheels) and the officer in charge. Ultimately the department will install 1500 belts in its vehicles.

The American Automobile Association applied pressure to the manufacturers in a resolution adopted at its 1956 annual meeting. "Ways and means of protecting the driver against his own mistakes," the AAA said, was the most pressing need of the moment. A resolution argued that reasonable reserve power was necessary for overtaking and passing, and for emergency conditions, but said that "power above that would seem to impose on the car user an unwarranted potential hazard.

"The American Automobile Association, therefore, urges automobile manufacturers to tone down their increasing emphasis on more and more horsepower and higher and higher speed potential in their new models, and devote more thought and emphasis to ways and means of protecting the driver against his own mistakes.

"It is also urged that increased efforts be made to develop and introduce new safety features into the construction of automobiles, and that automobile safety be emphasized."

Horsepower continued to go up, nonetheless.

One of the difficulties that Cornell had found in assessing the worth of new design ideas was the paucity of medical information on crashes. Said Dr. Hugh de Haven, director of the crash-injury research program: "Without medical data the engineers have been completely in the dark about many essential matters pertaining to safety. They have had to work without information as to what forces the head and body can tolerate and without statistical data on how often people are dangerously hurt and by what. Part of this lack of information can be attributed to inadequate investigation and reporting of accidents."

Standards of accident reporting in those states that have shown real awareness of the problem are rising rapidly today. Indiana and Connecticut, for example, make meticulously detailed reports on every serious accident, complete with diagrams, photographs, medical findings and texts, all put together by experts. To help the good work along, the Ford Motor Company and the Chrysler Corporation both made grants of $200,000 to Cornell in 1956. (In 1959 General Motors made a considerable grant for research in the relationship between exhaust gas and cancer in humans.)

The manufacturers were not the only ones to help. Tangible evidence of the Cornell program appeared in mid-1957 in the form of a virtually crash-proof automobile. This work was sponsored by the Liberty Mutual Insurance Company. The insurance companies have a big stake in highway safety, not only because of the number of injuries and fatalities but because of the fantastically high damage claims that juries are beginning to allow. Particularly in New York State, juries award six-figure damages at the drop of a hat. The attitude often is, "The defendant isn't going to have to pay for this man's broken back; the insurance company will put out the money, and they've got a lot of it." Naturally, every damage claim paid is reflected in the premiums we pay for accident protection.

The Cornell-Liberty automobile is a six-passenger, four-door sedan. The cost of the research that went into it was estimated at over $100,000. The seating arrangement of the car is unique: the driver sits in the center of the car, with two passenger seats beside him, one on each side, three inches or so behind him. A fourth seat, for a rearward facing passenger, is fastened directly to the driver's seat, back-to-back. (Most people *like* rear-facing seats once they try them. They enjoy the relaxed, living-room feeling they engender.) Two other passenger seats are in the rear. All seats are of the bucket type so long standardized on racing cars and the better sports cars, designed to prevent the user from sliding by retaining his thighs in place. Each seat is equipped with a safety belt which retracts under spring loading when it's not in use.

The driver does not steer with a wheel. A two-lever steering yoke, or bar, as on a child's sled, pulls out from the dashboard, and steering is done by pushing and pulling the levers. Three inches of movement is all that is needed for the sharpest turn. Again, this "quick" steering is a pickup from racing and sports automobiles. The yoke is, of course, padded and spring loaded to give reluctantly under the driver's weight if he's thrown forward. (Incidentally, the yoke form of steering is the easiest of all to learn. Consider how quickly a child learns to steer a sled. The wheel, as a steering device, is clumsy and dangerous. It was originally used because the multiplication of power it gave was helpful in handling the stiff pioneer automobiles. Power steering has removed the wheel's last excuse for existence. A single-lever universal control will ultimately replace the wheel. It will move forward to accelerate the car, backward to stop it, steer in left and right lateral movement.) The driver sits a long way back from the windshield, which offers a 180-degree field of vision. The windshield is duplicated in the rear.

The doors are two-section hinged doors, rather like those in a telephone booth, and open up practically the whole side of the car. Racing type "roll bars" are in the roof, and they are strong enough to support three and a half times the weight of the car in event of a turnover. An old, old idea—spring-mounted bumpers—has been revived, but instead of being used in front and rear only, they completely encircle the car, promoting glancing instead of direct impact in case of collision. The car's fresh-air intake is mounted in the roof, as high as possible away from concentrated highway exhaust fumes, and the instrument panel is color-coded to assist the driver in quick recognition of the various switches and controls. This last notion derives from aircraft practice. It was found that pilots made fewer errors if the lever controlling the landing gear, for example, were in the shape of a wheel, and so on. The Spanish Pegaso automobile, one of the world's most expensive, had its dashboard controls coded in symbols: light rays for headlights, a whirling spiral for the starter, and so on. So does the Swedish SAAB.

A 50 per cent reduction in the automobile injury and death rate would follow the universal adoption of this design, Cornell officials believe. I think they are demonstrating the typically cautious professorial outlook. I would expect adoption of this design to reduce the accident rate more drastically than that.

Granted, this car would not easily lend itself to sale by what we now think of as conventional means. It is not long, low, slinky looking; its engine, comparatively low powered, will not whisper seductively to be unleashed on the open road (what "open road?"), and its seating arrangement has been poorly thought out for lovemaking. All it will do is take you where you're going in comfort and reasonable speed, say 80 if you really need it, and keep your neck in one place while it's performing this simple and useful task.

I predict it will be coldly received at first, and I predict that it will be widely copied if the various state legislatures and the Congress enact the restrictive laws their individual members are now considering. For it is getting very late. There is an automobile accident about once every twenty seconds in the United States today. Imagine this vast country as silent as the plains, and imagine that we could all, each one of us, hear these crashes, and nothing else. Every twenty seconds, day and night, the demoniacal screech of metal grinding on metal, or wood, or concrete, then the tinkle of the odd bit of glass, the whuff! of gasoline going up in an orange sheet, and finally, the moans and the screams. If we were *all* listening, twenty-four hours wouldn't pass without stringent federal action being taken. Well, there are those who are listening; believe me, they're listening.

25 · Are You Warm to the Touch?

PRESUMABLY you are fairly alive, because if you're sufficiently interested in driving to read a book about driving, you must be a driver; and even the most backward states do not allow the moribund on the roadways. But a cursory search will turn up some remarkable borderline cases, never doubt it. You may be conscious by medical definition, but consciousness is a matter of degree. Most of us are only partly aware of what's going on in our immediate environment, and this lack of attention to pertinent detail is frequently fatal. I do not propose to cite individually the dozens of examples that come to mind. That sort of thing is available in various primers and textbooks on driving that are suitable for the very young. I am making in this book a number of perhaps unwarranted assumptions: that you know it's stupid to make a right-hand turn from a left-hand lane, and so on.

But think of the fellow you know—we all know one—who cannot speak, while driving, without turning to look at the person spoken to. This man is not conscious. He may not be in a true somnolent state, but certainly he is not conscious. Let us leave him as quickly as possible, so as not to be his guest at the accident, and consider the genuinely conscious driver. For an example we seek out a demonstrably expert driver, whom we call Mr. Sloane, and we hang on his person a microphone attached to a tape recorder. (If the fellow has been through analysis, that's good because, while the Freudian couch may not have improved his driving, it will have made it easier for him to deliver unto us his running thoughts.) We put a two-hour reel on the recorder and send him out to drive from here to there and back. Lo, the machine speaks:

"We start the engine and since it's cold we'll let it warm up for sixty seconds. That's enough, but it's important. You sit there and let it run for sixty seconds. Then you will not find yourself stalled half in and half out of the driveway, and a ten-ton truck loaded with concrete reinforcing rods about to contest the right-of-way with you. So. We are comfortable. Safety belt fastened. Windshield reasonably clean, and all that. Gas and oil. Since we're going to go a good little way, it would be smart to check the tire pressures. Three pounds too little air in a tire means a lot of extra flexing when the tire turns, a lot of heat, maybe a blowout. Maybe not this trip, maybe next trip, when your wife is driving.

"O.K. We put the go stick in Drive and move out. Something coming both ways. Gear lever in neutral to wait. Not necessary, just smart. You want to be real smart, put it in reverse. O.K., clear enough, blast off. Set the rear-view mirror. Nothing else to do. You did your fiddling with the heater, the radio, while you were waiting for the engine to warm up. So go. Three houses down, here's where that chasing dog lives. Lies beside the road and runs at the wheels. Get set for him, hold the course, don't give him an inch. When you think of it some day, have somebody ride with you, give him a shot of ammonia from a kid's squirt gun. Remember an Airedale who killed four people; ran at the car, the driver twitched the wheel to the left, got about four inches into a truck passing the other way. It was enough.

"Around this corner, not too close to the edge, somebody could be walking toward you, could be a kid on a bicycle. Now a mile straight, two entry roads to watch. Nothing this one. Guy coming up fast behind. I'm running 40, I figure he's doing 55, don't argue with him, but when he pulls out to pass, run up to about 45 just in case his judgment of forward distance isn't too hot. He's about 20 miles over the limit.

"Nothing in the second entry road. A bend down here, cows in the field on the right side. It's seven A.M., so consider the possibility somebody will be moving the herd across the road. Don't bet they milk at six in the morning; how the hell would you know? Who was it hit the cow with that Duesenberg in Georgia, years ago? Both very dead. No cows crossing. Downhill bend now, wet, in reverse camber, take a line and hold it, straight. Another bend, same thing, straight. Old lady in a Packard doing about 30. Get right by her; you're better off with her behind you. Two kids on the roadside, must be waiting for the school bus. Neither one of of them looking. Horn, until they do. Nothing coming, so move out and give them an extra two feet, for luck. If you see kids, watch for a ball in the road; if you see a ball, stand on everything. If kids run in the road, stop and talk to them. Be very sweet to them; say, 'Look, Mac, or Honey, *don't* go out in the road like that, you scared me half to death, I was afraid I was going to run right *over* you!' That's all, then beat it. They remember better if they get it from a stranger. There are some areas in the rural South where it's better just to wave a stern finger at them. There are also some areas where it's better not to do anything at all.

"All downhill now, wet leaves. Look well ahead, you don't want to have to do any hard braking here. Cluster of cars on both sides of the road down here, new house going up. Workmen. Could be a truck coming out. No. Three-point intersection, watch it, that yo-yo may be thinking of cutting across you for the right-hand fork. He was. Made it. Bully for him. Stop light. Stop, look behind to see if Mr. Cadillac intends to stop. Watch tight, hard to judge speed in depth. If doubtful, duck. Looks silly? Does, but not so much as plaster cast on neck. There goes the light. Turn right, three miles or so to the Parkway. Still 35-mile limit, but you'd better run 45 to stay with the traffic. Four car lengths to the fellow in front. Nothing you can do about the one in back, just watch him. You can sometimes cure a bumper rider, when you have a little clear space in front of you, by putting on brake light and hard gas simultaneously. This will open up three or four car lengths between you; and, if he's civilized, he'll leave it that way. Never try it twice, because if it doesn't work the first time the man has been certified a moron, and the second time he'll come right in with you.

"Trailer truck ahead, empty, now that the fellow in front has turned off. Watch this, his brakes are made to hold him loaded, and empty he can stop like a shot if he puts them on hard. He can forget. How do you know he hasn't been sitting there for seven hours? He could be a little tired and fresh out of benzedrine. He turned off. Long straight here, I can see seven kids walking, two on bicycles. Horn. They're building a store up here, could be trucks. No, but one pulled out a minute ago, here he is, enormous dump, loaded with dirt and rocks. We'll hang back good on him. If a rock falls off, watch it to the last possible minute, then duck. Better to pass him, unless a long downgrade coming. Never let a heavy truck get behind you on a long downgrade if you can avoid it. Probably nothing will happen except that you'll watch him too hard, worry, and maybe do something dumb.

"Parkway coming up, flip the turn signal, light the brakes once. Quick look, is the idiot behind slowing? Right, so turn. Ease up on it. Remember you've been driving only ten minutes or so, at 45, and this traffic is running 60–65, so wake up. Here's the hole, put it in Low and get out quick, no point in dawdling around, dump it into Drive at 30 and run it to 60. You want six car lengths now, and the chances are you can't have them, but do the best you can. Here's the first bend, watch it; the rule is you don't want anybody in it with you. Never pass in a bend, never let anybody pass you in a bend. Reason being the other guy is a moron, and he will not hold his line. He'll drift over toward you. No good. Speed up or slow down, but don't let them do it. After a while you never think of it.

"Gas station coming up. Watch for cretin in front to discover suddenly his needle says empty and dive in. Watch for chumps coming out of station. Get over to the left lane for a few hundred yards, it's the best way to cover both contingencies. Here's a sucker in front running on about 15 pounds of air in his near-side rear tire, and doing an easy 65. Get away from me, man! I belted it once and touched 75 to pass him. O.K., sue me, but he's going to have a blowout any minute now, and not beside me. It would have been nice to blow horn, point to tire, tell him to stop. Would have, if he'd been going slower. Not at 65; anybody too dumb to feel that soft tire might let go the wheel and stick his head out the window to look.

"Three kids just blasted by in a '36 Ford. What a paint job! First one I've seen in the East: flame painting. Beautifully done tongues of flame pouring out of the louvres all over the hood. Probably a dozen coats of lacquer, rubbed and rubbed *and* rubbed. They're doing about 80 and if there's a cop within ten miles he'll nail them for sure. The kid who's driving knows how, though; ran through that bend like a train, didn't get an inch off his line. Old story, terrific reaction time, no judgment. Best kid driver I know is sixteen, he's running a '41 Plymouth now, a junker, and he loses kids in new Fords. He can shift so fast it's hard to believe, and he never touches the clutch. How many times has he rolled? Who could remember? Actually, he's learning: he's trying to find out where the limit of adhesion is, and he finds out by going past it. If he lives, he'll be driving as a pro in four years' time. He'll live, too, that one. How do I know? I don't, but he'll live. He has six hours flying time, too. Some kid. If he was my kid I'd have a little talk with him, that I would. Wouldn't try to stop him, though, no use. I'd buy him a good hot rod, get him in a club, let the other kids hold him down. That's the only way for a kid who really and truly wants to go fast, and knows how. No good threatening him, no use taking his car away, none of that, you'll just kill him quicker. He'll get it in the middle of the night, driving somebody's car, strange to him. Either chain him to a post or get him in a club.

"Big convertible ahead now, fellow and his wife. How do I know she's his wife? They're fighting like cats and dogs, that's how.

He's waving one arm, she's waving both. He's in the left lane at about 50. I'm turning my lights on. Hit the dimmer switch a couple of times. No dice, he's too busy. Horn. So help me, he turned all the way around to look! He's so mad he's forgotten he's got a rear-view mirror. O.K., he jerked over. I'm by. Ooops, says 70; get off it. Right lane now. I took a look as I pulled over, sure enough, here comes the *polizei*. So. Not all the way, though, he's hanging back. I think he wants me for breakfast, maybe. I'm back at 57. Woof! There he goes, he must see something better up ahead. Remarkable how those big sedans handle now. They stick. They didn't used to. Long hill ahead and I see what he's looking at—a fire-engine-red something, low, Mercedes, I think, 190, no 300SL, and flying. Woof! He just ran by six in a string, uphill. Of course he can run away from the cop, but he won't. Conscience will get him. He's breaking the law when he runs, the officer is just doing his regular day-by-day job, and anything that happens isn't his fault. That's the difference. They're both out of sight now.

"Guy in the road, halfway, up here, changing a flat. He has room to move up off the road but he didn't do it. Must have had what appeared to be a reason, to him. Guess; he wanted concrete to put his jack base on. Sucker. He could carry a square foot of wood in the trunk for that, doesn't take a giant mind to think of that. Reminds me of a nice nineteen-year-old kid I saw in a hospital one time. Football player. Nice kid. He saw somebody stopped with a flat, stopped to help. Imagine what a nice fellow he must have been, to do that. So he was taking off the wheel and a standard bird brain came along and hit him. He picked himself up out of the bushes. He felt O.K., just dazed. He couldn't find anything broken. The guy he'd been helping was dead, though. An ambulance came. They wanted to load him. He said no, he felt fine, he'd walk over. He made it to the steps, about, and collapsed. Trouble? He had a broken vertebra in his back; and, when he bent to get into the ambulance, the edges clipped his spinal column, clean and quick. He's paralyzed, waist down, for good.

"Here's the red Merc off the road, and the police car ahead

of him. They're having a little conversation. The troopers in this state are very polite fellows. Doesn't matter if you just went screaming through a red light at 90, they'll be very polite and objective with you, generally. Sound principle. It's hard to argue with a man who won't raise his voice, just says, 'May I see your license and registration, please?' Saves wear and tear all around. It's a mean job, though, anyway you look at it. You sit there all day or all night, pushing it, looking for trouble. Very little that's pleasant will concern you. Put your neck out to chase some idiot; if you catch him in time, chances are he'll threaten you with the mayor's cousin. If you don't catch him in time, you have to pick him up and maybe his leg comes off in your hand. It's no picnic just doing the easiest part: walking up to the guy's window and asking for his license. Every cop who's been a cop for five years knows about somebody who did that and had a slug in him before he could say 'please.' I think if I was a cop I'd go up to the door with that thing in my hand, ready, every time. Five hundred guys would get sore, but the 501st I'd have a hole in him before he had one in me.

"Tollgate. Twenty cents now; used to be a dime. I expect to live to see it half a dollar. Easy out of here, look in the two nearest lanes both sides. Here's a cowboy, Olds 88. Yipes, look at that thing dig; that's not stock. Go ahead, chum, you'll get no argument from me. Cool, man, dig the sidesaddle stance, he's sitting with his back turned halfway to the door, left arm draped outside, cigarette going, radio coming in loud and clear, no sweat anywhere, girl friend sitting beside him. Beside him—what am I saying? There's room for two more people between her and the right-hand door. She's happy, she knows she's riding with a real chauffeur—hold it—I wonder if the screech came through on the tape. What happened was that somebody pulled out just after the Olds went by. This other guy was in the right-hand lane; he pulled out without looking; there was a station wagon coming through the slot. He locked up everything for a second, lost it, just did get it back, not by much. I was three lengths behind the wagon, heading for the right-hand lane. I got in all right, nothing happened. I'll put that down for the first incident of the trip. I figure to see one like that every 50 miles at least, one like that or worse or not so bad, but something that could have been a pile-up. Be interesting to know how many of those near ones there are every hour in this country, every minute even. Funny thing is that I'll bet the fellow who pulled out looks behind him 99 out of 100 times. For some reason or other he skipped it this once. My guess is that he was burned when the Olds blasted past him; pulled out quick to give him a contest. If there'd been an accident he'd have been tagged as causing it. Hardly fair. The character in the Oldsmobile has some of the credit coming, in my book.

"Hitchhiker coming up, suitcase beside him, arrow on it points to word 'Rochester.' I don't want him. Probably deserving fellow, trying to get home to see his sick mother for all I know, but I don't want him. I've got enough to do driving this lump and trying to stay alive, without wondering about some strange cousin sitting beside me. Off the Parkway here, a four-lane that turns into a three-lane down the road a way. The three-lane highway is the greatest killer since the machine gun. Name me something good about a three-lane highway. This is a beauty, fast mixed traffic, heavy trucks, motorcycles, everything but pogo sticks. Drop to 45 and watch it. Truck ahead loaded with construction steel. Those big girders bother me; I always think they'd come in so easy. I'll pass him, I'm looking, no dice, there's a blind hump there, back in; back out, no good, something coming, in, out, still clogged up, in again, woof! Guy behind me moved past, flying. I'm out, something coming against him but he'll make it, by a hair. The trucker lets him have four toots on the horn, dah dah-dah dahhh, very expressive if you do it right. It's clear now and I go. Yellow light ahead, get on the brakes; yellow means red, never green.

"Here we go again, I'm sandwiched between two trucks now, driving on the front one's brake lights because I'm boxed on the outside, too. Outside is clear now, so I move out, but still in the same relative place. I don't want to move up until I know I can run around the truck in front; I don't want my slot closed if I have to duck back into it, so I don't go completely out. Clear again and I can run for quarter of a mile.

"It's raining now, hard, too. The road is running into a town, crossroads every long block or so, most of them stop signs, no lights. Keep your eyes moving from side to side, it's good for 'em anyway. Downhill to a big clover-leaf complex now, real slippery blacktop here, watch it on these sharp bends, big tractor trailers on three sides, guardrail on the other. What you do, you stay absolutely in station, let everybody around you figure you're sensible, won't do anything stupid. Keep the same distance from the truck ahead, maintain a rigid line around the bends. You're better off if they don't have to wonder about you because that way they'll pay more attention to their own driving. That's part of what keeps race drivers alive: their ability to predict the behavior in almost any situation of everybody else on the track. Wet steel plates on the bridge now. Watch this, you can lose it very easily on this stuff. Over. Trucks to the right, I'm left toward the Parkway, heavy traffic on the approach up ahead.

"This is ten minutes later and I'm still not on the Parkway. There's been an accident here. I'm almost up to it, they're going around now in single line. Big sedan, too smashed to see what kind for sure; anyway three people, there are three blankets spread over them, and I mean all over them. Easy to see what happened: the road approaching the Parkway here curves downward and runs under a bridge. This car came down there too fast, he lost it; and, since turning *into* the skid, the right thing to do, would have meant pointing the wheels *at* the bridge, he must have lost his head altogether, turned *away* from the skid. That way he really set it up good, the car went into the bridge wholly broadside, hit the curb, tripped, hit the bridge pier *top* first. That way they all flew into the top of the car head first, and since by now the top of the car was against the concrete bridge . . . woof. Belts would have helped, I imagine, although the car looks like a total.

"Out on the Parkway now, 60 again, still raining hard. I'd like eight car lengths in this rain, I won't get it. I'm in the right-hand lane, and I'm staying there as much as I can. You have a little better percentage going for you in the inside under any circumstances. You have to remember that anybody who is dying to pass fast in a real rain storm is either a yo-yo or in a real big hurry and in either case it's better to stay away from him.

"Since everything went automatic transmission I've ridden

left foot on the brake pedal. It takes a long time to get used to it, a real long time, and only a professional should do it if he is also doing much driving of three-pedal cars, but most people don't these days, they drive automatics alone. You can do yourself some good using your left foot for the brake. I think some people might make a whole second doing it, a panic stop. A second isn't much, but it can mean three car lengths at 60 miles an hour and that's a great deal, can be the difference.

"I was over this road a few months ago, five o'clock in the morning. It was winter, cold day, there was nothing on it, not one car every five miles, and believe it or not I came to an overpass bridge, set in a little bend, and there were two cars stacked up there, one man dead, another just about. A simple thing did it: the road was clear so they were flying. The road was dry, no snow or ice—except under this one bridge. It was at the bottom of a sort of little valley and water had gathered there and frozen; the shade of the bridge kept the sun from melting it. That was all it took; these fellows thought that if the road was dry in one place it must be dry all over. They hit the ice, the road had a tiny little bend there, woof! It was all over once they started to slide. The one who lived later admitted he'd been over 95 and he felt safe as a church. He would have been, too, if he'd known how to drive, if his car had been O.K., and if he'd had something to think with. If there's going to be ice anywhere it'll be under a bridge, why should you have to tell anybody anything as simple as that? Like having to tell somebody to look behind before pulling out to pass. They'd kick a fourteen-year-old kid out of school if he was too dumb to know that much.

"Two cars ahead now, a wagon and a sedan, running side by side. I'm on them now, they're doing about 63. The one outside won't go faster to get by, the one inside won't back off. I should think their chances of trouble are about six, seven times what they would be if they were running alone like sensible people. I'm dropping way back now, ten lengths isn't too much if they slide into each other. You couldn't pay me enough to make me light a cigarette right now, I'm watching these cousins. They're coming up on another guy now, something will have to give, the one inside I guess. No, he flashed his lights, probably blew his horn, too, I couldn't hear, and the dope moved over to the left, right in front of the other contestant. So Mr. Inside got on by. Now Mr. Outside is cutting around and chasing. They're running tandem again now. Bully for them.

"Sign says restaurant 1000 feet ahead, that's for me, I'll get some coffee. Set the signal. Guy behind keeps coming, light the brakes for him a couple of time, but without putting the brakes themselves on, how do I know the lights are on? I've got an extra light wired into the system, on the dashboard. If the stop lights don't go on I want to know about it. He moved over. I'm off the gas now, and a quick look at the speedometer; I want to get down to 20 before I turn in, and when you've been running at 65–70, 40 miles an hour can seem slow enough to jump out, you should check the gauge to make sure. Speed is relative, you drive at 140 for an hour and 65 seems so slow you wonder why you bother to stay awake for it, O.K., 20 it is and we slide in, get on the brakes, 5 miles an hour through the slot between the pumps and the gas station, 3 would be better, barely moving, because you have no way of telling when anyone is coming out, and park it and shut down. . . ."

That's how it is with the conscious driver. Our hero is forty-five, has been driving since he was sixteen, figures he has driven 750,000 miles, has had two tickets in that time, one for parking, one for speeding, and one accident, a five-dollar fender scrape. He figures he has driven over 150 different makes of steam, electric and gasoline automobiles, the fastest speed he remembers is 201 miles an hour. He drives absolutely smoothly, so smoothly in fact that after a long ride with him you have the impression he never varied his speed at all. He holds the wheel in both hands, always, either at ten and two o'clock, if things look lively, or at eight and four o'clock if he's relaxed. He won't smoke, and if you shot off a gun in the back seat he wouldn't look around. He talks, he sees the countryside he's passing through, he enjoys himself, but in one corner of his head separate business is being done, every minute, and much more than he put on the tape, too.

"You think so much faster than you can talk," he said after

he'd heard the tape. "You have time to mention one factor in a given situation, but there may be two or three others. Like that business with the kids beside the road, there are different things. A kid who's going to run across the road, he takes a certain stance that a man wouldn't, he kind of gathers himself. And I remember one time I saw a kid on a lawn running for a slot between two parked cars. I had plenty of time to get there before him, but I backed off on principle. What do you know, *another* kid popped out in front of me. *He* was the kid the kid *I* saw was chasing!

"But all those examples are just frosting. All that matters is that you have to drive from a quarter of a mile to a mile ahead of yourself, and you have to believe that every other car you see is in the hands of a moron who is also your worst enemy. It's a lot of trouble learning, I'll give you that; it's months before it's automatic; and for most people it's too much trouble. But I've seen more wrecks than most people, and it's a messy way to die. That's what I always think of. It's so messy."

26 · The Expert's Expert

Most people do not know what incredibly bad drivers they are because they have no standard of comparison: they don't know what *good* driving is. The average shirt-sleeved American male, beer in one hand, cigarette in the other, watching Ray Robinson fight on TV, understands that he would not be able to handle Robinson in a street fight. He *knows,* in other words, that he, Joe Blow, is not much of a fighter. But because he has never seen any really good driving, and hence does not know what is possible in an automobile, he is hampered by no such modesty when he assays his ability behind the wheel.

There are about 76,000,000 Americans who are licensed to drive automobiles. Of this number, 2 per cent—1,500,000—concede that they might be better drivers than they are. All the rest, as far as we can tell, believe themselves to be experts of the first rank. This is incredible, but try to accept it, because it's true. Or is it incredible? Think about it for a moment. You're a pretty good driver, aren't you, pal? Sure you are. Isn't much left for you to learn, is there? You bet not.

Of course, if you went out with a really good driver who was in a hurry, you'd probably die of fright. You would be struck numb with terror because, being totally ignorant about the driving of an automobile, you would be totally unable to understand what was going on.

Let us consider, for example, a ride with Stirling Moss, as this is written the leading racing-car driver in the world. Moss is not a more *careful* driver than Mr. Sloane of the previous chapter, but his sheer technical ability is greater, to the level of virtuosity. Moss is the expert's expert. In 1956 Moss won the Italian Mille Miglia race, run over 1000 miles of *open road,* at a record speed: nearly 98 miles an hour. This record will probably stand forever, because the Mille Miglia race, the world's most dangerous, may never be run again for really fast cars. Moss carried a passenger, Denis Jenkinson, former motorcycle sidecar champion of the world, a most cold-blooded and knowledgeable man. Jenkinson's job was to read a seventeen-foot-long strip of paper unrolling from a plastic case on the dashboard and, using 13 hand signals, tell Moss what the road was like just ahead. This he did, so successfully that Moss has said repeatedly that he could not possibly have won the race without him. Afterward, Jenkinson told what the ride had been like in *The Racing Driver* (italics mine):

". . . On the straights to Verona we were getting 7500 revolutions per minute in top gear, which meant about 170 mph . . . we could keep at *170 over blind hillbrows, even when overtaking slower cars.* . . . Entering *the main street of Padua at 150 mph,* we braked for the right-angle bend at the finish and suddenly I began to realize that Moss was beginning to work furiously on the steering wheel, for we were arriving at the corner much too fast. . . . I sat fascinated, watching Moss working away to keep control. . . . With the wheels almost on locking point, he kept the car straight to the last possible fraction of a second, making no attempt to get round the corner, for that would have meant a complete spin and anything could have happened. Just when it seemed we must go head-on into the straw bales, Moss got the speed down low enough to risk letting go the brakes and try making the corner. As the front of the car slid over the dry road, we went bump into the bales with our left-hand front wing, bounced off into the middle of the road, and as the car was then pointing in the right direction, Moss selected bottom gear and opened out again. . . ."

"Up the Radicofani [Pass] we stormed, with the car bucking and slithering about to such an extent that I should have been frightened but for my complete faith in the masterly driving of Stirling. . . . On the winding road from Siena to Florence, physical strain began to tell on me, but I gave myself renewed energy by looking at Stirling, perfectly relaxed beside me, working away at the steering as though we had only just left Brescia instead of having driven for nearly 700 miles in a broiling sun.

"The approaches to Florence were almost backbreaking, as we bounded and leaped over the badly maintained roads. Down a steep hill in second gear, we went into third at peak revs, making me think that it took a brave man to unleash about 300 horsepower down so steep a hill and change into a higher gear while doing it. At speeds sometimes *exceeding 120 miles an hour we went through the streets of Florence,* over the great river bridge, broadside across a square, over tram lines and into the control. . . .

"Up the long straights through Modena, Reggio, Emilia and Parma we went, not wasting a second anywhere, cruising at 170 mph, cutting off only where I indicated corners or bumpy hillbrows. Looking up, I suddenly realized we were overtaking an airplane, and then I knew I was living in the realms of fantasy; when we caught and passed a second one my brain began to boggle at the sustained speed . . . the car was going perfectly and reaching 7600 rpm in fifth gear in places, which was as honest a 170 mph plus as I'd care to argue about. . . . In one village we had an enormous slide on some melted tar, and for a moment I thought we would hit a concrete wall, but with that absurdly calm manner of his, Moss tweaked the wheel this way and that, caught the car just in time, and with his foot hard down we went on our way as if nothing had happened. . . ."

Moss and Jenkinson entered the 1957 Mille Miglia, the one which was so marred by the death of the Marquis de Portago and a group of spectators. They were the last car to leave the starting point at Brescia, and they had the shortest ride of the race—less than 10 miles. Entering a bend at high speed, Moss felt the brake pedal come loose. The bend was solid with spectators—men, women and children lining the edge of the road—and the ordinary driver would have killed himself and fifty of them. Moss told me about it in a letter:

"I was approaching the corner at approximately 130 mph. I estimated that the corner could be taken at about 90, therefore it was a fairly sharpish curve, to the left. I lifted my foot off the accelerator and put it on the brake and, on increasing pressure on this pedal, it suddenly shot forward and in fact broke off. More or less at the same time I was dropping the car down into fourth gear. I glanced quickly down at my feet, realized there was a big gap between the accelerator and the clutch. I didn't have time to be afraid. I pulled the hand brake on, which was useless; pushed the car into third, immediately followed by second. I can remember the car fish-tailing a little. At the same time as all this I attempted to put the car into a bit of a broadside to lose a little speed. I managed to get the car around the corner and then dropped it into first gear. Finally Dennis Jenkinson and I had to jump out and stop it manually. When I tell you there were absolutely no brakes at all it is no exaggeration: the car was so free-running that when we turned it around by hand we had to be careful that it did not run off the camber into the ditch. . . ."

That is the kind of thing that can be done with an automobile by someone who knows how. Moss and other professionals of his caliber handle automobiles as if they were toys being pushed around on the dining-room table. The next time you slide up to the narrow edge of an accident because you've been doing 50 miles an hour on a wet road, remember that Stirling Moss would probably be perfectly safe on the same road at 125 miles an hour. The conclusion is inescapable: you aren't a very good driver. You don't know very much about automobiles, how they handle, how they work, what to do with them. You don't realize how hideously dangerous they are. You don't pay attention, and in short you don't know what the hell you're doing. That's why your chances of being involved in an accident this year are so good.

I remember remarking to someone that Moss had said that one of the hardest parts of learning to be a racing driver was acquiring the ability to concentrate on driving, without a second's lapse, for the whole length of a race, three hours at a time.

"Guy must be stupid," my friend said, taking both hands off the wheel to light a cigarette. He steered with his knees, more or less, the car edging inexorably to the right. "Driving ain't that hard." The fellow is no longer with us, having been gathered to his Maker in an odd fashion: he ran into another car in the approach to a toll gate. The police theory was that he had dropped his quarter and was looking for it on the floor and had let the fact that he was in a moving automobile slip his mind, as it were. Ludicrous? Nothing like that could ever happen to you? I wouldn't bet on that proposition. It was the $65,000-a-year head of an international widget corporation, not an idiot, who started his stalled car by putting it into gear and then asking a couple of passers-by to help him push it. The engine caught nicely—and the car ran downhill and smashed in the screened porch of a house, killing two children.

A high-grade moron makes a good driver, in point of fact. James Stannard-Baker, research director of Northwestern University's traffic institute, was first to advance the theory. The intellectual, Baker said, won't take driving seriously enough to concentrate on it, and the driver who has a really low I.Q. *can't* concentrate. But the high-grade moron, if he has been carefully trained and is alert and fairly mature, is the safest, most careful of all drivers.

Are you as bright as a high-grade moron?

In the opinion of many police officers, no, you're not. For example, in the mountain country of the West, state police and rangers grow hoarse telling drivers to stop and cool off their brakes before they lose them altogether. The officers know which cars are heading for brake trouble because of the smoke coming off their wheels. Why is smoke coming off their wheels, Daddy? Because they are so incredibly unlettered in things mechanical that they think the safest way to descend a long hill is to put the gears into neutral and go down on the brakes.

When a driver comes up behind you at night and leaves his high beam on, so that the light reflected from your rear-view mirror truly blinds you, is he being deliberately rude? Almost never. He's too stupid to realize what he's doing to you, that's all. If someone comes up behind *him* and does the same thing, he *may,* in a few minutes, make the connection with what he's been doing to you, and push his dimmer switch.

When a driver doing 30 miles an hour in a 50 mph zone ties up traffic until there are a dozen cars strung out behind him, is he deliberately trying to provoke an accident? Almost certainly not. He's too dumb to realize that he ought to pull over, that's all.

It is as well to bear things like that in mind. Remember: No one ever got hurt on the highway by underestimating the intelligence and the ability of the average American driver. He's a real dope.

27 · Nevertheless, You Too Can Learn to Drive

As THIS BOOK was being written, one Robert W. Mausolf of New York City unburdened himself of an appeal in the letters-to-the-editor column of one of the automobile magazines.

"Call this a confession if you like," Mr. Mausolf wrote, "but I seldom travel at 'legal' speeds because I feel that they must be designed for the incompetent. If I were hard of hearing, or if I wore glasses half an inch thick, or if I drove a refugee from a junk heap, then the legal speed limits would be fine and dandy.

"Don't get me wrong, under special circumstances I believe in going much slower than the legal speed—it works both ways—but when the road is straight and open, and weather and visibility good, why not burn out the carbon a little?

"It's time we all faced a few facts. As long as people believe that driving is a chore that anybody can do, we are going to continue to have 'highway homicide' at an ever-increasing rate. 'Anybody, with a little training, can drive a car,' is the misconception and the rule of thumb.

"For a few dollars and a drive around the block anybody can get a driver's license and, as long as it is renewed, a person can keep his license till the day he dies, whether or not he continues to see, hear or even think properly after the initial 'vision, written and driving tests.'

"The only real solution to the mounting traffic fatality rate is to cure the trouble at its source. What I'm driving at is that driver's licenses should be issued only to people who can really drive.

"First prerequisite should be a complete physical. The second should be a written test to determine not only knowledge of rules of the road but also general intelligence level. Finally, before getting a license, a person should be required to pass a road test that is worthy of the name. Once around the block, parking the car, and starting off on a hill are some indications of driving ability but what may be good enough in city traffic could be pure murder on a parkway.

"Too many accidents are chalked up to 'excessive speed' when the real reason is simply BUM driving."

Mr. Mausolf's earnest, if somewhat lengthy, exposition reflects a position more commonly held than most of us realize. For the competent driver *must* be appalled by the standard of performance he sees on the roads around him. It *is* true. Most of us *are* bad drivers because most of us have been badly taught. Ideally, driving instruction would begin in nursery school and kindergarten with traffic-signal indoctrination, proceeding to thirty hours of classroom and field work in high school, some of it on Aetnacans and other training devices.

A venerated folk belief in Shaker Heights, Big Sur, Beacon Hill and Ninth Avenue is that a husband cannot teach his wife to drive. He cannot, the old saw goes, because he will lose patience with her, he will shout, she will weep, and a bill of divorcement is as likely to result as a driver's license. There is much sad substance to this legend.

Are you a husband, obliged, perhaps, to teach your wife to drive? Attend. Are you a wife, dreading the first period of instruction? A daughter or a son, edging toward your first license? Listen to me. I know about this.

My own wife has an attitude not unusual among women: she loathes machinery and all things mechanical. Before I taught her to drive, she had been flunked out of two New York City driving schools, institutions whose boast it was that if the pupil could read one-syllable words he could be taught to drive. My wife's savage hatred of machinery overcame their vaunted skills in short order. Hardened as only New York City entrepreneurs and Marseilles saloon keepers can be, nevertheless they conveyed to her that they were unable in conscience to take her money, and asked her please to go away. I cite all this merely to validate my right to brag after I've stated how well my wife drives today, which is very well indeed. I want you to know that this was a *difficult* case. If your own little trainee, whether related to you by blood, vow or mere money, seems a trifle difficult, take heart, and don't give up.

It is necessary, of course, that you, the teacher, not be an absolute cretin. You ought to know at least a little bit about teaching, which is, after all, something of an art. It is not enough to be a good driver to teach driving, any more than it suffices to be good at anything else in order to teach it. I used to know a man who was one of the best drivers in the country. He was mechanically a very much better driver than I was, and I often longed to ask him to check me out in a few things. We were close friends at the time, he was of a generous nature and would have refused me nothing I cared to ask him for, but I never asked him for a driving lesson because I knew he couldn't teach me anything. He was totally incapable of understanding how another person felt, of getting into another's mind; and, this being so, he would obviously be quite incapable of teaching. No one can teach successfully who cannot expunge from his mind everything he knows about the subject being taught for long enough fully to understand how the pupil feels. Most amateur teachers, emphatically including most of those who teach others to drive, have the attitude often attributed to the American tourist abroad: Because someone can't understand English, he assumes the man is deaf and begins by shouting at him; he is soon angry at the fellow's obvious stupidity and in due course loses his temper. The reason most husbands fail when teaching their wives to drive is easy to grasp. The husband understands how a gearbox works, he has understood it for years. Refusing stubbornly to place himself in his wife's position, he can find no other explanation except willful stubbornness and congenital stupidity to account for her inability to shift gears like a master.

Let us ponder the methodology. And let us brush aside, right at the beginning, the *wrong* way to go about it. This is the typical scene:

Jason Thumbdumb, having risen sufficiently high in the economic scale to move his family from the city to the country, finds it imperative to teach Mrs. Thumbdumb how to drive, so that she can take him to the station in the morning and cart the squalling young from home to school to scout meeting during the rest of the day. Accordingly he sets aside a bright Saturday morning, rolls out the station wagon and summons his helpmeet. He speaks:

"Now, look, Hettie, there's nothing tough about learning to drive a car. It's simple. Here's what you do. You move this lever here until the little pointer points to 'N.' Then you turn this key. When the engine starts you take off the brake—that's this gimmick here—and you move the lever over to where the pointer says 'D.' Then you push down on the gas pedal—that's the one on the right—and the car will move. The harder you push on the gas, the faster it'll go. When you want to stop you take your foot off the gas, push down on the brake—that's the other pedal there—and the car will stop. Got it? Now you try."

Mrs. Thumbdumb, all elbows and exposed nerve endings, gets behind the wheel. Holding the gear lever like a surgeon's scalpel, she pushes it to "N." Then she turns the starter key. The engine fires right away, but she keeps the key hard on. There is a moan from the starter and an anguished howl from Jason.

"Let go of it!! Let go of it!! For God's sake, don't hang on it after the engine's started! You want to tear the Bendix apart? Jesus!"

With the engine running, Mrs. Thumbdumb moves the lever over and treads delicately on the accelerator. Nothing happens.

"More gas, more gas!" declaims her teacher. "Push on it a little, you won't break it, it's no eggshell, you know."

She pushes. The engine stalls.

"No wonder, you birdbrain," Mr. Thumbdumb informs her, "you forgot to take the hand brake off. How in hell do you expect the car to move with the rear wheels locked? Try it again."

This time, the brake off, Mrs. Thumbdumb pushes vigorously on the gas, no less vigorously than she did before. The car leaps like a startled goat. Completely unclued about steering, Mrs. T. misses the old apple tree by a hair and her husband just does manage to throw the car out of gear before they climb the stone wall.

"You trying to kill yourself, and me too?" Mr. T. inquires. "Do you know it would have cost $150 to fix this lump if you'd hit that wall? Can't you pay the *least* attention to what I tell you? Well, *can't* you?"

At this point, without a word, Mrs. T. gets out of the car and goes into the house. Later, her husband will find that she is in the bedroom, the door locked. Eventually they'll make up and try again, and some day, unlikely as it seems, she'll learn to drive —after a fashion. Because she must, Mrs. Thumbdumb will accept her husband's instruction, but the minute she has her license, the minute the state has certified her competence to handle a 200-horsepower machine under all conditions of wind and weather, at that moment she'll stop learning, and from then until the day she dies, there'll be very little improvement in her driving technique. She may never have an accident. She may never even cause one, but she'll be a dreadful and a dangerous driver all the days of her life.

That's the wrong way. The right way?

The right way starts with paper and pencil and the dining-room table. First lesson: What makes a gasoline engine go?

One of the commonest sights, when all automobiles had manual transmissions, was the stalled woman driver. Nowadays, with most new cars mounting automatic transmissions, one sees less of this, but it still happens, and the reason is the same. No one ever told the poor girl how an internal-combustion engine works, and why it has no torque, or twisting power, when it's turning slowly. Draw a crude vertical section of an engine and explain the Otto cycle to her: intake, compression, power, exhaust. (Even if you're teaching her on one of the increasingly popular foreign two-stroke cars, the SAAB or the DKW for instance, explain it as a four-stroke.) The essential point to convey is that the power stroke, the one that does the work and moves the automobile, is very violent and of very brief duration. Therefore, if power is to be continuously applied, you tell the good woman, there must be very *many* such strokes, the engine must be turning fast. If you once get this point across, she'll almost never stall an engine.

Next show her that the clutch pedal makes or breaks the connection between the engine and the road wheels. Using the palms of your hands, show her how the clutch plates rub together to take up the drive. The essential point is that if this rubbing is severe or prolonged, it will wear out the plates. When this point has been grasped, you have given her a lifelong indoctrination against slipping the clutch. Nearly all women abhor waste.

Next explain the gearbox. Start with the fact that it is harder to put a heavy object into motion than it is to keep it moving. Explain the individual gears in terms of levers: first gear is the longest lever, therefore the most powerful, and so on. Remind the learner that the engine produces most power when it's turning fast. Therefore, it must turn fastest, in relation to distance traveled by the car, when hooked up to first gear, less in second, and so on. Then you will find it easy to convince the learner that the combination of high gear (short, weak lever) with slow (weak) engine will certainly result in stalling. Take your time. Tell the tale slowly and with good humor and it will stick forever.

Now—and this is harder—obtain a toy automobile with steerable front wheels and explain skidding and skid recovery. Once over lightly is enough for a starter, you'll have to do this many times before it's understood. And do not prolong the entire lesson beyond a half hour. She won't take it.

First time actually *in* the automobile you never move it. Adjust the seat so that it's perfectly comfortable. Then, starting with the ignition switch, force the student to memorize the location of every control, emphatically including heater and radio controls, window winders and door locks. Keep at it. Not until the learner can unerringly touch every control on the car while blindfolded do you turn on the engine. This is very important. If the learner, moving, is forced to take her eyes off the road every time she adjusts a control, she will learn slowly and with difficulty because she will be trying to learn ten things at one time, and concentrating on no one of them. Additionally, of course, it's dangerous.

When the controls have been learned you can start the engine and move the automobile. It should be a manual-transmission car. Manual-transmission cars will be on the roads for many years. There is no point in teaching a novice driver on an automatic transmission. Do it the other way around. Why? You *need* to be told? Well, consider the case of the wife of a friend of mine, Mrs. Goodwife. She learned to drive on an automatic-transmission Studebaker and for three years drove nothing else. One day when her husband had the car, a friend, Miss A., called for her, drove her to her own rather isolated house. Miss A.'s car was a manual-shift station wagon. Miss A. made some tea, but before it was poured she staggered to a couch and fell on her back in the grip of an angina attack. Mrs. Goodwife called the doctor's office. His nurse said he was out, but that she, the nurse, could help if Miss A. were hurried to the office. Mrs. Goodwife dragged her, somehow, to the wagon and stripped the gears out of it trying to drive it. Mrs. Goodwife then dragged Miss A. back to the house and they waited for the doctor. Miss A. died that night. Of course, you're right, she might have died anyway. Are there any further questions of a similarly penetrating nature?

When you first move the car with the learner at the wheel,

do not do it in a driveway or any other constricted place. Go to a park, a ball field, a parking lot, a freight-loading yard or some such open place. Ask the learner to do only two things at first: move the car and steer it in a general way. That's quite enough. And keep your big fat mouth shut as much as possible, and keep your voice down when you do speak. Remember, if you were being taught to ride a unicycle or pilot an airplane, you might not look like such a ruddy genius either. And remember, too, that the United States Army, on the basis of thousands of tests, believes that women make better and safer drivers than men. They even have faster reaction times. So curb that feeling of superiority.

After a couple of hours of starting, stopping and steering, the average learner should be ready to essay a quiet street. But be sure it's a quiet street, and be sure the learner is panic proof. You must know that if you see a child and say "Brake!" brake is what you'll get.

In steering, try to remember this: the wheel, as we've remarked before, is a poor device for directing a moving vehicle, and it's hard to learn to use it. Be patient. The learner will nearly always wait for the car to show where it's going *before* turning the wheel. Remember this, and allow for it. The *anticipation* of turning that marks the competent driver is not instinctive and must be learned by trial and error. The first time your pupil starts around a corner you may be sure you'll think she's going to miss it. Be brave and hang on, she's doing only 15 miles an hour, and let her get around it in her own way, which will be a series of saw-tooth lines. Anticipation and smoothness of steering come only with practice.

If you've gone along this far, you're over the hump. Now enforce endless practice over all kinds of terrain, plus all the theory you can get into her pretty little skull. Be pleasant about it. Be gay. And don't ask her to remember fifteen things at once. One bulletin a day is plenty.

For example: "You know, lamb-pie, in slippery weather lots of people hit things head-on quite needlessly. They're in a bend, for example, and decide they're going too fast. Of course, if they'd remember the rule, slow before a bend, accelerate *in* it, they'd be all right. But they didn't, and they're in a bend too fast on a slippery road. So they put the brakes on hard, and all of a sudden they find themselves going straight off the road, not around the bend, but straight in it, and off the road. They put the brakes on harder, and they go off just the same. Why? Because they locked the front wheels and locked front wheels act like sled runners. They slide straight ahead. If the front wheels are allowed to turn, even a little, they'll steer the car as they should. So, if you're ever on a slippery road with the brakes on, and find the car going where it shouldn't go, remember, take your foot off the brake and let the wheels steer. Then, when you're going straight, brake again, but lightly, gently, repeatedly, and not locking the wheels."

All theory can be taught in this way. Just use a little kindness, a little imagination. After all, this *is* your wife, let's say. Therefore, you *do* want her to drive with reasonable safety. You do want her to live to see your next anniversary, don't you? If not, be a man and shove her off a cliff, but don't let her take four other people with her, as she very well may if you turn her loose on the Boston Post Road badly taught to drive.

One thing can't be taught in theory and that's skidding and skid recovery. For this you've got to skid. Where? That's your problem. If you live in cold country you can find a frozen lake or pond or river. Some parking lots are badly drained and get pretty slippery. Something can be done on a slippery ordinary road provided you can use it when it's empty, say at five or six in the morning. What, get up at five A.M. to teach a dame how to skid? That's right, better she should learn from you than from the back end of a ten-ton trailer. A perceptive pupil can learn quite a lot from sitting beside a good driver who is deliberately provoking and correcting small skids—quite a lot, but not enough. To be safe on the road in any weather, the learner must be able to provoke a skid at will and come out of it safely. The driver experiencing a skid for the first time will almost surely "lose" the automobile altogether.

A month of intelligent instruction should make a reasonably safe low-speed, around-town driver out of anyone. After that, competence depends upon practice, the absorption of theory through reading, and willingness to go on learning. A period of considerable danger occurs when the driver first experiences full confidence. It varies in the individual, and is comparable to the sensations of the airplane pilot who has five hundred hours in the air. At this point the driver knows enough to know he's pretty good, but doesn't know enough to know how bad he is. When this happens you have an incipient accident case on your hands. Sometimes it helps to take the subject to a good sports-car road race. (A track race won't do it because the races are special and the round-and-round circuit is too far out of range of normal experience.) The driver who's beginning to think he's pretty hot stuff will often become quite thoughtful after watching the experts take a few bends at 120 miles an hour.

Perhaps the worst mistake husbands make in teaching their wives to drive is an error of omission: once a girl has a license, they never watch her drive again. When they go out together, Papa drives—always. His former prize pupil may have picked up every bad habit in the book, but he'll never know it until the day she hits the town steamroller. At least once a month the sensible teacher will take a ride as a passenger. And remember, no shouting. Control the temper. Quiet, please.

28 · Stand Well Back, There!

A FEW YEARS AGO the staid *Journal of the American Medical Association*, no sensation-monger, characterized the automobile death toll as "Our Number 1 public health problem." A logical point of view, since only cancer and heart disease destroy more useful years of life among us. Still, automobiles knocked off 38,500 people last year and put about 1,000,000 into the hospitals.

Bad judgment did most of them in, of course. Going fast where it wasn't safe to go fast, hitting a curve a little too hard, forgetting that there might be a child behind that tree, and so on. But a good many of them went for a lack of a few cents' worth of nuts and bolts.

There are about 800 places on an automobile where two parts are joined together, usually by a nut-and-bolt type of fastener secured by a lock washer. These fasteners are constantly trying to work themselves loose, and they often succeed, with unhappy results. The state of New Jersey recently discovered that 1262 accidents within its boundaries had been caused by failed fasteners. It's a safe bet that at least 1200 of the people driving those cars had never thought of tightening a nut or of having someone else tighten one. To be really secure, you ought to tighten every nut on the car every ninety days. Crucial connections, such as steering system fasteners and wheel nuts, should be seen to more frequently. Uncritical readers of automobile advertising might be excused for believing that the cars aren't *built* at all, but are delivered from on high by celestial conveyors. The facts are different. The American automobile is put together by labor nearly all of which is rated "unskilled." These men do not have to work today, as they used to have to work, at a pace so fast that it bordered on cruel and inhuman treatment, but the production line is moving, it stops for no man, and a lick and a promise often has to do. These men are kindly and goodhearted, most of them, but they are *not* craftsmen, and they do *not* love their jobs. One of the biggest automobile dealers in this country told me that he spent on an average $80 to prepare new cars for delivery, and most of the time involved was spent in tightening things up, replacing lost nuts, and so on.

The only way to insure quality production is to use a high inspector-worker ratio. The Mercedes-Benz automobile, next to Rolls-Royce the best-made car in the world, is the end product of a system using one inspector for each eight workers. In the production of the high-performance models of Mercedes-Benz, every nut is tightened with a torque wrench, and it is the boast of the management that a car cannot get past inspection with even a slight burr or wrench-mark on one edge of a nut. No U.S. automobile is built to such standards.

In the years immediately after the Second World War, people who were really knowledgeable about automobiles inclined to prefer foreign cars to domestic on the ground of superior handling qualities. They were right. Until fairly recently American cars handled very badly: they were loose and sloppy on the road. In 1947, for example, a little TC model MG Midget, all 54 horsepower of it, could run away from almost anything made in Detroit, given a bit of winding road. Our cars are very much better now, but only the best of them—say Chevrolet's Corvette—can compare with the best of the Europeans. My own conviction is that a small, quick-steering, high-powered car is best and safest: something like a 1600 Porsche, a Gran Turismo SAAB, an

Alfa-Romeo Guillietta. The small amount of research that has been done on the problem seems to indicate that a big car is *very* slightly safer in an accident than a small car, but that the small, agile, over-engined, over-braked car is less likely to get into trouble in the first place. The high-performance or sports car is safe, among other reasons, because it keeps its driver busy, and therefore alert. He has numbered instruments to read, quick steering and a manual shift. The present trend to automatic everything, with even instruments replaced by lights that come on only in the instance of trouble, is dangerous because it's soporific. Analysis of parkway and turnpike and toll-road accidents indicates that the *primary cause* of trouble is the driver who has fallen asleep! The long, fast turnpikes are dangerously hypnotic. Safety engineers are now considering such makeshift safety devices as strips of noise-making concrete every few miles, and fog horns set in the center strips. These things may help, but until the fully automatic automobile is with us, the turnpikes will continue to be dangerous.

Even the fully automatic automobile will have accidents, but they will be due to malfunction of the mechanism, not errors in judgment. Impressive beginnings have been made in attacking the two big automatic automobile problems: guidance and collision-control. General Motors already has a workable guidance system: a wire buried in the highway broadcasts a weak radio signal to two antennas mounted on the car. A computer figures which radio is getting the stronger signal and sends corrective instructions to the steering apparatus. The only drawback to the system is the necessity of cutting open the nation's highways with diamond-tipped saws and burying a few million miles of cable.

Radar would seem to offer the best means of making it impossible for a car to run into anything, but it works too well: radar not only senses a car ahead and orders the gas pedal lifted and the brakes applied, but it does the same thing in a corner —it "sees" a tree standing there in a straight line ahead. Straight radio or infrared light seems to offer better hope. Whatever the method, it's a certainty that the fully automatic automobile will ultimately be with us, the "driver" sitting there reading the paper if that's his pleasure, secure in the realization that electronic servants are watching out for him.

Until that happy day, however, you've got to drive the thing yourself, like it or not.

29 · What Happened to Old Man Harsch?

1

ON THAT MORNING in May, the millions were on the road, moving in the routine madness of travel across the land, moving in every wheeled thing that could be driven by burning oil: little two-stroke engines hung on bicycles, scooters, motor bikes, three-wheeled and four-wheeled and six- and eight- and ten-wheeled things, drinking a Niagara of gasoline for pleasure and profit, for the greater glory of Allah and the owners of tanker fleets, but mostly for the fun of moving about, singly, freely, at will—that, or the earning of a living. Some scores of them would be dead by midnight, some hundreds would be bent, broken, bloody, but most of them would get away scot-free and live to ride another day.

Some were sheep and some were shepherds, but it is a peculiarity of the game that the risks are almost equally divided.

Among the sheep:

Thomas A. Jeremy, age fifty-one, salesman of hats, resident of

Norwalk, Connecticut, husband to Martha, father of Tom, Jr., and Edith.

Sybil James, thirty-six, resident of Providence, Rhode Island, schoolteacher. Helen Davison, thirty, the same.

Tony Volos, resident of Arth, Switzerland, twenty-eight, occupation: traveler, sometime photographer, sometime automobile racing driver.

The Hamil family, consisting of Hugh Hamil and wife Inez, and Hardy, six, Peter, four, and Esther, eighteen months, all residents of New York, New York.

Among the numerous shepherds:

James Agnatelli, forty-one, resident of Ridgefield, Connecticut, occupation: state police officer.

Peter Harsch, fifty-three, resident of Katonah, New York, employee of the State of New York, specialist in the maintenance of highways, and Jerry Murray, twenty-five, Fritz Speyer, twenty, Homer McEvoy, forty-eight, and Redd Murphy, twenty-five, variously truck drivers and laborers in the employ of the State of New York.

Mr. Jeremy, on that late morning in May, was in the pretty country of upstate New York, the Finger Lakes country, driving from Ithaca to Elmira on business.

The Misses Sybil James and Helen Davison were driving their mutually owned station wagon from Providence, Rhode Island, to Hyde Park, New York, to visit the ancestral home and the burial place of Franklin Delano Roosevelt.

Tony Volos was not driving at all. He was sitting on the porch of a friend's estate in Pound Ridge, New York, drinking tea and soaking up the sunshine.

The Hamil family was intent on visiting Mr. Hamil's mother, who lived in Brewster, New York, and before they saw Mrs. Hamil they intended to stop in New Canaan, Connecticut, and see a college friend of Mrs. Hamil's. Their car was a new hardtop.

James Agnatelli was patrolling the Merritt Parkway in a standard interceptor.

Peter Harsch and the Messrs. Murray, Speyer, McEvoy and

Murphy were rolling in two state trucks on Route 137, New York, in search of a guardrail reported broken through.

None of these people had had, as yet, the pleasure of the acquaintance of the others. That was to come.

2

The street in front of the hotel was wet from a sweeper that had just gone past and it steamed in the sun. This was a bright, crisp day; a good day in May. Tom Jeremy stood on the sidewalk in front of the hotel, on State Street, and stared up the hill.

A bellboy jogged down the steps carrying Jeremy's luggage: the leather two-suiter, the big sample case and the little canvas carryall.

"Car'll be right around, Mr. Jeremy," he said. He looked down the street and eased the bags to the sidewalk. The old black sedan came sliding up as if he had called it. It was a '55 with 46,731 miles on it. The boy piled the stuff in the back for his dollar and Jeremy pushed off.

He ran down State Street and out of town, past Buttermilk Falls, and headed down 13 toward Elmira. He was in no great hurry. He ran at his regular sixty. He turned the radio on, got his cigar going good and leaned back in the seat, his left arm out the window on the roof. The May air rushed warmly around his wrist. He would finish his calls in Elmira that morning and be in Binghamton by midafternoon. He had three calls there, and early in the morning he'd be out and heading for Connecticut and home, down through Deposit and Roscoe and Monticello to the Bear Mountain Bridge across the Hudson and then over to Norwalk.

The tires sang on the road under him, paying for the push with the microscopic bits of rubber they left on the surface. They were good four-ply nylon tires and Jeremy had no worries about them. He didn't worry about anything. He wasn't a worrying man. Bad things didn't stay with him long. Just outside Ithaca, for instance, the ash had fallen from his cigar into his lap, he had let go of the wheel to brush it away, and the car had pulled a little to the left toward a passing ten-wheel tractor-and-trailer rig. For a split second, his left arm out there on the roof had felt sickeningly vulnerable, and he had pulled it in quickly; but he forgot the feeling and the incident within a mile.

Tom Jeremy sometimes quarrelled with his wife because she could not or would not persist in the cheerful view of life that he insisted reflected the only normal attitude.

"Only sick people remember unpleasant things," he'd say, "and it makes 'em sicker, too. They die sooner. *I* don't let myself think about anything but nice things, and you'll see, I'll live forever."

He believed that he was a good man, that he set a good example, and that even if his children were not able to understand and emulate the wisdom that moved him, still it would affect them. It would seep into them; they would remember, knowingly or unknowingly, how their father had done things, how he had reacted, behaved, marched in the little narrow part of the world that had been his, and they would be the better for it. He tried to look ahead to that revelation, which he saw as a sudden, thunderclap sort of thing; he tried to see Tom, Jr., and Edie receiving the ultimate message, but he got a fuzzy picture, for two reasons: the projection required that he think of himself as dead, which he found unpleasant, and he was a man of low imaginative resource. He abandoned the effort. It would all work out with the children, he was sure it would. They were good kids. Tom, Jr., was a sophomore in college at eighteen; you had to admit that was good. He was going to be an electrical engineer. Edith, too, was a wonderful little girl, a gorgeous thing at fifteen, and as bright as her brother. She got good grades in everything, but in chemistry she was apparently something astonishing. She had never had anything worse than an A since her first course in junior high.

His children amazed Tom Jeremy a bit, and frightened him, too. He found it hard to account for their intelligence, and its unaccountability worried him. He would have liked to flatter himself that the brightness of his offspring sprang naturally from his loins, but he knew better, he was an honest man, and, even more unusual, never more so than with himself. He knew that characteristics sometimes skip a generation, and he was inclined to credit his father, a dear good man who'd taught school all his life, and had made pretty heavy weather of it. Certainly Jeremy had to put down any suspicion of his wife. Martha was a dear old girl, and she had smoothed out his life and said a blessing over it and he adored her although he would never have said so, but intelligent she was not.

In Buffalo, two days and 137 miles before, Tom Jeremy had bought something for Martha, a salad bowl of a strange yellow-brown wood, not that he did that very much any more, he didn't; the time for that sort of thing was gone, or he thought it was gone and Martha didn't seem to mind. When he'd first started on the road of course he brought back to her more goods than he sold every trip, but that was different, everything was different then, particularly the being away from her was different. It was a wildness, then, it really hurt; he could feel it and it was a pain as real as toothache or any other he'd ever known. It had been a long time going down, too.

Now he felt near to Martha when he was far away, and far away from her when he was near to her, and it all evened out into a simple acceptance of their life, pleasing to both. He sometimes wondered how it would be when he retired, and they were together for the rest of time. He thought very seriously about such things in his quiet and mostly unspoken determination to live the good if unspectacular life. His life had taken a turn toward goodness about the same time it had been revealed to him that he was not going to be one of the immortals of salesmanship nor very wealthy either, but he did not think he was any the less worthy for that. One day, in his forty-second year it had been, things came clear enough for him then, not so clear that he had to admit it with finality, but he knew it all the same. Not that he really lacked either money or reputation: he could make $15,000 a year most years. *He* could sell hats if anybody could sell hats.

He rolled into the outskirts of Elmira, down to 40 miles an hour, the wheel jerking under his hand, the suspension thudding over a new excavation. His foot came heavily down on the brake as a light went red, and the car moved off almost by itself, almost automatically, when it showed green. Jeremy never thought about driving any more, hadn't for years; it was all unthinking mechanical movement to him. After all, counting his driving mileage in units of ten thousand he couldn't remember how much there'd been of it and he was still waiting for his first bad accident.

He let the car drift up to the Mark Twain Hotel and got out of it. He looked around a bit before he went in. He didn't like this town as much as Ithaca, but it was all right, and the day was still a warm fine day and he appreciated that. It was exactly 11:04.

3

At 11:04 that morning Sybil James was snuffing out the day's first cigarette. She stuffed it into the yielding grill of the station wagon's ash tray and pushed it shut before the wind could get into it.

"Boy, you really ate that one alive," Helen Davison said to her. "Every time you took a drag on it it came down half an inch."

"I suppose so," Sybil said. "It gets harder every day. Maybe I ought to abandon all these systems and just quit."

"I would," Helen said, "but then it's easy for me to say, never having smoked. But I should think this business of having the first one hour later every day would be murder. Doesn't it get harder every time?"

"Yep, does," Sybil said. "Dammit."

Helen giggled. "I was just wondering," she said, "when it gets up to midnight, are you going to stay up that night, no matter what, so as to have it?"

"If it gets *that* bad," Sybil said, "I might as well start taking it in the arm and get it over with." She slowed the car. "Do you want to drive a while?" she said. "I could pull into this gas station."

"No," Helen said. "But we could have some coffee. There's a place across the street that looks presentable."

They left the car at the pump for gas.

The coffee was pretty bad and the cruller that Sybil took was a veteran. She gnawed on the end of it and considered the propriety of dunking.

"You know," she said, "we really ought to tell them how lousy this is. Maybe they don't know. It would be a kindness."

"You're kidding," Helen said. "Of course they know. They just don't give a damn."

Sybil giggled. "Do you remember a boy named Hassan?" she asked. "Toby Hassan? He was expelled a couple of years ago. I had him in English II for a while. One Saturday morning I'd been shopping and I went into a little place for some coffee. He was there. He was eating a piece of lemon pie. He called the man over and said to him, he said, 'Tell me, have you got any pie that was made since last Tuesday?' He got a short answer, of course, and all of a sudden he picked up his piece of pie and hit the man right in the face with it. It was very funny. Then there was a fight, naturally, and a policeman came in and dragged him off. I admired him for it, I must say I did."

"Stout fellow," Helen said. "What was he expelled for? He wasn't the one who slugged old Thorgesen, was he?"

"No," Sybil said, "I don't think so. Hassan was expelled over a slight case of pregnancy. They wanted him to marry the girl and he said he'd never heard of anything so outrageous. I've often wondered what became of him."

A lean and hairy young man was hovering over the station wagon. He looked about seventeen and his arms came an incredible distance out of the sleeves of his coveralls, stiff with a month's grease.

"That left front is pretty soft, ma'am," he said. "There's only twenty pounds in it. Ought to be twenty-six, anyway. Maybe you've got a slow leak."

"I don't think so," Helen said. "We just haven't paid any attention to it for a while. If you pump it up I think it'll be OK."

He dragged out the air hose and bent to it. He checked all the tires and put air in all of them.

"I put in twenty-eight," he said. "That's better for tubeless, run 'em a little hard they'll last longer."

Helen thanked him and paid him and they moved off.

Sybil James was a good enough driver. That is to say, she was all right, competent enough, as long as nothing happened. She stayed in her own lane pretty well, she didn't tail-gate, she was careful to make signals and if anything she drove too slowly. She had learned to drive a long time back, when 100 horsepower was a lot, and she was a little bit afraid of the power in the new engines. She treated the accelerator with exaggerated respect, and her tendency was to brake pretty hard when she had to brake at all. By paying attention, refusing to be distracted, she had driven a long time without ever getting into any kind of trouble worse than a crinkled fender.

Her brother had taught her to drive; she adored him and tried very hard to please him. He was her only brother, her only close relative if it came to that, and she thought he was surely the best driver who ever lived. He was indeed very good, strong, with quick reactions, and he had made a good fighter pilot and had three confirmed kills when he died 14,000 feet over Korea. His body had been returned and Sybil had buried him in the little family plot in Kansas. It had been a small funeral; there were only twenty-one people in all, including the squad from the air base, and Sybil had been thrown into so deep a depression that her friends had thought it fortunate Denny's body had come back in the summer-vacation time. They doubted she could have gone on teaching otherwise.

As it was, she didn't want to stay in Kansas and she left that autumn. She was not a pretty girl, but she was wonderfully pleasant company, and there was a neatness about her, a shiny look, that some people might value over beauty. No one with that taste in women had happened along, however, and anyone familiar with the statistics of the great American marriage grab bag could have told her, if she needed telling, that her chances were steadily declining. She didn't often think about it; she was just waiting it out, pretty sure that if she could last long enough, the pain—it was really a controlled hysteria, not a pain, but that was the handiest tag for it—would fade away and leave her in peace. In the meantime she was grateful for her work and for Helen.

Helen seemed to Sybil much younger than thirty, and she was in her eyes enormously pretty, too. Helen was not really and truly a teacher. She did not have, in Sybil's view, a teacher's mentality or outlook. She wasn't *academic.* She taught physical education and of course she was frighteningly healthy and strong, wickedly strong. Helen was never tired, never depressed, never anything but her best: cheerful, ready to go, ready for anything. She was warm, she was generous, it was impossible to be deeply depressed when she was near; she made even introspection pointless. Sybil counted that day blessed that she had found Helen, and she thought nothing of her occasional stubbornness, her wish to have her own way. Sybil was happy, for the most part, to do what Helen wanted done, and what Helen wanted her to do, and as time passed the things that had seemed hardest to accept became not only easier and acceptable but even pleasant.

"You might go a little faster, dear," Helen said. "The limit's 50 here and you're barely over 40. We'll be all day at this rate."

Sybil bore down a bit on the gas pedal and automatically squeezed the wheel tighter and sat up straighter. She didn't mind doing 50, she didn't really mind 60 but she wanted nothing whatever to do with 70 and that was the way it was with her. Helen, on the other hand, had no qualms about 75 or 80 and she liked to look at 100 for a few seconds every once in a while. She drove like a man: easy, relaxed, confident. She'd been driving since she could remember, and she'd had only one accident. "That one was a rouser, though," she'd say. "The car was what the insurance people call, in their gruesome way, a 'total.' There wasn't enough left of it to make it worthwhile hauling it to the junk yard."

The sun was high and hot and they ran along Route 84 in Connecticut in light traffic. Helen noticed that the car was putting out a harder ride. She could feel the bumps in the road, the expansion joints when they were on concrete, and she told herself to remember to look at the tires when they stopped for lunch. Twenty-eight pounds might be too much for such a hot day; they were probably actually running well over 30 now.

She slid down the seat until her neck was hooked on the back of it, resting, and she nudged up the radio volume with her knee.

It was a nice day, they were alone, it would be interesting to see Hyde Park, and you could even argue, if you wanted to, that it wasn't altogether a vacation; it would be professionally worthwhile. She was glad they had thought of it.

4

Tony Volos lay stretched on a deck chair in the sun, not really awake but not sleepy. There was a pot of tea on a table beside him and the rinds of a quartered orange. He looked out over the long lawn, over the little lake to the laurel-covered hills of the Pound Ridge Reservation. There was no one else in the house, the air was still and warm and quiet. Tony had nothing to do. No one could make a demand on his time. The day was his own and he wondered what to do with it. He was limp as *pasta*, his chest barely rose and fell with his breathing.

I am, he told himself, a hibernating bear. The idea amused him and he began to try to close off all the sounds of the world one by one, hypnotically. To do this he had first to listen, and what had been velvet silence began slowly to turn into bedlam. In the thin woods across the lake a crow shouted a rasping warning to the flock. Far away, on the road, a horn sounded, and close by a war-strength squadron of yellow-and-brown Italian bees raped a patch of clover blossoms. Overhead a Constellation rumbled and thudded, climbing westbound for California, and even when it had passed and there was no overt sound, he could hear the noise of the world itself, the jostle of the universal molecules one against another—that, or the whisper of his own blood in its veins. He gave up the exercise, rolled over and poured more tea. In the house, the phone rang. He derricked his legs over the edge of the chair and went in. He was very tan. He was wearing white linen slacks and nothing else. He did not hurry.

He picked up the phone and listened.

"My dear girl," he said. "Nothing. . . . No one is home. . . . I was loafing in the sun, thinking about you. . . . Certainly I'm lying and it's ungracious of you to ask. . . . Well, I might, if I could get up enough ambition to drive in. . . . Yes, we could, couldn't we. . . . I know it was. . . . It would be better this time, too. . . . OK, I will, I'll see you at five, something like that. . . . Sure. . . . Right. . . ."

He hung up. Standing, he looked down at the phone in its cradle, and ran his fingers back and forth along the spine of it. It was colored a bright lemon yellow and the cord was yellow, running into the wall and then, if you wanted to think of it in that way, running out of the house and all the way to New York and the coffee-brown wall in Rosa Martin's bedroom. The wall stood straight and warm in his memory, butting the white ceiling, and that prospect moved him, but against it he had to balance the quiet pleasures of this house and a peaceful afternoon in it, and the drive to town as well. The driving was a chore, really, an hour and fifteen minutes of demi-boredom.

There were three cars in the garage, none of them his, but all of them his to use. The cars belonged, like the house, to his host, his friend Hartnett: one Lincoln Capri, one Ferrari Testa Rossa, one Porsche Carrera. He tried to make a little diversion for himself of deciding which car to take, but the decision was obvious: the Lincoln had a flat, someone had run over a beer bottle on the garage floor; the Ferrari was a semiracing car, too fussy for traffic; so it would be the Porsche, a nice little car, and fast.

The ride would be fun were it not for the speed limits on the parkways. Volos had grown up driving on the Continent, and only the Italian attitude toward speed on public roads seemed reasonable to him. He could see no point in driving slowly, he truly enjoyed fast driving, enjoyed it as few men ever do; he liked riding as a passenger almost as much as he liked driving himself. His certification in this particular was complete; he had three times ridden as a passenger in the Mille Miglia race in Italy. There were men who had driven in that thousand-mile open-road madness, and won it, who swore that no money and no option on fame and glory would persuade them to go as passengers in it, sitting there hanging on for life over blind bumps at 170 miles an hour, screaming over the long straight highways at 185 in pouring rain, feeling the wheels bite desperately for grip on the absurdly unguarded mountain corners—but Tony was enchanted with it; he could sit there relaxed, every pore in his body open, sensation-inviting. So honest was his hedonism that he was not sure he didn't prefer riding as passenger to driving, for the passenger's duties were usually insignificant, his responsibility slight for the winning or losing and he could thus concentrate on the joy of movement. Tony was not eager for fame, and he had no ambition.

His father had disinherited him for that failing, and with rare thoroughness he had cut him out of his will, forbidden him the family house in Athens, burned all his possessions, the toys of his childhood and the books of his maturity, made it impossible for him to support himself in Greece and forbidden all members of the clan to violate the excommunication under penalty of equal sanctions. Until this blow had fallen on him in his nineteenth year, over his refusal to study accounting in preparation for a career of supervision of the ancestral industries, Tony had not thought often about money; now that he had none, he still did not often think about it. For most of his life he had lived in houses that were cousins to palaces, but he was not less happy in a country inn. He had had good horses and fine cars of his own, but he was unable to understand those who claimed a greater pleasure in personal property than in the use of someone else's. He found the two sensations precisely the same. He was not much impressed by ownership in any form. He would approach a woman sitting next to her husband and make fervent love to her if he felt like doing so, and he often did, and he was somehow, inexplicably, inoffensive in the effort, so that he rarely came to trouble by it, and his success-to-failure ratio outraged probability.

He went to the kitchen, a cubist arrangement of white porcelain studded with enough dials and switches, it seemed to him, to outfit a small Balkan-sized atom pile, and undertook the preparation of a lunch of bacon and toast. By cooking the bacon very slowly he managed not to burn it. He made more tea and ate another orange. He had shaved and showered earlier, so he sluiced himself with cologne, pulled a striped shirt over his head, took a jacket off the back of a chair and walked along the inside passage to the garage. He had decided to go into town early, as long as he was going at all, and see some other people before he visited

Rosa Martin. He opened the garage door in front of the Porsche, stared at the car for a moment and opened the next door as well. He stuffed his jacket through the window into the Porsche and turned to the Ferrari. He snapped off the brake and pushed the car out of doors.

The shovel-nosed little red car started with the frightening bare-metal clatter of its breed and he sat at the wheel, letting it idle fast for a few minutes, staring at the dials that recorded its workings. When it was warm he put it into gear and moved off on the winding driveway, blipping the engine up and down, bouncing on the seat as the hard springs resisted the ruts. When he came to the highway he looked both ways, dropped his foot on the accelerator, snapped the clutch out and braced himself. The rear wheels screamed and smoked as they spun, the car hesitated for a second, then blasted down the road, two straight scars of black rubber behind it. This was a good road, New York 124, and not much traveled, and Volos ran down it to the junction with Route 35, the speedometer needle flickering between 90 and 125 miles an hour. At the junction he turned and came back, a little faster, drifting the bends, braking very hard for the corners. Down and back he hadn't seen another car. He backed the Ferrari into its place and shut it off. He felt much better. He warmed the Porsche, turned on the radio and started for New York. It slid along the road at 75 miles an hour and he felt that he didn't even have to steer it.

5

There was a reason, or at least an explanation, for the mild little burst of speeding Hugh Hamil did on the Merritt Parkway that day, but it was no reason he could cite, certainly not before his wife. It had to do with a girl who passed him somewhere north of Greenwich, in a white Corvette. She had brown hair of the color inadequately described as chestnut; she was tanned and lean and all that, a white sweater with a little black jacket, a green wisp of scarf on her head; and she sat very prim and upright at the wheel.

But girls who would fit, key-in-lock, that description, are no great rarities. It was an intangible that moved Hugh, finally. She made him think of Ned Jordan's legendary advertisement, cited, as Holy Writ, wherever hucksters gather and martinis are drained and trumpet-loud brags are bragged. Like every other copywriter, Hugh Hamil had had Jordan well dinned into him at one time or another: He could remember the picture of the Jordan Playboy, a nice clean pen-and-ink sketch, the wild-haired girl at the wheel, the line, "Somewhere West of Laramie. . . ." The ad ran on about the girl, and what a bright-eyed, strong-limbed heller she was, and about the car: ". . . There's a savor of links about that car—of laughter and light—a hint of old loves—and saddle and quirt. It's a brawny thing—yet a graceful thing for the sweep o' the Avenue. . . ." That was the ad that sold 10,000,000 automobiles, not Playboys, to be sure, but scores of other makes that followed it, hustled by men who knew, with Jordan, that it was much better, saleswise, Joe, to plug not the car but what the car could be made to mean for a man's ego.

The trouble was, the real trouble, she reminded him of Marion. Marion was The Almost One for Hugh. Every man has a girl like that, a glorious anachronism usually, running in memory across lawns long withered, in bright dresses gone to dust years past, or glowing warm in some candle-lit restaurant since scraped off the earth to make a parking lot. Marion Dellany was the one he almost married, would have married if she'd have had him, and couldn't marry when she would. It had been a college-time love, and the war had spoiled it, although she was going to wait, she said, she promised, and she had said she'd prove it the whole of the last week before he went away, and if that was proving it, prove it she had, gloriously, he thought, magnificently, knowing then no better. At any rate he truly had not wanted another woman for a long period afterward, but in the fullness of time he got his Dear John letter.

He was still unmarried when she divorced the man, but he and Inez were engaged, and although Marion obviously wanted him then, he could come to no decision, and in time events took the decision for him. He had seen Marion only once at that time, for dinner on a cold October night, and what he had chosen to interpret as the gallant sadness, or the sad gallantry, in her dear little face had haunted him ever since. He thought of it as "ever since," but in truth the pain had come on a schedule of diminishing frequency as the years knitted themselves together.

Something in the face of the girl in the Corvette brought the image to him now and he wanted to see it again, and bruise himself and suffer just a little. He decided to catch up. He couldn't get out of his lane immediately, and when he did there were five cars between him and the white two-seater, which was, what was more, being driven with considerable enterprise. He flashed his lights at the car just ahead and it moved into the right-hand lane at once; the next in line was stubborn, and speeded up instead of giving way. It took 65 to stay with it. Hugh wished it would get up to 80 and really cut a path. He was strangely excited, on the edge of mild hysteria even, and he felt that he was alone, although Inez was dozing close enough to touch him and the children were noisy in the back seat.

The car finally pulled over and Hugh passed. The Corvette was a long way ahead now, he could see it rushing up a slope half a mile in front of him, but there were only two cars between them, and he was sure he could catch up. He had been too excited to look into his mirror, but something flickered in it now and he looked: a black sedan, headlights snapping up and down. For a second he thought of running away from the fellow, but the realization that it was a police car caught his foot on the pedal and he pulled aside. He was surprised when the officer looked over and waved to the side of the parkway.

"Daddy! Are we arrested?" Hardy asked, his voice high with excitement.

"I don't think so," Hugh said. "We'll see."

Hardy had waked Inez, and she looked at Hugh wide-eyed.

"Were you speeding?" Inez asked.

"Maybe a little," he said. "But it's nothing to worry about." He ran the car over the curbing to the grass and rolled down the window. He didn't look around, but in his side mirror he could see the officer approaching with the traditional firm unhurried step, tucking a pair of sunglasses into a breast pocket as he came. Hugh felt a rising sensation to which only genuine bloody-handed criminals are immune. He found to his extreme annoyance that for a moment he couldn't remember in which pocket he had carried his wallet for twenty years.

James Agnatelli looked bored, but he was not. His work never really bored him. There were details of it that he didn't like but he was never bored. He was a cop who preferred being a cop to anything else. He was one of the so-called "new" policemen, which is to say that he was a serious-minded fellow who did not believe that all law was resident in the end of a night stick. He knew a considerable amount of psychology and a lot of law. He had read the books. He had done the course at Northwestern. He was forty-one, a sergeant, fourteen years a trooper. Like all police officers, he really and truly did dislike criminals, although he would try to understand them and make every due allowance. Since his specialty was traffic, the criminal he most frequently dealt with was the speeder and he honestly hated speeders. His distaste and his anger varied according to which of the two classes they put themselves into: the under-70's and the over-70's. The under-70's he was inclined to think of as perhaps amiable idiots who needed mostly instruction. The over-70's he felt should be awarded mandatory jail sentences to be spent picking jute in the bag mill.

He stopped just a little behind the door of Hugh Hamil's car and looked in. Man, woman, three kids. The edginess he always felt on approaching a car died down, a little.

"May I see your license and registration, please?" he said.

Hugh fished his license out of his wallet. Inez had already found the registration in the glove compartment. He handed the two papers to Agnatelli.

"You were going a little fast, weren't you?" Agnatelli said.

"Maybe a little," Hugh said. "I don't think I was speeding." The officer shrugged his shoulders ever so slightly.

"I had you doing 65," he said. "That about right?"

"I didn't think I was going quite that fast," Hugh said.

Agnatelli walked to his own car and got in.

"What's he doing now?" Inez said.

"Oh, he's calling in to find out if the car's stolen or if I'm wanted for arson or mopery or anything," Hugh told her.

Agnatelli came back. "You didn't tell me *why* you were going that fast," he said mildly.

"Really no reason, officer," Hugh said. "I saw someone ahead of me whom I thought I knew, and I was trying to catch up, that's all. Not a very good reason, you see. Not a reason at all."

Agnatelli handed the papers through the window. "You ought to take it a little easier," he said. "I don't think you knew how fast you were going. Better watch it, before you find yourself doing 80 along here." He nodded shortly and walked away.

"He didn't give you a ticket?" Inez said.

"Nope," Hugh said. "No ticket."

He watched the police car pull on ahead. He was seriously grumpy and out of sorts. He really had wanted to see the girl again, and now that he could not, the deprivation annoyed him. Being caught speeding humiliated him and it was worse for Inez and the children being in the car. He was angry and he felt less of a man than he liked. He looked at the speedometer; it was sitting at 60 and he deliberately dropped his foot and let it run to 65 for a bare instant. Then, frightened by his temerity, he dropped to 55 and stayed there, fuming.

"Were you really trying to catch anyone?" Inez asked him.

"I made that up," he said.

Back on the road, Sergeant Agnatelli settled down to patrolling at 50 miles an hour, building up another kite tail of cars behind him that were afraid to pass. Since his speedometer was an accurate one, and since only the best German and the very best British cars provide such instruments as a rule, he knew that most of the drivers behind him believed they were doing 53 or 54 miles an hour. So some stayed behind, while a lesser number, gluing their indicators to 55 exactly, inched on past, feeling brave.

Agnatelli wondered, now that he'd let him go, if he had been quite right in letting Hamil off without a ticket. He had based his decision on the comparatively low speed, the obvious dismay of the driver and his disinclination to argue or get fresh, plus, probably, the fact that his wife and children were aboard. Nothing would have helped had his speed been two or three miles an hour greater, or if Agnatelli had held him at 65 for a long distance; but the Parkway was full of people doing 65 in spurts; you couldn't get very excited about that.

It took something quite unusual to excite Agnatelli now, but still, what it took to excite you, you could find. He remembered entering the Parkway one December night in a fog so heavy that 10 miles an hour was risky. He was sitting in an entrance road, peering into the drifting mist for headlights when a sedan came past doing an easy 80. Agnatelli tried to chase, but he'd lost the taillights before he could get going and after that it was no good, he couldn't catch up. It wasn't fear that stopped him, it was the certainty that he'd go off the road. He'd had one glimpse of the car as it passed. He believed it was red and of the peculiar style of coachwork the British call "razor-edge," so he called ahead to the next tollgate and they sorted the car out and held it for him. The driver turned out to be in his fifties, conceded that he'd been doing between 80 and 85, but said he considered it perfectly safe because his eyesight was abnormal, there were few cars on the road, and he knew it very well indeed. He was seriously annoyed at being given a ticket and Agnatelli remembered he'd held it in his hand for a long time, as if trying to decide whether to keep it or tear it up then and there.

Agnatelli pulled into a filling station and drifted through to the far end of it to park. As he got out of the car, Hamil's blue hardtop went past, in the inside lane. One of the children saw him and recognized him and pointed.

6

Peter Harsch and his crew found the guardrail, not broken, as had been reported, but bent and pulled out of one of its posts, and had it replaced and everything tidied up within an hour. They went around then, the long way back, and it was a mile or so from the site of the guardrail trouble that Harsch noticed the break in the paving. A pie-shaped piece of concrete, eighteen inches to the side, had cracked out of the shoulder of the road. Old man Harsch had a wonderful eye for that sort of thing, and he spotted it a long way off.

"Slow down a little, Fritz," he said. "We'll want to stop for a bit up here."

He pointed out the place and climbed down when the truck had stopped. It was easy to see what had happened. A stream ran beside the road and it had been in flood. Strong-running water, coming over its banks, had burrowed under the roadway at one point, washing away the dirt, rolling down the stones that made the base of the road, until a little concrete-roofed cave had been dug under the roadway. Then something heavy had come along, probably a truck, and the weight of one of its great wheels resting for just a second of time on the pie-shaped piece of concrete over the dug-out hole had broken it through.

The crew got down from the other truck and they all fell to work. They built up the base with solid fill and patched in the broken slab. To protect it until it could set up hard, they erected a small barricade and put a kerosene torch beneath it. They cleaned up the site and went away. At five o'clock or so, on their way home, they'd stop and light the torch. As for now, it was time for lunch. It was necessary to stoke the machines.

Farther west in New York State, Tom Jeremy was lunching at a roadside stand. He had done no business in Elmira: the city was shut up tight for some kind of a Mark Twain celebration, nothing was open but a drugstore or two. Jeremy was too old a hand to try to sell the day after a celebration, and the day after that would be Sunday. Since he would have to come back to Elmira in any case, he decided to skip Binghamton, too, and go home. He was making good time and he expected to be in Norwalk by six o'clock.

Sybil James and Helen Davison were in New Haven because Sybil knew a woman in the French department at Yale. It was a pleasant break in the trip and they could have lunch in company, walk about for a while and still be in Hyde Park by nightfall.

Hugh and Inez Hamil were relaxed in Exurbia. They sat on the determinedly picturesque lawn of their friend's house in New

Canaan drinking mead-and-soda. Some months before, their host had come upon a recipe for mead and had been intrigued by the fact that this was man's oldest alcoholic beverage—and by the simplicity of its manufacture, as well. Fermented honey and water, nothing to it, in a month's time one had liquor. He had experimented widely, he had sage-honey mead, white-clover-honey mead, Hymettus mead. They were all rather sickly sweet, and it was hard to think of the bearded Vikings, beating across the North Atlantic in their little longboats, fueled by such stuff, but it was intriguing, too, and the Hamils dutifully drank it down while the children bickered among the swings and sand piles.

They had set themselves a quarter-of-five departure time and they would stick to it.

7

Tony Volos was back in Pound Ridge. He had gone twenty miles on his way, happy as a swallow on the wing, when he discovered that he had no money with him. He had left his wallet in the house. He remembered where: in a Shetland jacket he'd worn two nights before. Ordinarily a shortage of currency bothered Tony very little. He didn't need much money; ten dollars, twenty, was enough to take to New York. And he didn't need to take it with him, he could cash a check at any one of a dozen places.

But he was in worse case: there were tollgates to pass, and he hadn't a nickel in change. He ran the Porsche off the road and made a pocket-by-pocket survey. Nothing. He emptied the glove compartment in search of stray coins. Not a bean. He slid the seats back and investigated the floor. After all, one never cleaned a car without finding a quarter or two on the floor. It was not true. He considered the matter. After all, one could go into a tollgate, make a determined and protracted search, display hideous embarrassment—what could the man do? He certainly couldn't say, turn around and go back—why couldn't he? He could, of course. And even if it did work, once was one thing, but doing it three times over was something else again; it became a career.

Tony ran down the road a mile to the next exit, crossed and

went back. He was soon happy again. After all, maybe it was good. The day was sunny and warm, lovely in the country and probably unpleasant in town; the people he'd intended seeing were not the world's nearest and dearest to him, they could wait; he wasn't due to see Rosa until five. He went along to Pound Ridge and when he burbled up the long driveway, the busy little engine behind him working away in second gear, he was disinclined to turn around and start out again. He made a quart of tea, poured it over a trayful of ice cubes, and went to the porch again. He set a sunshade over the chair and looked around for something to read. He found a book. It was a green-bound paperback copy of Forster's *Howards End* and he had been reading it for ten days. It bored him for the most part, but it had a certain soporific appeal, like the buzzing of bees or a steady wind in poplars, and, besides, it was a classic work, woven through with symbolism and he wanted to have read it. He began to read chapter XXI, waiting hopefully for the rich symbolism to declare itself to him. He looked at his watch. He wanted to give himself seventy-five minutes for the trip to New York, and he meant to be a decent half-hour late. There was lots of time.

8

The wind was of no consequence at 5:19 that evening. It was no more than a breeze, five knots in gusts. The temperature was 60°. There had been no rain for two days. During most of the day, no shadow of cloud had lain on the southern Connecticut-New York border, but now, as day's end neared, a low bank of cumulus rolled up in the west and reddened in the sun.

In the next hour, in the ordinary way of things, something more than 1,000 automobiles, trucks, motorcycles would pass the intersections of Routes 57A and 139. Those coming from the east would round a bend and have disclosed to them the intersecting highway on the right, and, on the left, the yellow-and-black barrier marking the small broken place in the pavement. Those coming from the west would have slightly more time in which to see these things, for the curve on the western approach was farther from the intersection. Those coming up 139, south-bound, one would expect to come cautiously because 139 curved very hard into 57A and in addition climbed steeply.

Tom Jeremy ran from the west, at just over 60 miles an hour. He was tired, he slumped in the seat, he had let his cigar go out. Sybil James and Helen Davison were running west-bound at something around 50 miles an hour, at any rate not going really fast. They had stayed longer in New Haven than they intended to stay, but no one was waiting for them in Hyde Park, and they had decided that if they saw a nice place, they would stop for dinner, a good long dinner, and then look for a motel. They were full of vacation's ease and quite at peace.

Tony Volos was coming down 139 and he was coming fast. Rosa Martin had phoned to say that she'd be late at her hair-dresser's and he had overstayed even that extra leave, searching, page by page, for the concealed wisdom of E. M. Forster. He drove earnestly, hugely enjoying an engine that would turn 6,000 rpm without strain, a suspension that stuck as it should.

Hugh Hamil felt a little better for the alcohol he had had in New Canaan, but he was still seriously out of sorts, anxious for night and sleep to put a period to the day. He felt burdened with his woman and his squalling young; he yearned back to the care-free tripping of bachelordom. The girl in the Corvette had set him down, and Sergeant Agnatelli had somehow emasculated him. He drove west on 57A, holding the wheel loosely at the bottom, tail-gaiting a station wagon with Rhode Island plates. The driver, he noticed irritably, was a woman, and so was the passenger. He edged up closer. He looked at his speedometer, which read 50. He thought of the old rule, one car length for every ten miles an hour and one more for luck. Who needs such non-sense, he said to himself, and he kept his foot down.

James Agnatelli had gone off duty at four o'clock. Now at 5:19, he was sitting on the back porch of his house in Ridgefield, drink-ing lemonade. When his son Toby came back from the store, they were going to drive to a farm a little way into New York State to look at some puppies. One night in the January past, Mr. Agna-telli, in an excess of enthusiasm, had promised the boy a dog if he achieved an eighty-five average in school for three straight months. The third month's report was in and the dog was due; there was no way out of it.

Peter Harsch was stepping out of a truck. Redd Murphy had lighted the torch by the barricade and they were about to call it done when old Harsch declared for one more look at the patch. He pushed the torch aside because its open flame was leaping about in the breeze, and it was the moving light, that bit of flame, that Tom Jeremy saw first. He had come hard around the bend and, probably because he was sitting slumped in his seat and a little bit to the right of the center line of his wheel, he had missed seeing the barricade. He was driving straight for it, and sure to catch it with his right fender, when the moving light caught his eye. He reacted slowly. Moving the wheel with his right hand alone was slow business in itself, and a sliver of time was eaten up in getting his left hand in off the roof to help. He was slow getting his foot off the gas, and the car was already turning to the left when he found the brake pedal. Inevitably he skidded, so that he took the barricade with his right door instead of his fender, and as he looked that way he saw the surprised face of Peter Harsch—apparently he was trying to look into the window, at least that was how it appeared to Tom Jeremy—and the next he knew, if he knew anything, Harsch was through the window altogether and flying for him.

The black image of the big sedan filled the whole windshield in front of Sybil James. An instant before, she had heard what she thought was the sound of a low-flying airplane and she had turned her eyes to the right to look. When the sedan loomed ahead she simply froze. She had never considered the eventuality of a head-on collision in any hard, particularized way, and so whatever she did would not be automatic, but could result only from consideration. She considered, for half a second, considered as best she could in terror and absolute silence; she could not even hear the scream of Jeremy's four wheels ripping sideways across the rough concrete, and then the cars came together at an impact speed of around 100 miles an hour. Hugh Hamil, four car lengths behind Sybil's car, had just time to get the brake on and throw his right arm across his wife's face. He threw his arm out in the natural way, that is, palm to the rear, and as his hardtop bored into the rear of the station wagon in front, he felt his elbow break.

Tony Volos had shifted from fourth to third gear a couple of hundred yards from the corner, doing just under 90 miles an hour, and was down to 50 and in second gear, the engine blatting through the exhaust pipes, just before the apex of the corner, when he saw Jeremy's sedan fly tangentially across the road toward the intersection. He did no thinking. It was plain that if the present relative courses of the two cars were maintained, they would meet. If he braked, they would still meet. Tony's orientation was professional, and the professional's rule is: "When in trouble, accelerate, nine times in ten. The tenth time, pray." Tony dropped his foot flat on the gas and hoped the wheels wouldn't spin too much. He threw himself toward the right side of the car and hung on as it jumped and the black mass of the big sedan threw itself behind and, it seemed sure to him, over the Porsche. He heard a tremendous rending crash. As soon as he could get the car in hand again he stopped and ran it up on the grass.

Running back along the road he heard a voice off left shouting, "Call the police! Call the police!" The road seemed to be full of automobiles, it looked like a junk-yard corner. One edge of the stack of junk was burning brightly and Tony was surprised to notice that the flame was blue-white and electric looking. A horrifyingly loud scream, high-pitched but still plainly male, was splitting the air of the whole world right down the middle. There were two trucks beside the road which Tony hadn't noticed before and he saw a man jump off the tail-gate of one of them, a six-foot-long crowbar in his hand. They ran together to the cars. Then Tony saw that there were two in the jagged cluster and a third, a hardtop, on its side and twenty feet off to the right. One of its front wheels was spinning.

The man with the crowbar said, "Jesus! Get 'em out, the whole thing'll go up any minute!"

A boy ran across the road, dragging a big soda turn-up fire extinguisher. It bumped on the road, the little red hose flopping around. Tony had grabbed a door handle and pulled savagely.

He had it in his hand, looking down at it. He dropped it and helped the boy turn the fire extinguisher up to rest on its crown-shaped base.

Someone yelled, "Don't use water on that fire. Don't use water!" The boy dropped the hose and ran. Tony reversed the extinguisher again to turn it off. He couldn't find the fire they'd been fighting.

One of the sedan's doors was off now and a big red-headed man in farmers' blue overalls backed out of the crumpled wreck, tugging something after him. His arms were blood to the elbows and there was blood on his face. What he had in his arms was Harsch and he was dead. They could not move Tom Jeremy because he had taken the steering wheel in the middle of his chest.

Men to help were suddenly crowding the scene. They appeared, they materialized. Tony heard one of them say impatiently that he was a doctor. Smoky crimson flames were burning far down the highway and Tony remembered distantly that he had lighted two of them himself. A wild-eyed man, his face smudged with black, had run to one of the trucks for them and had shoved two of them at Tony, shouting, "Just scratch 'em on the road and stick 'em into something!"

A siren sighed into silence and two New York State troopers ran into the light. There was a wrecker down the road, marked by two unbearably bright red lights riding on poles over the cab. The screaming had stopped. Everywhere underfoot the roadway crunched with glass, and gasoline was puddled on the shoulder, seeping down the crown of the road.

One of the troopers, a short, heavy man, was out of sight in the wagon that had mated, head-on, with Jeremy's car. "One is alive," he yelled out. "I don't think the other can be."

The other trooper was grunting directions to seven or eight men trying to lift the overturned hardtop. Tony ran to it and grabbed.

"One big one, now," the trooper said. The car came up and someone rammed a three-foot-thick piece of firewood under it. It held. "That's enough," the trooper said. "Can you get in there now, Doc?" The screaming began again, very close. The doctor, stern and young looking in the strange light, dropped to his belly and wriggled halfway under the side of the car. "Everybody on it," a voice said. "Don't trust that stick." The screaming stopped again, not quickly, but it stopped, it became a sigh and a moan. You could hear the baby crying then, a teen-age girl was holding it tightly in her arms. She was barefoot.

"There were three kids in there," somebody said. "Where's the other two?"

"Bill MacDonald took the one kid in to Saint Mary's," a voice said. "The other one's over under the tree."

There were four lumpy-looking mounds under the big tree, covered with blankets and what looked like half a pup tent.

James Agnatelli ran into the light. The first man he saw was the short trooper. "Jimmy," the trooper said.

"Can I do something?" Agnatelli said.

"Sure can," the trooper said. "Move some of 'em off the road before somebody lights a cigarette. We've got everybody out but the one under here."

Agnatelli moved around the back of the hardtop and looked, in habit, at the license plate as he went. He stopped and read it again. He ran down the list of numbers he kept in his memory. It didn't come up stolen. . . . He looked at the car again and turned to a man braced under the bumper. "Were there three kids in this?" he asked.

"That's right," the man said. "Man and his wife, I guess, and three kids."

Agnatelli moved into a knot of people. "All right, folks," he said, "move off the road. You can't help any more now. Let's clear it up." They straggled away. There was a fire hose flooding the road now and, when it was well wet down, the wrecker hooked on and dragged Jeremy's car down the road. The station wagon came with it for the first few feet, then, reluctantly, it let go and the front end dropped, the sound it made was a reprise in miniature of the great rending shout of so short a time ago. A headlight lens fell and shattered with a silly tinkle.

Tony walked away. A local officer was standing beside the Porsche, waving a flashlight at the traffic now beginning to trickle through the scene. He saw Tony reach for the door.

"This yours?" he asked. Tony nodded.

"Get it out of here."

"I saw this thing," Tony said. "I was coming out of 139 when it happened. I thought maybe I should stick around."

"Do you live near here?" the man asked.

"Couple of miles," Tony said.

The policeman pulled out a notebook. "Give me your name and address," he said. "Let me see your license. Come around in the morning."

"OK," Tony said. He lowered himself into the car and, for the third time that day, moved off for New York. He didn't feel terribly like going, now, but he was damned if he wouldn't. He knew that the man who had almost hit him was dead. He knew he was lucky, and he knew, too, that he had done the right thing to save himself.

"The way these crazies drive," he said to himself. "It's all unbelievable." He was going to be late for Rosa now. He ran down the chain of lights that marked the backed-up traffic, and when he was clear of it he dropped the car into third, belted it good and hard for a start and then began to run.

Tom Jeremy did not come home that night, and Ithaca knew him no more. Not Ithaca, nor Elmira, Binghamton, Buffalo, Utica, Johnson City, Endicott, Auburn, Syracuse—none of them saw him again. He was remembered in those places, though. His wife remembered him well, his children less well, and it would have saddened him to know that it never came to his children, in a flash of revelation, that he had been a wise man in his life. He had been a good man, they knew that, but they never did know that he had died, and killed, because he was a stupid man.

Sybil James had three broken ribs—what was thought at first to be a frontal skull fracture was not. She endured tearing headaches for a long time, but she was not physically handicapped in her profession. Perhaps she taught as well as she ever had, but she had no conviction she could go on doing it for long. Her loneliness was in itself insupportable, and she could not put out of her consciousness the searing certainty that it was self inflicted, that Helen had died through her fault, through her omission. She didn't know what she had done that was wrong, but this lack of evidence in no way lightened the indictment.

She threw away hundreds of hours of her life in review of the accident: if she had not been distracted for that second by what she still thought had been an airplane; if she had reacted quickly enough to turn the car, and hit the one ahead a glancing blow instead of directly; if she had taken the trouble to know the wisdom of driving a two-pedal car with the left foot on the brake. She had never heard of the technique before the accident, but now she tortured herself by estimating the distance she could have saved with an extra half second of braking time, the diminished speed with which they would have hit the Jeremy car, the difference it would have made to Helen. She was perfectly aware of the futility of all this and so sometimes her persistence in it frightened her badly. She did not buy another car. She never drove again.

Tony Volos remembered the accident only when he passed the 57A intersection. It was not a notable incident in his view. For his own part, he had had much closer calls, and in company more distinguished. He had seen worse accidents, he had seen eighty-four people killed by a single automobile. He told the police what he knew, giving himself only ten miles an hour the best of it when he stated his speed through the corner. There was some curiosity on the part of the troopers about one of the tire marks, the tread of which matched the car he had been driving. They indicated, the police said, a speed in the 70's. Tony argued that these were not skid but spin marks, that he had been accelerating, not braking. They asked him to please prove it, and he was able to do so. In July he got an assignment from an Italian house to do a book of color photography on mountain climbing and, what with one thing and another, years passed before he came back to America. He never knew, of course, that Sybil James had thought the blatting over-run sound of his Porsche had been an airplane's exhaust, and if he had he would, perhaps properly, have attached little weight to it.

Hugh Hamil died. The coroner found that the upper part of his body had been projected through the window, although the seat belt had held the lower part firm. The car, in rolling, had pinned him, but his death, freakishly, was due not to head injuries but to visceral damage. Inez Hamil lived. Her head jackknifed through the base of the windshield, but it had carried her husband's arm before it, and thus she could believe, and it was true, that he had saved her life. Peter died. There was no mark on him, but his neck was broken. As far as Inez knew, he had been just as tightly tied down as the other two children, who were only frightened and shaken. The trooper who took her deposition in the hospital told her that it was new in his experience for any living thing to survive such a crash, and, being a wise man for one so young, he led her to think kindly of her husband for having installed seat belts in the car. Inez had some money saved, there was insurance, including a company policy of Hugh's she had not known of, and so she could manage for a while. After six months she went back to work. It seemed to her that to think much about it would be somehow disloyal, but she was sure she would eventually marry again. She did not really know what had happened that night in May. How could she know? Only one man knew that anger had played a part in it, and immaturity and bravado, and he was dead.

James Agnatelli had stayed on the scene until he could be of no more use. Then he and Toby had driven on to the farm. He bought for the boy the best puppy on the place. He thought about the accident a long time that night. This was no new thing for him, and he knew the two New York State officers weren't sleeping well either. He tried to decide the question, would a ticket have slowed him, or not? He knew it could not be decided, but he felt the weight of argument lay with the positive. Before he had been out an hour the next day he gave a man a ticket for doing 61 miles an hour.

"I believe you," he said. "I believe you were barely over 60, but the limit here is 55."

"They must have raised your quota lately," the man said, clearly furious.

Agnatelli looked at him. "Here you are," he said. "It's returnable Tuesday in Westport." He started away, but before he'd reached his own car he turned and came back. "Look," he said, "I don't want to have an argument with you, and I'm not going to explain anything, but if I were you, I'd sit here for five minutes, and have a cigarette, and simmer down, before I started to drive again. You don't have to, you understand. It's just advice."

Peter Harsch had been a bachelor, and when it came time to bury him people who had lived near him for most of the twenty-seven years he had been in America were surprised to find how little they knew about him. His estate comprised a neat little six-room frame house on half an acre, more or less, of land, a '50 Chevrolet coupe and $2,181.09 in cash. No one ever came forward to claim it.

ACKNOWLEDGMENT is made to the following publications for chapters that appeared in somewhat different form:

Chap. 2, copyright 1957 by Ziff-Davis Publishing Company (*Sports Cars Illustrated*); chap. 3, copyright 1959 by Ziff-Davis Publishing Company (*Sports Cars Illustrated*); chap. 6, copyright 1957 by Atlantic Monthly Company; chap. 8, copyright 1957 by Curtis Publishing Company (*Saturday Evening Post*); chap. 9, copyright 1952 by Atlantic Monthly Company; chap. 10, copyright 1959 by The New York Times Company; chap. 11, copyright 1959 by Ziff-Davis Publishing Company (*Sports Cars Illustrated*); chap. 12, copyright 1959 by Ziff-Davis Publishing Company (*Sports Cars Illustrated*); chap. 16, copyright 1959 by H.M.H. Publishing Company (*Playboy Magazine*); chap. 18, copyright 1957 by Hillman Publishing Company (*Pageant Magazine*); chap. 19, copyright 1958 by Atlantic Monthly Company. The excerpt from *The Racing Driver* by Denis Jenkinson on page 194 is reprinted by permission of B. T. Batsford, Ltd., London.